The Global Financial Crisis in Retrospect

Anthony Elson

The Global Financial Crisis in Retrospect

Evolution, Resolution, and Lessons for Prevention

Anthony Elson
Chevy Chase, Maryland, USA

ISBN 978-1-137-59749-6 (hardcover)   ISBN 978-1-137-59750-2 (eBook)
ISBN 978-1-349-93735-6 (softcover)
DOI 10.1057/978-1-137-59750-2

Library of Congress Control Number: 2016959375

Cover design by Tom Howey

Printed on acid-free paper

This Palgrave Macmillan imprint is published by Springer Nature
The registered company is Nature America Inc.
The registered company address is: 1 New York Plaza, New York, NY 10004, U.S.A.

In Memoriam
Georgina Emily Mackinnon
Robert Truscott Elson

PREFACE AND ACKNOWLEDGMENTS

In certain respects, this book is a sequel to my earlier book *Governing Global Finance: The Evolution and Reform of the International Financial Architecture*, which was published by Palgrave Macmillan in 2011. That book examined the global financial crisis of 2008–09 in the context of the history of financial crises in the post-WWII era and the efforts by governments since 1944 to establish and maintain a stable global monetary and financial order free of major financial disruptions. This book focuses more directly on the causes and consequences of the global financial crisis with the benefit of additional hindsight and the efforts of scholars to explain and understand the key factors behind the crisis and the special challenges it has posed for policy-makers in dealing with its after-effects. In this connection, it is remarkable to realize how little weight was given to the possibility of a global financial crisis arising from the credit bubbles in housing finance in a number of advanced countries and the extent of improvisation and experimentation that has been required in policy-making to deal with its shockwaves.

The slow pace of global economic recovery, the persistent threat of "secular stagnation" and the significant distance of the major central banks from a normalized monetary policy stance provide dramatic testimony to the enduring negative effects of the crisis and the still uncertain timing of a full recovery. In this context, I provide an assessment, which was absent in the previous book, of the influence of mainstream macroeconomic thinking in (unintentionally) setting the groundwork for the possibility of the financial crisis and its lack of relevance for policy formulation and implementation in the period since. Given the international dimensions of the financial crisis, I also examine the defects in the international financial architecture in terms of its role in crisis prevention in the period leading up to the crisis, as well as the more positive role it has played in crisis management since late 2008.

One entirely new perspective raised in this book is the role of the financial sector in exacerbating the problems of income and wealth inequality in the United States and other advanced countries prior to and since the crisis. Before the crisis, the growing problem of inequality was not a major concern of macroeconomic policy-makers and academics, but since the crisis it has become an important topic of public debate.

Given the enormous impact of the global financial crisis and the continuing problems of dealing with its after-effects, issues of reform from an intellectual, institutional and policy perspective have been a major topic of concern in academic and policy debates. Accordingly, this book attempts to address some of the issues relevant to this debate in an effort to contribute useful ideas. Of particular concern to me as an economist have been the reform of financial regulation, the reform of the international financial architecture and reforms in the theory and practice of macroeconomic policy. These are big topics and have been and will continue to be in the years ahead the focus of important academic and policy debate. Clearly, the emphasis they have been given in the period since the crisis represents one of its major legacies. In this book, my intent has been to highlight some of the key aspects of these topics and to suggest possible new approaches that could be considered in the various reform efforts that are needed. In view of the extent to which financial globalization has become a dominant feature of the present-day international economic order, I believe that the greatest challenges for policy and institutional reform relate to the international financial architecture.

At the end of the book, by way of a summary, I identify a number of lessons and conclusions from the experience of the global financial crisis that need to be addressed and considered if future crises of this magnitude are to be avoided.

Many people have contributed to my thinking on the issues raised in this book since the outbreak of the crisis. In this connection, I would like to express my appreciation for the valuable fellowship of colleagues and students at the Duke Center for International Development and the Johns Hopkins School for Advanced International Studies, where I have been teaching for the last decade or so. These academic centers are dedicated to the highest standards of professional training for graduate students and young government officials from around the world in an inter-disciplinary approach to public policy and international affairs, with a strong emphasis on international economics and economic development. My interactions in and outside the classroom have provided numerous opportunities to reflect on the ideas expressed in this book.

I also wish to acknowledge the invaluable work experience I enjoyed at the International Monetary Fund, where I was a senior staff member for many years. This institution plays a central role in the international financial architecture and epitomizes the meritocratic and technocratic ideals of an elite international organization on a par with the best national traditions of public financial administration. This book could not have been written without the work experiences I had in its regional and functional activities. Again, my interactions with colleagues of the Fund during and since my tenure there have influenced my thinking on many of the issues raised in this book. Needless to say, none of the three institutions mentioned above should be implicated as endorsing any of the views expressed in this book.

Finally, I wish to acknowledge the very able assistance I received from Xiaoxiao Zhang, a recent graduate of the School for Advanced International Studies, in putting together the charts presented in this book and on its cover.

Anthony Elson
Chevy Chase, MD, USA

PREVIOUS BOOKS BY THIS AUTHOR

Governing Global Finance: The Evolution and Reform of the International Financial Architecture

Globalization and Development: Why East Asia Surged Ahead and Latin America Fell Behind

CONTENTS

LIST OF CHARTS

CHAPTER 1

Introduction

This book deals with the stability of the global capitalist system and how it can be made to work better. Few if any persons alive today can remember the Great Depression of the 1930s, but that event has been recalled many times since the onset of the global financial crisis of 2008–09, which brought about the Great Recession. The impact of the recent crisis in terms of lost wealth for households and corporations has been enormous. Moreover, seven years after the onset of the crisis, its effects are still being felt in many advanced countries, as output and employment in the European Union remain below pre-crisis levels, and real wage stagnation, low inflation and weak economic growth have been continuing problems in the United States. Except for the extraordinary government intervention and expansionary monetary and fiscal policies, it is quite likely that a repetition of the Great Depression would have occurred in the aftermath of the 2008 crisis. However, as a result of the government's rescue operations, there has been a sharp increase in the public debt of the countries most affected by the crisis. There has also been an unprecedented expansion in the balance sheets of the central banks of the countries most affected by the crisis, as they have aggressively pursued unconventional monetary methods to promote economic recovery with only moderately successful results. Moreover, it will take a number of years for these fiscal and monetary positions to be stabilized or normalized, with uncertain economic effects as that process is carried out.

© The Author(s) 2017
A. Elson, *The Global Financial Crisis in Retrospect*,
DOI 10.1057/978-1-137-59750-2_1

Both of the crisis events noted above were preceded by a speculative activity (first in the stock market and more recently in housing), which was supported by excessive and high-risk financing by banks and other financial institutions. These phenomena have come to be known as "bubble" activity, which have not been uncommon in capitalist economies because of the effect of herding behavior among buyers of real or financial assets. In these events, risk is inappropriately priced in financial markets, with the result that investment is misallocated. (In the second half of the 1990s, the "dot-com" bubble was in plain sight as market participants were coming to terms with some of the financial spillovers from the IT revolution.) At some point, a change in market expectations occurs, partly induced by a tightening of monetary policy, and a crash in asset prices ensues, which causes severe losses in the banking sector and for indebted households. The drop in household and corporate wealth, together with a sharp decline in bank lending, leads to a severe cutback in economic activity. Why these financial excesses (booms) and retreats (busts) at the national and global level take place and what can be done to diminish their likelihood in the future is the subject of this book. In a world of uncertainty, an economy based on decentralized markets and private decision-makers is subject to a variety of shocks (both natural and technological) and changes in investor sentiment, which can lead to cycles in the pace of economic activity, but near-catastrophic events that lead to a complete breakdown of the system as in 2008–09 should not occur.

It is important to be clear about what is meant by a capitalist or global capitalist system. Capitalism is usually defined to mean an economic system in which the means of production are in private hands (private property), as distinct from socialism, where those means of production are under public control such as in the form of state enterprises and/or worker cooperatives. In this book, the term is also intended to carry the connotation that the economic system operates on the basis of decentralized markets in which changes in relative prices for goods and services determine the allocation of resources in the economy, as distinct from the decisions of a central planning authority under socialism.

Since the mid-1980, it has been fashionable in the social science literature to refer to "varieties of capitalism" to capture the idea that there is not one single model of capitalism, as reflected, for example, in the different roles that the government plays in the liberal market economy of the United States compared with the coordinated market economies of Germany and Scandinavia and the mixed-market-based and state-run economy of China. Apart from their role in setting the rules and regulations for the operation of markets and conduct of business activity, governments can differ in the degree to which they play a direct role in investment, production and trade or in capital-labor relations and social welfare arrangements.[1] In this book, I will not dwell on these differences, as the contemporary global economic and financial system has tended to minimize differences among capitalist economies through the effects of global competitive forces arising from trade and financial integration and the impact of multinational financial and non-financial corporations, at least among those countries of the North Atlantic region where the effects of the crisis were most virulent.

It needs to be recognized at the outset of any discussion of the capitalist economic system that this system has been the greatest engine for economic prosperity and reduction of poverty in the history of mankind to date. From the middle of the nineteenth century until 2007, the year prior to the outbreak of the global financial crisis, real per capita income for the leading economy in the global system (the United States) expanded at a compound annual rate of 1.8 percent a year, which raised average real per capita income (in 1990 US dollars) from US$1849 to US$31,655 over that time span. During the previous four and a half centuries, income levels on a comparable basis were virtually stagnant, growing at a compound annual rate of 0.17 percent.[2] Notwithstanding such gains, global capitalism has produced substantial inequality in the distribution of income and frequent bouts of boom and bust, with the development of a financial system that has been essential for the expansion of investment needed to improve productivity and living standards. What is at stake, then, in the discussion that is laid out in this book is how the global economic and financial system can be made to work better so that the negative side effects of its growth and expansion can be minimized.

Economic and financial crises were largely absent in the immediate post-WW2 era. During the third quarter of the twentieth century, national economies were relatively closed in terms of trade and financial flows and banks were subject to tight regulation. Then, with the onset of globalization in the late 1970s and the growth in international capital flows, there has been a series of financial crises that have affected both emerging and advanced countries alike. The most recent one of 2008–09 has been the most severe and global in scope and has raised major questions about the stability of the global economic and financial system. In terms of foregone output, the economic cost of the global financial crisis for the US economy on the basis of actual and forecast GDP through 2018 has been estimated at nearly US$11.5 trillion, a staggering sum. This calculation includes the loss in output due to a reduction in potential GDP as a result of the financial crisis (US$3.6 trillion) as well as the loss in output with respect to a lower trend line of potential GDP (US$7.9 trillion). In addition, it has been estimated that the additional loss in output that would have occurred in the absence of the fiscal and monetary interventions of the government could have amounted to at least US$9 trillion.[3]

The growth in economic and financial globalization in the last four decades has been truly remarkable. A standard way for measuring the growth in globalization is to look at the increase in the global stock of financial assets and liabilities as well as the annual flows in trade and finance in relation to global GDP all measured in US dollars. All of these four aggregates have grown sharply since 1975, and in particular since the late 1990s, but the growth in financial aggregates has far outpaced the growth in trade (Chart 1.1). In the former case, the stock of global financial assets and liabilities—reflecting mainly debt, portfolio investment, foreign direct investment and financial derivatives—has expanded from around US$6 trillion in 1980 to somewhat more than US$200 trillion in 2007, just prior to the onset of the global financial crisis. Most of this growth took place among the advanced countries, rising from around 68 percent of

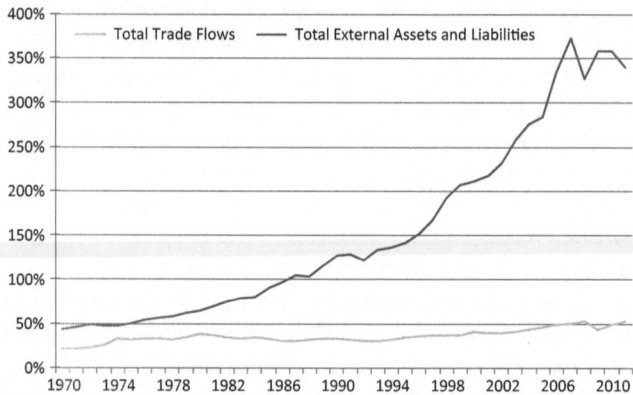

Chart 1.1 Total external assets and liabilities and trade flows as a percent of World GDP (*Source*: World Trade Organization and External Wealth of Nations Database (http://www.philiplane.org/EWN.html))

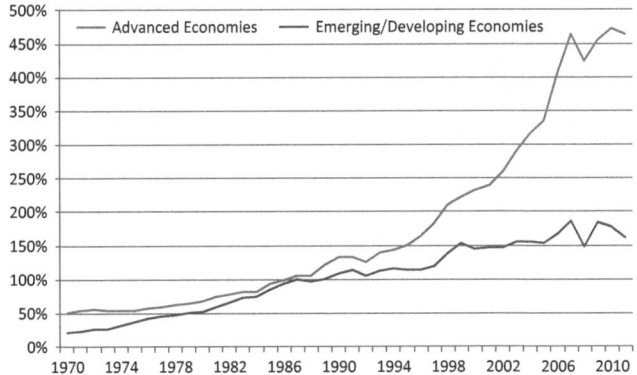

Chart 1.2 External assets and liabilities as a ratio to GDP (*Source*: External Wealth of Nations Database (http://www.philiplane.org/EWN.html))

their combined GDP to 463 percent in 2007 (Chart 1.2). During the period 2000–07, which represented the period of housing bubbles in the US and selected European countries that preceded the crisis, this ratio doubled. Most of the expansion in global financial assets and liabilities has been reflected in an increase in international debt stocks as a result of the growth in cross-border banking and flows in international debt securities (Chart 1.3). Again, this growth was particularly strong in the period of the housing bubble preceding the global financial crisis, during which international debt stocks rose by a factor of more than three times.

The aggregate flows of goods, services and financial transactions at the global level provide another striking image of the expansion in globalization. From 1980 to 1995, these flows represented on average around 22 percent of global GDP, mainly because of the impact of global trade in goods. However, over the next 12 years, including in particular the seven years leading up to the global financial crisis, these flows as a share of GDP more than doubled, mainly because of a surge in global financial flows, reaching a peak of 53 percent of GDP in 2007. The largest component of these flows was in the form of cross-border bank loans, reflecting a major expansion in the scale and scope of large multinational financial institutions.[4] By 2009, there was a substantial reduction in the size of these flows, amounting to 22 percent of global GDP, thus completing the cycle of boom and bust that accompanied the global financial crisis during the first decade of the new century.

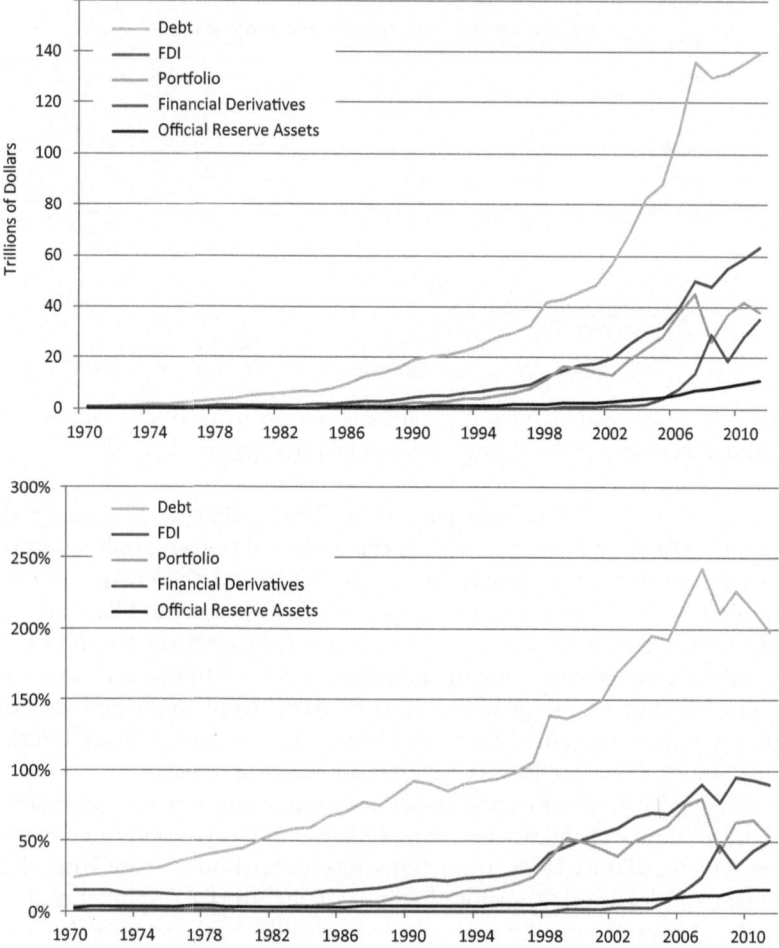

Chart 1.3   (a) External assets and liabilities by instrument (in trillions of US dollars). (b) External assets and liabilities by instrument as a ratio to GDP (*Source*: External Wealth of Nations Database (http://www.philiplane.org/EWN.html))

The decade preceding the recent financial crisis was seen as a relatively benign period of financial globalization, as the countries involved in the Asian financial crisis of the late 1990s were recovering and reforms had been made to strengthen the international financial architecture (IFA), which comprises the institutional arrangements charged with overseeing the global financial system. In addition, a broad consensus had developed about the potential benefits that economic and financial globalization could bring. The expansion in foreign trade and direct investment since the mid-1970s had proved to be a powerful force in promoting economic growth among the advanced and emerging market economies alike. More generally, the growth in the global financial system has provided a number of indispensable benefits in support of the global capitalist system. First, global finance has made possible the extraordinary growth in the cross-border flow of goods, services and capital through international banking and capital market operations. Second, it has improved the allocation of investment through the identification of new business opportunities and ventures beyond national borders. Third, the growth in international capital markets has expanded the scope for improved risk management for savers and investors within national borders. Finally, it has increased the possibilities for consumption smoothing of agents in individual countries in the face of shocks or volatility in the flow of their income.

Notwithstanding these important benefits, however, the global financial system has also demonstrated its capacity to foment cycles of boom and bust in the financing of asset price bubbles and to increase the risk of financial crises because of the volatility of short-term capital movements and the phenomenon of "sudden stops" in capital inflows. In addition, there has been a rapid growth in financial trading activity, related in part to the advent of high-speed computer transactions, that goes beyond the socially useful functions of finance identified above and represents a misallocation of resources and a threat to the efficiency of capital markets. In order to maximize the benefits of global finance and minimize its risks, it is essential that governments establish and maintain an effective set of arrangements for the IFA that is discussed further below and in Chaps. 5 and 7 of this book.

In the period leading up to the recent crisis, three fundamental tenets about the global capitalist system were widely held in academic and policy circles, which have now been largely discredited. The first was that market-based, free enterprise economies had the capacity to maintain a relatively steady pace of employment and output growth, and in the event of periodic departures from that trend, they had the flexibility to be largely self-correcting such that they could recover that pace mainly through the effect of natural economic forces. In a global system, these tendencies were thought to be mutually reinforcing if the major economies operated close to their potential output level with low inflation by means of each country's focus on domestic macroeconomic stabilization and a flexible exchange rate policy.

The second tenet was that financial markets were efficient in the sense of their ability to reflect quickly all relevant and available information for the determination of asset prices so that investment flows could be allocated to their best use on a sound basis and risks could be well diversified. In a globalized economy, this tendency was to be enhanced through the free flow of capital and market-determined exchange rates.

The third and final tenet was that economies based on capitalist principles did not display any systematic bias in the determination of income distribution and that factor rewards were largely determined according to the relative contribution of labor and capital to output growth. At the global level, it was expected that with the free flow of capital, especially foreign direct investment, a process of economic convergence would unfold, so that over time disparities in real income per capital among the advanced and developing countries would be reduced.

The basis for each of these three tenets, and how they have come to be challenged, is explored in subsequent chapters. The following paragraphs highlight some of the main points of that discussion.

The notion of the national economy as an equilibrium system, under which deviations from trend growth would be naturally self-correcting, is an old notion in economics. In the wake of the Great Depression, this tenet of "classical" economics originating in the nineteenth century was the focus of attack by John Maynard Keynes in his celebrated book, *The General Theory of Employment, Interest and Money*. It is interesting to note how frequently his name and this book have been mentioned since the onset of the recent financial crisis, as both academics and policy-makers have struggled to understand its origins and deal with its effects. However, with the advance of macroeconomics as a discipline since the time of Keynes, his name and work had largely been set aside by both mainstream academics and policy-makers as more sophisticated theoretical frameworks were developed. In the course of that work, a modern or New Classical paradigm became very prominent in the period leading up to the crisis that reinforced the idea of the national economy as an equilibrium system.

In practical terms, this notion was reinforced by the success of "inflation targeting" and the experience of the "Great Moderation", which led to a significant reduction in the variability of output and inflation since the late 1980s. This experience led many policy-makers to believe, consistent with the prevailing academic paradigm of the economy prior to the crisis, that severe disruptions associated with business cycles were a thing of the past.

A key element in understanding the dynamic of periodic booms and busts is that banking and financial activity typically plays a vital role in promoting both phases of these economic cycles. Such booms and busts are contrary to the predictions of the efficient market theory of finance noted earlier. Thus, it is important to understand why banks operate in the way they do and what role the governmental framework of regulation and supervision can and does play in augmenting or dampening that source of instability. In a world of globalized capital flows, it turns out that contrary to the second tenet explained above, the potential destabilizing forces of banking and finance can be augmented and transmitted rapidly from one country to another. As shown in Chart 1.4, the growth in cross-border banking positions was particularly strong in the decade leading up to the global financial crisis, rising from a stock of around US$20 trillion in 2000 to around US$60 trillion in 2007, mainly among the advanced countries. Because of the development of dense cross-border networks among financial institutions engaged in international financial transactions, instability

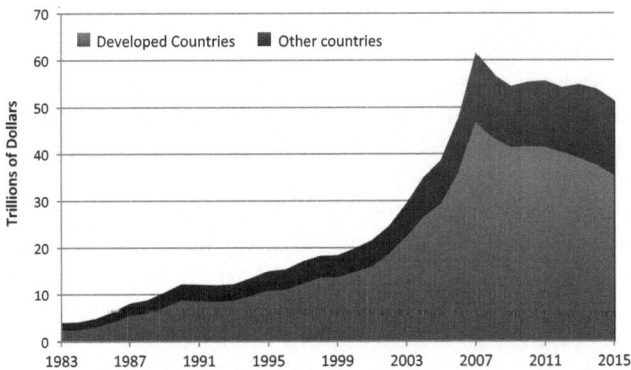

Chart 1.4 Total assets and liabilities for banks' cross-border positions (in trillions of US dollars) (*Source*: Bank for International Settlements, International Banking and Financial Statistics)

in the financial markets of one country can be quickly distributed across borders through the linkages of these networks. This phenomenon was in full display in the global crisis of 2008–09. As a result, the resolution of the crisis of necessity has had both national and international dimensions.

At the international level, efforts have been made since the establishment of the International Monetary Fund (IMF) in 1944, and in particular since the onset of financial globalization, to reinforce and expand what has been called the international financial architecture (IFA). The IFA represents the collective effort among the major economies to establish a network of cooperative arrangements, both formal and informal, to promote stability and sound functioning of the international monetary and financial system. Some of the main tasks of the IFA have been to exercise oversight of global financial stability, to promote international policy coordination and cooperation on financial regulatory standards and to provide an international lender of last resort (ILOLR) mechanism. Obviously there were major defects in these arrangements in the period leading up to the global financial crisis. Accordingly, in understanding the origin of global booms and busts and to limit their occurrence in the future, one must identify the defects in the IFA and develop a multilateral reform agenda for the future. Such a process has been under way in the wake of the crisis, but it is not clear that it will be sufficient to resolve the problems that contributed to the crisis and bolster global financial stability on a lasting basis.

The issue of income inequality in the United States and other advanced economies was largely ignored in public debate prior to the crisis, even though it had been a growing problem for many years. The burden of adjustment on many lower and middle class families in the aftermath of the crisis, however, has aroused particular concern about the major disparities in income distribution that have developed over the last 30–40 years. This concern has been heightened, in part, by the research and publication in 2014 of Thomas Piketty's book, *Capital in the 21st Century*, which clearly documented the deterioration in the distribution of income in the advanced countries, especially since the onset of globalization. This book, the title of which is reminiscent of Karl Marx's famous book of the nineteenth century about the capitalist system of that era, has demonstrated that contrary to the predictions of modern growth theory, there are certain tendencies (or "laws" in Piketty's terminology) in the global economic and financial system that give rise to a skewed distribution of income. Rather than simply the result of an abstract notion of factor rewards, Piketty argues that institutions and political power have a significant impact on the distribution of income. One manifestation of these forces may be reflected in the decline of labor income as a share of total income in a number of advanced countries. From the 1950s to around 2000, this share was relatively constant at around 65 percent, but after that year it declined to just below 55 percent by 2013.[5]

At the global level, it seems that the forces of globalization have exacerbated income distribution within countries to a significant extent with the growth in financial market activity and the demand for high skilled labor in IT-based industries. By the same token, one can observe that there has been some convergence in GDP per capita between the advanced and certain developing countries (witness the growth of China and East Asia). Nevertheless, the disparity in income per capita between the richest and poorest countries has increased with the growth of globalization. For the purposes of this book, it needs to be understood that financial globalization and income inequality were intertwined in that the former played a role in exacerbating income distribution in the advanced countries and that the latter was a factor in the bubble phenomenon that preceded the crisis.

One additional flaw in the global capitalist system that needs to be recognized is the problem of climate change. Patterns of industrialization and the use of fossil fuels to support the growth of manufacturing have led to an unsustainable rise in carbon emissions, which pose a serious threat to all the natural habitats and patterns of life on the planet. The most advanced economy in the global system (the United States) and the fastest growing economy (China) are in fact the two largest polluters. In basic economic terms, the problem of climate change reflects a massive market failure, in the sense that the cost of carbon emissions has not been properly reflected in the relative prices of goods and services dependent on the use of fossil fuels for their supply. It can be argued that globalization has exacerbated the problem of climate change as the growth of manufacturing has spread throughout the global system along with the growth of trade and foreign direct investment. However, the issue of climate change will not be addressed directly in this book as it has not had a significant impact on or been impacted by the problem of global booms and busts, which is central to this book. Nevertheless, there is a role for the financial system in supporting the development of renewable energy sources and mitigating the impact of economic growth on climate change in order to promote a more sustainable pattern of economic development, which is noted briefly in Chapter 5 of this book.[6]

The three tenets described above and the empirical reality that contradicts them will be explored in more detail in the subsequent chapters. These issues are central to any evaluation of the stability and efficiency of the global capitalist system. First, one needs to understand how these distortions and departures from idealized norms arise and then determine what kind of government intervention is appropriate or feasible. In such an analysis, it needs to be recognized that the power and influence of special or vested interests play an important role in determining the government policy that may make it possible for pre-crisis conditions to develop. One example of this tendency was the repeal of the Glass-Steagal regulation in 1999, which limited commercial banks from engaging in the trading of securities and other financial instruments typical of investment banks. At the time, officials in the US Treasury Department and leaders in the US Congress, under intense lobbying from the major banks in the New York financial community, believed that the repeal of this legislation would remove an important barrier to an improved operation of the banking system and financial markets. Among other things, the legislation repealing Glass-Steagal (the Gramm-Leach-Bliley Act) allowed large commercial banks such as Citibank to become even larger universal banks with operations spanning insurance, investment and commercial banking operations. This reform also expanded substantially the scope for financial activity outside the perimeters of traditional banking activity in what has come to be known as the "shadow" banking sector through innovations in the use of securitized instruments. Consistent with the tenets of the efficient market theory of finance, these developments were seen as an improvement in the financial system, which did not warrant close supervision and regulation. In the event, however, these changes paved the way for the major banks to engage in reckless, speculative behavior associated with the housing bubble that preceded the recent financial crisis. Because banks like Citigroup incurred major losses as the crisis unfolded and were considered "too big to fail", the US government ended up providing close to US$500 billion in liquidity support, capital injections and loan guarantees from the Federal Reserve and the US Treasury for that bank alone, the largest amount for any financial institution.[7]

In the wake of the crisis, issues of political economy, as revealed by the influence of powerful interest groups in the financial community exercised on Congress or directly on government agencies, also played a role in determining the nature and scope of the government intervention. In the field of monetary policy alone, the challenges faced by governors of the Federal Reserve have been unprecedented. The problem of dealing with the zero lower bound for policy interest rates for a sustained period of time, the uncertain effects of quantitative easing and the threat of a significant reduction in potential output (or "secular stagnation") for an indeterminate time in the future have put an unusually heavy burden of experimentation and uncertainty on central banks not only in the United States but in Europe as well. This burden is more troublesome, given the fact that the use of quantitative easing and liquidity creation in order to lower long-term interest rates to promote investment and spending has had the unintended effect of exacerbating income inequality via the capital gains it has promoted with higher yields for a variety of financial assets which are traded mainly by high income groups. In addition, the search for yield in this low-interest-rate environment has meant that financial transactions have focused on more risky investments with the potential for new bubbles and financial instability to develop.

An examination of all the aspects relevant to an understanding of the issues raised above would be beyond the scope of one book. My intent is to examine the global financial crisis of 2008–09 as an example of the extreme tendencies of the global economic and financial system and to understand why they exist and what can be done to moderate them. In the course of the study, I will attempt to identify the main ideological, institutional, policy and political economy factors that affect the stability of the system, which the reader can pursue by means of the various references and sources cited in the footnotes to the text. On the basis of this analysis, I will identify the main lessons of an analytical, institutional and policy nature that should be drawn from the global financial crisis and its aftermath in order to minimize the possibility of a similar crisis in the future.

The main topical content for the remaining chapters of the book is as follows. Chapter 2 examines the origins and consequences of the global financial crisis of 2008–09 in more detail. While unprecedented in the post-WW2 era in terms of its scale and reach, this crisis shared certain features common to other financial crises that have occurred in the age of globalization with regard to its origins and propagating mechanisms. In particular, the chapter discusses the links and chain of causation across a number of advanced countries: from an asset bubble in housing to severe distress in financial markets and then to a major downturn in economic activity. In this context, the unprecedented growth in "shadow" banking activity outside the purview of normal regulatory oversight and the widespread cross-border distribution of securitized financial instruments and other derivatives will be examined. The global dimension of the financial crisis cannot be fully understood without an appreciation for the role of international capital flows, as reflected in the problem of global imbalances and the complex web of gross capital flows among the advanced countries. At the same time, the chapter will show how the crisis could not have occurred without a complete breakdown in the formal and informal institutional mechanisms for the supervision, monitoring and control of financial activity, which are essential for the stability of modern capitalist systems. The chapter will also examine why the recovery from the crisis has endured so long and why it has been deeper and more long lasting than recoveries from normal recessions.

Chapter 3 highlights the development of orthodox and mainstream thinking in the advanced countries since the middle of the last century regarding the stability of market-based economic systems and the efficiency of markets for financial assets. While these issues have been subject to continuing debate among academic economists and policy-makers, what is striking is the degree to which a benign consensus on these issues had been reached in the period leading up to the financial crisis. This consensus was reflected in the widespread support for the economic and financial globalization, liberalization of financial markets, promotion of derivative trading and primary focus of monetary policy on inflation targeting. The strongly held belief in the underlying stability of modern capitalist systems was, to a large extent, grounded in the presumed efficacy of principal-agent relationships underlying business and financial contractual relationships and the soundness of their internal risk assessments. The stability of a market-based economic system was also grounded in the prevailing macroeconomic models used by many academic economists and policy-makers, which made no allowance for financial instability and sustained departures from macroeconomic equilibrium.

Chapter 4 examines the unprecedented challenges for macroeconomic policy in the wake of the economic and financial crisis that have persisted far longer than any other downturn since the Great Depression. In the field of monetary policy, these challenges have been reflected in the emergence of the zero lower bound for short-term policy rates of the major central banks and their experimentation with "quantitative easing". Much less consensus has been formed for the conduct of fiscal policy, with broad political support initially for a counter-cyclical fiscal stimulus, followed by unproductive debate and some withdrawal of fiscal support of economic recovery on both sides of the Atlantic. A sustained decline in medium- to long-term interest rates in real terms has raised concerns about the possibility of "secular stagnation" as a continuing challenge for the regularization of fiscal and monetary policies.

Chapter 5 focuses on the complications for managing an economic recovery, given the global dimensions of the crisis affecting Japan, Western Europe and the United States. The particular problems facing the euro zone arising from its currency union, the defects of its Stability and Growth Pact and the debt problems of its southern tier (and Greece in particular) will be examined. The chapter will also highlight the defects of the international arrangements that governments have put in place (i.e., the IFA) to promote international policy coordination, global financial stability and a harmonized system of financial regulation, which contributed to the onset of the global financial crisis and have frustrated its resolution. Clearly, financial globalization had expanded at a pace that far exceeded the capacity of the IFA to manage.

Chapter 6 examines the impact of modern capitalist systems on income distribution and the problem of income inequality in the advanced countries, which was largely ignored in public debate prior to the crisis, even though it was clearly becoming more distorted in the period of time beginning well before the end of the last century. A view that income distribution would improve as countries develop, which had been formulated in the 1950s and 1960s, remained largely unchallenged. The focus of debate has shifted since the outbreak of the crisis in view of its significantly negative effects on low- and middle-class incomes and because of the landmark study on the long-term evolution of income and wealth inequality, noted earlier, by Thomas Piketty (*Capital in the 21st Century*). The chapter explores the connections between events leading up to the crisis and the exacerbation of income inequality as regards the contribution of public policies and the growth in the size and scope of financial sector activity. The chapter will also identify a number of public policy reforms in the financial sphere that have the potential to halt or partially reverse the trend of income inequality, most of which will require some time to have an effect.

Chapter 7 evaluates some of the major regulatory and institutional reforms at the national and international levels that are needed to minimize the risk of economic and financial crises in the future. At the national level, these involve an expansion in the scope of monetary policy beyond the short-term employment and inflation goals to include financial system stability. This change also requires an adjustment in the scope of regulatory policy from one that focuses primarily on the prevention of undue risk-taking by individual financial institutions (micro-prudential supervision) to one that promotes overall stability in financial market operations (macro-prudential supervision). At the international level, the chapter will explore the efforts that are needed to improve the governance and functioning of the IFA so as to promote greater stability of the international monetary and financial system. In particular, the roles of the IMF in international policy coordination and as an LOLR are highlighted. The case for a sovereign debt restructuring mechanism is also examined.

Chapter 8 focuses on the criticisms that have been triggered by the crisis on the role of mainstream macroeconomics in promoting ideas that contributed to the onset of the crisis, such as the notion of the national economy as an equilibrium system and the efficient market theory of finance. While there has been much debate on the veracity and relevance of these two conceptual paradigms to macroeconomic analysis and policy, there has also been a strong appeal for the consideration of alternative frameworks for economic analysis. The chapter considers two such frameworks, namely the approach of behavioral economics and the implications of complexity theory. The chapter will also review the growing interest in alternative approaches for the teaching of economics, which would involve both mainstream and heterodox ideas and conceptual frameworks, and a greater emphasis on economic history and the history of economic thought.

Chapter 9, the concluding chapter, summarizes the main conclusions and lessons of a policy, institutional and ideological nature that can be drawn from an analysis of the factors giving rise to the global financial crisis and of the challenges of dealing with its consequences and aftereffects. This discussion will also highlight the main challenges that need to be overcome and reforms that need to be instituted in order to put the global economic and financial system on a more sustainable basis. Many of the reforms that are being implemented or need to be formalized, particularly in regard to the IFA, will require careful monitoring and review on a sustained basis for a number of years to ensure that they are having their desired effects. This requirement poses perhaps the greatest challenge for democratic political systems in which the focus of debate is on a range of short-term policy issues and the impact of long-term goals are discounted until another crisis occurs.

SUMMARY AND CONCLUSION

The global financial crisis of 2008–09 was a near cataclysmic event that involved major economic and financial costs on a scale that had not been evidenced since the Great Depression of the 1930s. Both of these events have revealed the extreme tendencies of global financial capitalism and the challenges of maintaining financial stability so that the potentially strong benefits of the capitalist system can be maximized. These challenges have become more difficult with the enormous expansion of financial globalization since the 1970s, whereby the growth of cross-border financial flows and linkages among financial institutions has far exceeded the growth in the international trade of goods and services. During the first quarter century following WW2, financial crises were relatively rare events because of the tight controls that governments maintained on financial activity, both nationally and internationally. But with a shift toward financial liberalization during the last quarter of the twentieth century, financial crises became more common, mainly among the developing and emerging market economies, as these countries struggled to develop the institutional arrangements and policy tools to deal with financial globalization. The global financial crisis was the first such event to involve the advanced countries on a major scale. The spread of financial crises has been a continuing challenge for the IFA, which represents the cooperative institutional arrangements (such as the IMF) that the governments have put into place to promote global financial stability. The failings of these arrangements and the need for further reforms are a major focus of this book and will be examined in subsequent chapters.

The global financial crisis has also revealed significant flaws in the mindset of many economists and policy-makers in the period leading up to the crisis, which projected a benign view of the inherent stability of a market-based capitalist system and the efficiency of a liberal financial order. The first of these two ideas had been the focus of attack by John Maynard Keynes in his analysis of the causes of the Great Depression. However, the framework of his thinking had largely been abandoned with the development of alternative macroeconomic models that supported a policy of inflation targeting, as validated by the experience of the Great Moderation, which preceded the global financial crisis. The notion of efficient financial markets was viewed as essential for the promotion of sound investment and fostered a relaxed attitude on the part of financial regulators regarding the self-regulating capacity of financial markets. This posture largely ignored the important role that financial markets and institutions can play in promoting economic booms and busts.

The role of the capitalist system in promoting income inequality was also largely ignored prior to the global financial crisis as economists had tended to view economic growth and income convergence as coincident trends. This view has changed in the light of the economic effects of the crisis and the impact of a major study by Thomas Piketty on the long-term trends in income distribution in the advanced countries. These three elements in thinking about the aggregate economy prior to the global financial crisis are also examined in the subsequent chapters of this book.

NOTES

1. The "varieties of capitalism" is a vast topic in the political economy literature which is beyond the scope of this book; see Peter Hall and David Soskice, eds. (2001) *The Varieties of Capitalism: The Institutional Foundations of Comparative Advantage* (Oxford and New York: Oxford University Press) for a sample of this literature.

2. The estimates of real per capita income levels are taken from the Maddison database maintained by the Groningen Growth and Development Centre, which is available at www.gdgc.net/maddison. The growth rate in real income for the period from 1400 to 1850 is based on estimates for the United Kingdom.

3. These estimates are based on a report by Better Markets "The Cost of the Crisis: $20 Trillion and Counting" (July 20, 2015), which is available at www.bettermarkets.com.

4. These data are taken from Exhibit E1 in McKinsey Global Institute "Digital Globalization: The New Era of Global Flows" (New York, March 2016).

5. The phenomenon of the declining share of labor in total income is discussed in Roc Armenter, "A Bit of a Miracle No more: The Declining of the Labor Share" Federal Reserve Bank of Philadelphia Business Review Q III, 2015; pp. 1–9.

6. A recent study that examines the role of finance in promoting sustainable development is UNEP "The Financial System We Need: Aligning the Financial System with Sustainable Development" The UNEP Inquiry Report (October 2015).

7. The details of this assistance package are presented in the Final Report of the Congressional Oversight Panel (March 16, 2011).

CHAPTER 2

The Financial Crisis of 2008–09: Fragile Banking, Economic Bust and Deflationary Consequences

Much has been written about the recent financial crisis since its emergence in 2007, as analysts and commentators have tried to come to grips with its causes and linkages with the Great Recession. The simple fact that problems in the relatively small sub-prime category of the US mortgage market could spiral into international financial chaos was testimony to the enormous spread of financial globalization in the years preceding the crisis. Many of the features of the cross-border financial networks and the nature of global financial flows that laid the groundwork for the transmission of shocks from one country to another were not well understood by regulators and policy-makers prior to the crisis. Additionally, public and private forecasters in 2008 were not expecting an economic downturn of the magnitude that occurred in the wake of the financial crisis.

In an attempt to shed light on these issues, this chapter focuses on three aspects of the financial crisis. First, how did the specific causes of the recent crisis relate to financial crises experienced by other countries in the past? While there were unique conditions and characteristics of the crisis in terms of the role of "shadow" banks and new forms of securitization, certain commonalities with other financial crises can be identified. Second, the chapter tries to elucidate the fragility of the financial structure and the inverse pyramid of risk that had built up within that structure, which was at the center of the crisis. In particular, the crisis revealed the perils of an unregulated system of financial operations in which there was a complete failing of the private commercial market arrangements that

© The Author(s) 2017
A. Elson, *The Global Financial Crisis in Retrospect*,
DOI 10.1057/978-1-137-59750-2_2

normally safeguard the integrity and stability of the economic and financial transactions in a capitalist, market-based economic system. Third, the chapter focuses on the chain of links between the outbreak of the financial crisis in late 2008 and the immediate downturn in economic activity that followed. The problems in promoting a recovery from that downturn are taken up in Chap. 4.

The Ingredients of a Financial Crisis: What Was Unique and What Was Common?

Financial crises have been a feature of capitalist systems for hundreds of years. In their seminal book on the history of financial crises (*This Time is Different*), Carmen Reinhart and Ken Rogoff identify more than 500 financial crises that have erupted in capitalist-based economies since 1800. Most of these have taken place in North America and Western Europe. However, since the modern age of globalization began in the mid-1970s, financial crises were mainly associated with developing or emerging market economies until the global financial crisis of 2008–09. Financial crises essentially can emerge in three ways: one is a banking crisis, involving the insolvency of a large number of a country's banking institutions; a second form is an exchange rate crisis, involving the breakdown of a fixed exchange rate system or a collapse in the value of a flexible exchange rate, and a third is a public debt crisis involving the government's default on its domestic or foreign bonds. Quite often these crises can occur simultaneously, or in close sequence. For example, if a government defaults on its sovereign debt, which is widely held by domestic banks, this action by government can lead to a sudden loss of capital in the banking system and the insolvency of one or more banks, potentially giving rise to a crisis of confidence in the banking system. Alternatively, if a banking crisis occurs, this can follow or lead to a rush in capital flight, which can threaten a government's exchange rate peg or capacity to meet the demand for foreign exchange, thus giving rise to a sudden drop in the external value of the domestic currency and an exchange rate crisis. And if the government intervenes to bolster the capital position of banks considered "too big to fail", this action may lead to a significant increase in the government's debt burden. If the government's debt position is considered by market participants to be unsustainable, then it may confront a sudden jump in the risk premia on its bonds and difficulties in servicing its debt, and a debt crisis may develop.

The financial crisis of 2008 evolved essentially in the form of a banking crisis, although it involved non-bank financial institutions or "shadow" banks instead of the regular banking system.[1] In this regard, as explained below, the crisis in the United States erupted among financial institutions that operated completely outside the safety net or regulatory frameworks which apply to the traditional banking system. Because of the heavy commitment of public funds to bolster the capital position of banks considered "too big to fail" in both the United States and the European Union (EU), doubts about public debt sustainability were raised soon after the crisis erupted, in particular for a number of countries on the periphery of the euro zone. In these countries (especially Greece, Ireland, Portugal and Spain), what evolved as a banking crisis quickly turned into a public debt crisis, following a typical sequence from a banking crisis to a public debt crisis noted earlier. This second stage of the global financial crisis is examined in Chap. 5.

Why is banking so prone to crises? The business of banking is inherently risky as it involves the conversion of typically short-term liabilities (e.g., private sector demand deposits) into longer-term assets in the form of long-term loans to support purchases of homes by households (mortgages) or investment or commercial operations of businesses. In undertaking this activity of maturity transformation, banks play an indispensable role in capitalist systems. The development of a sound banking system is an essential ingredient in the economic growth of developing countries; studies have shown that finance leads economic growth in developing countries.[2] In the advanced countries, banks have facilitated the growth of commerce and serve as a common source of funding for the activities of large multinational corporations. In the economist's abstract world of perfect markets, banks are not needed, as savers and investors can deal directly with each other as they share full information and can cover the risks of borrowing and lending through market instruments that cover all sorts of contingent risks. However, in the real world, complete and perfect markets do not exist and thus banks are needed to facilitate the transfer of funds from savers to investors. On the liability side, banks offer a nominal return to individuals or businesses for their short-term deposits that provides a liquid asset for their cash requirements and payment needs, while on the asset side, banks search for the best investment outlet that offers a good rate of return, which in the aggregate can improve the allocation of investment.

There are risks for banks on both sides of their balance sheet, as depositors may decide to withdraw their funds without much notice or in large amounts if they fear that one or more banks may be in trouble. On the asset side, bankers cannot know with certainty how borrowers will use the proceeds of their loans. To mitigate these risks, governments have developed deposit insurance to give confidence to individual depositors and more stability in the funding for banks, while banks typically require borrowers to provide collateral assets as a guarantee for the repayment of loans. At the same time, governments have created central banks as the lenders of last resort to provide liquidity to banks in the event they suffer a sudden withdrawal of deposits and are unable to find willing buyers for their investment assets in order to raise cash to meet depositor demands. These two forms of public support to promote the stability of the banking system at the same time create a "moral hazard" for banks, in that with the benefit of this safety net they may be more willing to pursue risky investment ventures in the hope of higher financial rewards. Accordingly, a proper regulatory framework and active bank supervision are required to minimize that moral hazard.

It should be noted that the inherent risks for banks in their act of maturity transformation is compounded if a bank is internationally active and may be involved in currency transformation as well—that is, borrowing in one currency and lending in another. If a bank borrows short-term funds from a foreign financial institution denominated in a currency different from its own to make a domestic currency loan, the bank may face capital losses in renewing that funding in the event of the depreciation of the domestic currency. In these circumstances, a bank is facing what is called a "double mismatch" of risk on its balance sheet—one of maturity and the other of currency—which greatly increases the potential risk of insolvency involved in its operations. In an age of financial globalization, double mismatches of risk have been an important factor in most financial crises.

In the traditional textbook version of money and banking, banks are heavily reliant on deposit accruals (or retail funding) to fund their commercial lending operations and must maintain a certain proportion of those deposits as reserve balances with other banks or the central bank to meet reserve requirements or liquidity needs in the event of deposit withdrawals. In this environment—which best typifies the situation of a small-town thrift institution, credit union or commercial bank—the money supply and stock of bank credit is determined by the central bank through its issue of so-called base money or high-powered money (i.e., currency issue and bank reserve deposits) and the cost of borrowing reserves in the inter-bank market that it determines through its open-market operations. The money supply (narrowly or broadly defined) and thus bank credit are determined by the interaction of base money and the money multiplier or the ratio between the money supply and base money. The latter, in turn, is determined by the reserve deposit ratio or reserve requirement of the central bank and the currency-deposit preference of the public. However, in a world of large commercial banks that are active in the capital markets and "shadow" banks that are fully reliant on funding in the capital markets, this textbook view of banking is inadequate and misleading. In such a world, the stock of bank credit and money or liquidity is determined mainly by the lending activity of banks, and the central bank has only indirect control of bank credit through its influence over short-term interest rates in the inter-bank market for reserves. In this view of banking, a commercial bank seeks out lending opportunities or responds to the demand for funding by investors by creating loans, as a result of which it creates counterpart deposits that borrowers use in the course of the commercial activity for which bank funding was sought. Within this framework of analysis, the money supply increases as bank lending grows and banks borrow reserves from other banks if they face a deficiency of reserves for purposes of reserve requirements. This alternative view of the process by which the growth in money and credit is determined is consistent with the shift in central bank policy over the past few decades: from a focus on quantitative magnitudes such as base money and the money supply to one focused on the cost of credit through variations in the central bank's short-term policy rate.[3]

In the case of the "shadow" banking system, which does not provide bank deposit services for individuals, funding for investment banking operations is provided by other non-bank financial institutions in the form of short-term repurchase agreements (or "repos") or commercial paper (wholesale funding). In this system, the risk of maturity mismatch is accentuated as the investment activity of the non-bank ("shadow") financial institution is long-term in nature and the funding is typically of an overnight maturity that has to be renewed on a continuing basis with the pledge of collateral linked to the asset being financed. Short-term borrowing or leverage tends to be maximized, given the tax advantages of interest payment deductions and the goal of maximizing returns on invested equity in the institution. As discussed below, leverage played a very key role in the development of conditions that led to the global financial crisis.

In virtually every case, a banking crisis has been associated with an economic boom or "bubble" phenomenon typically in the housing market, in which households or businesses engage in a frenzy of activity and banks get involved in the prospect of easy profits. Among emerging market economies, banking crises have often been associated with a program of financial liberalization, involving the lifting of interest rate controls or lending restrictions on banks. In these conditions, a banking crisis develops because of two fundamental problems. One is that banks become eager to lend but do so without the proper internal controls and risk assessment procedures that banks need in order to operate successfully in a liberalized market environment. The other is that the government fails to put in place an appropriate regulatory or supervisory environment to assess the riskiness of bank operations in a more liberalized environment and to ensure that banks are adequately capitalized. In the case of the Asian financial crisis of the late 1990s, these conditions were fully at work in the banking crises that Korea and Thailand experienced. In addition, governments in those countries actively encouraged their banks to borrow short-term funding from abroad to finance domestic lending operations, thus exposing them to the potent risk of double mismatches noted earlier. The banks were relaxed about the risk of a currency mismatch in their lending operations as they believed that the government was committed to maintaining a fixed exchange rate or would cover their losses in the event of any currency depreciation.

The role of financial institutions in fomenting a housing or stock market boom and the critical funding mechanism of leveraged finance or borrowed funds as distinct from equity capital in supporting such a boom point to the essential feature of rapid credit or asset growth of financial institutions as the main predictive indicator for a financial crisis. In fact, in the course of examining the features of banking and financial crises over a number of decades, academic studies since the outbreak of the crisis have identified a boom in the growth of financial credit as the most important predictor of a financial crisis.[4] In the case of the United States, for example, the growth in mortgage debt was particularly strong in the years prior to the financial crisis, rising from US$3.9 trillion in 2000 to US$9.1 trillion in 2007 (see Chart 2.1)

One important analyst of financial crises whose work has pointed to the critical role of bank credit expansion is Hyman Minsky. According to his "financial instability" hypothesis, banks play an inherently destabilizing

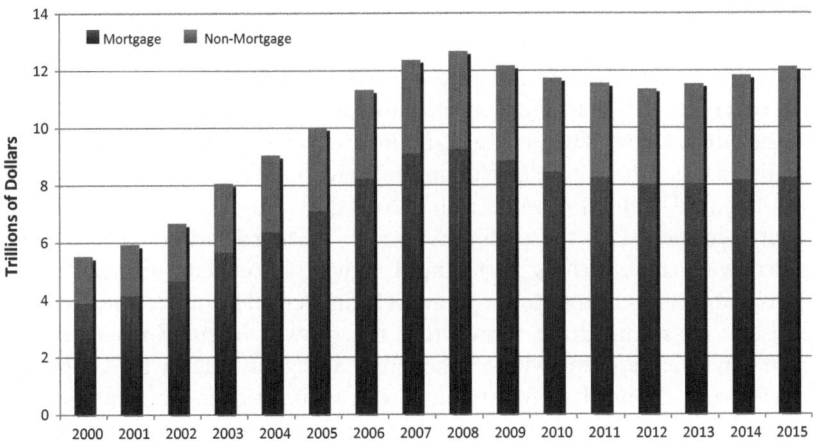

Chart 2.1 Total US household debt 2000–15 (in trillions of US dollars) (*Source*: New York Federal Reserve Bank, Consumer Credit Panel)

role in the economy in the absence of effective bank regulation and supervision.[5] This tendency is most clearly in evidence during periods of relative calm in economic activity, when banks are under increasing pressure from shareholders and boards of directors to increase their profits and return on equity. Accordingly, bank managers seek out increasingly risky ventures and investment opportunities in an effort to improve their profitability. Over time, banks take on higher risk in their lending activity, especially in the context of herding behavior, which inevitably leads to losses and the possibility of a banking crisis as banks reach a stage of what Minsky called "Ponzi finance", in which they make loans simply to enable the debt service on existing loans to be repaid. In the lead up to the global financial crisis, this behavior was clearly evident in the refinancing of mortgages during the housing bubble and in the operations of the major US banks, which participated in the securitization boom through the mechanism of off–balance-sheet special investment/purpose vehicles (SIVs/SPVs). The oft-quoted statement of the former Chairman of Citibank (Chuck Prince) that "while the music is playing, you have to get up and dance" speaks perfectly to the motivations underlying Minsky's "financial instability" hypothesis.[6]

More recent research has shown—consistent with Minsky's "financial instability" hypothesis—that the financial sector can expand in ways that are destabilizing for the overall economy. As noted earlier, a grow-ing financial sector is clearly correlated with economic development and is an important contributing factor to the economic growth of nations. However, according to the work of Thomas Philippon, in the decade prior to the Great Depression and again in the lead up to the global financial cri-sis, there was a sharp acceleration in the growth of financial intermediation and financial sector profits as a share of GDP.[7] Some of this growth has been identified with the phenomenon of "financialization" that is asso-ciated with the churning of financial activity as reflected in high-speed transactions and momentum trading. Of further relevance to the financial crisis, other studies have shown that the growth of the financial sector itself can reach a point where it becomes a negative factor for economic growth and financial sector stability, as it is likely to have been the case in the United States on the eve of the financial crisis.[8] As noted earlier, financialization was also a factor in the exacerbation of income inequality in the United States prior to the global financial crisis, which is examined in Chap. 6.

THE PYRAMID OF RISKS PRECEDING THE GLOBAL FINANCIAL CRISIS

In the case of the global financial crisis, one can see the typical case of the growth of financial activity associated with a bubble phenomenon. In the early 2000s, a boom in housing sales developed in the United States in part with the encouragement of two large government-sponsored entities (GSEs-Fannie Mae and Freddie Mac), which were created to refinance mortgage lending by private institutions through their long-term borrow-ing in the capital markets. The US Congress was particularly interested in promoting home ownership among low-income families and thus man-dated that Fannie and Freddie refinance the so-called sub-prime loans originated by savings and loans or other mortgage lenders with little or no down payment on the part of their customers. Then, with the assistance of Countrywide Financial, the largest and most active lender in the sub-prime lending category, the two GSEs created so-called mortgage-backed securities (MBS)—which were financial assets comprising both regular and sub-prime loans—that were sold as a securitized financial instrument with the underwriting of investment banks. These were the initial steps involved in the creation of a financial boom that operated completely out-side the scope of the traditional banking sector and the purview of any regulatory structure. Both the GSEs and institutions like Countrywide were subject, in principle, to regulatory oversight by specialized agencies, but both of these agencies exercised a very light touch and limited inspection in their supervisory activity.

The creation of securitized instruments such as MBS was an example of useful financial innovation as it expanded the scope of financing for home-buyers and mortgage lenders and created a new long-term investment vehicle for investors in the capital market. It also changed the nature of mortgage lending in that what was traditionally an operation of "originate to hold" for the asset side of a mortgage lender became one of "originate to distribute". Instead of holding a mortgage for the duration of its term as an investment of the lending institution ("originate to hold"), that institution simply became an intermediary in the creation of mortgage loans and their sale to another financial institution ("originate to distribute") that was specialized in the packaging of these loans in a new financial derivative instrument (or MBS) which was sold to investors in the capital markets.

What turned out to be problematic with this example of financial innovation is that it became subject to fraud and abuse and was not exposed to the careful risk assessment that would normally accompany securities sold in the financial markets. The fraud and abuse that set in at the stage of "originate to distribute" is that lending institutions began to lower the credit standards that they applied to sub-prime and other loans for low-income borrowers (so-called ALT-A loans)—because of the buoyancy of prices in the rising housing market—and did not disclose these defects in the loans which were sold to the packagers of MBS. These agents, in turn, did not properly disclose the quality of the underlying mortgage loans that they blended together in the MBS.

As the market for MBS and for other securitized instruments or derivatives such as collateralized debt obligations (CDOs) developed, other financial institutions became involved. CDOs had developed as hybrid derivatives or structured financial instruments that a large bank would typically create using a pool of its financial assets such as credit card interest due, student loan payments and often other receivables which it would transfer off its balance sheet through the device of these instruments. During the housing bubble, CDOs were used mainly to package together different tranches or pools of mortgages from different MBS that were judged to carry different degrees of risk. The fact that many different mortgages were pooled together in these tranches minimized the risk of the overall security, it was thought, as the risk of default of an entire class of mortgages was viewed as unlikely. Cash flows to CDOs were ranked from senior to junior, with any losses allocated first to the junior tranches as a form of protection to the more senior ones. As the market for these derivatives grew, further adaptations were introduced in the form of "synthetic" CDOs, which did not actually contain any mortgage-related assets but were designed to replicate their structure by means of another form of derivative known as credit default swaps (CDS; see below) as a means of speculating on the value of the original CDO or MBS.[9]

During this rapid expansion of the securitization process, the credit rating agencies (CRAs) failed to exercise due diligence in their assessment of the risk of these securities as they would for other securities (stocks and bonds) sold in the capital markets. In part, this failing can be attributed to the lack of full disclosure about the underlying elements packaged in the MBS/CDOs and the absence of experience as to their performance in the markets. More importantly, however, the CRAs were under great pressure from investment banks and other underwriters for the MBS/CDOs to assign a high credit rating to these securitized instruments (AAA in most cases) in order to attract buyers and to promote their appeal for financial institutions. Put simply, under the prevailing regulatory framework, AAA securities held by banks were not subject to any capital charge in the determination of their capital adequacy. An important institutional and fiduciary deficiency within these private market arrangements was that the CRAs were subject to a major conflict of interest as they were paid by the investment banks and other financial institutions that traded in the securities they rated. Thus they were under great pressure in the case of the MBS/CDOs to give them high credit ratings if they wanted to maintain a good business relationship with these firms. As a result, the first tier of a fragile pyramid of risk was created with these securitized instruments.

Money market funds were prominent providers of short-term funding for the purchase of these securities, which banks in the United States and Europe held either directly on their balance sheet or in off–balance-sheet SIVs/SPVs (special investment/purpose vehicles). The attraction of the latter legal entity is that it was not subject to normal regulatory oversight or minimum capital requirements except for the condition that any assets held in SIVs in the case of a withdrawal of funding or their illiquidity had to be transferred to the balance sheet of the parent financial institution, in which event they would become subject to regulatory scrutiny. Typically, SIVs would be established with minimal capital and would borrow very short-term loans from a money market fund in the form of REPOs or commercial paper to invest in medium to long-term MBS and CDOs, which served as the collateral for the SIV's funding instruments. Major investment banks such as Bear Stearns, Lehman Brothers and Goldman Sachs also became significant buyers and sellers of securitized assets, and these institutions, while nominally subject to the oversight of the SEC, had become essentially exempt from supervision. As a result of its rulings in 2004, the SEC in effect exempted investment banks from formal capital adequacy requirements and allowed each of them to determine their net capital requirements for market and derivatives-related credit risk on the basis of their own internal, mathematically based risk models.[10] The intent of this change was to put large investment banks, such as Bear Stearns and Lehman Brothers, on the same footing as regards the proposed requirements of the new Basel II capital accord, which established that the large commercial banks could determine their capital requirements on the basis of internal risk models. In effect, this change allowed these banks to substantially increase their leverage in the trading and acquisition of MBS and CDOs.

As a result of the minimization of equity requirements in the operations of these financial institutions and SPVs, a very profitable business was developed on the basis of heavy borrowing or leverage, the proceeds of which were used to invest in securitized instruments. Prior to the crisis, the degree of leverage in this non-bank or "shadow" banking sector of the financial markets—that is, the ratio of total assets to capital—typically rose to around 30:1 and even as high as 50:1. The fragility of this mode of operation, as a second tier in the fragile pyramid of risk leading up to the global financial crisis, was revealed by the fact that most of the borrowing was extremely short-term, typically overnight in the case of REPO financing from money market funds. In addition, with leverage ratios of 30 to 1, any impairment in the value of MBS/CDOs of, say, 3–4 per cent would eliminate the equity of the entity, using mark to market accounting rules, and push it into insolvency. In such a situation, the only safeguard against this fragility was an expectation on the part of the funders of SPVs that in the event of any impairment in the value of MBS/CDOs they would be brought back onto the balance sheet of the originating bank. What is remarkable about the lending or investment operations of "shadow" banks prior to the crisis is the rapidity with which these institutions were able to gear up to high levels of leverage for purposes of participating in the housing finance boom, and then unwind these operations as funding began to disappear.

The third tier of the inverse pyramid of risk that developed with the financing of the housing boom prior to the financial crisis of 2008–09 was the development of credit default swaps (CDS) as another form of derivative instrument related to MBS, CDOs and other securitized instruments. As in the case of CDOs, CDS contracts were traded over the counter—or directly with counterparties—instead of being traded on an exchange and cleared through a clearinghouse, as in the case of swaps and options for stocks and bonds.

CDS were developed by investment banks and large insurance groups, such as the American International Group (AIG), as a form of insurance against the possibility of any loss in the value of MBS and CDOs. At the end of the 1990s, senior officials in the US Treasury Department recommended that trading of these derivatives should not be subject to any regulation, as distinct from derivatives sold on exchanges. This recommendation was maintained over the objection of the Chairman of the Commodity Futures Trading Corporation, who predicted that the absence of any regulation of derivative trading would expose the financial system to undue risk. Subsequently, this recommendation was endorsed by Congress and embodied in the Gramm-Leach-Bliley Act of 1999, cited in Chap. 1, which also repealed the Glass-Steagal provision that prohibited commercial banks from engaging in the activity of investment banks. Nor would issuers of CDS need to hold any reserves to cover the possibility of their redemption in the event of a default in the underlying components of these securities. In effect, these provisions encouraged the use of CDS for purely speculative purposes. Those in support of the Congressional action, such as Treasury Secretary Lawrence Summers and Federal Reserve Chairman Alan Greenspan, argued that the creation of CDS was another useful innovation in modern finance in the direction of creating a more complete set of financial markets that would allow for improved risk management on the part of traders and investors. The only problem in this underlying faith in the efficiency of financial markets was that risk was severely mispriced in the issue and trading of securitized instruments and their associated derivatives, either because of improper disclosure about the risk of the underlying components of these instruments or misinformation on the part of traders who wanted to promote their sale. As a result, the purchase and trading in CDS became attractive to speculators who had no underlying position in MBS/CDOs but wanted to take bets on the safety of these securities.

What was remarkable about AIG's operations is that it was not only substantially involved in the sale of CDS but also involved in the purchase of CDOs through its securities-lending activities. Securities of AIG's life insurance subsidiaries, mainly in the form of corporate bonds, were loaned to banks and broker-dealers in exchange for cash collateral, which was then invested in a variety of other market-based financial instruments in which it was expected that AIG could earn a higher yield than that paid on the securities involved in its lending activities. In the period prior to the crisis, AIG steadily increased the share of its securities-lending activity based on the assets of its domestic life insurance companies as well as the share of those investments in CDOs of the kind described above. By 2007, that share is estimated to have reached 65 per cent. As a result, AIG was making bets on both sides of its balance sheet on the safety and soundness of new, untested securitized instruments related to the housing boom that ultimately proved to be disastrous to its financial solvency.[11]

Prior to the crisis of 2008, there had been a significant run-up in the value of housing and in the size of the "shadow" banking sector which had developed to support the housing boom. According to data collected by Economics Nobel Prize winner Robert Shiller, one of the creators of the Case-Shiller house price index, the median price of home sales in the United States rose by more than 80 per cent between the beginning of 2000 and the peak of the housing bubble in July 2006. Chart 2.2 shows the median house price in real terms, as well as the house-to-rent ratio, for the period 1983–2015. Both series show clear evidence of a bubble phenomenon during the period from the late 1990s through 2005. During this time period, there was also an explosion in the issue of non-agency based mortgage-backed securities, CDOs and CDS, as the funding vehicles for this bubble. According to data collected by the Securities Industry and Financial Markets Association (SIFMA), the outstanding value of non-agency MBS and CDOs rose from less than US$1 trillion in 2000 to US$4.1 trillion in 2007.[12] Meanwhile, the notional value of the outstanding stock of CDS rose from just under US$1 trillion in 2001 to US$58 trillion at the end of 2007 according to data collected by the International Swaps and Derivative Association (ISDA), which is illustrated in Chart 2.3.[13] The rise and then fall in the stock of CDS is perfectly consistent with measures of the housing bubble derived from the Case-Shiller home price index referenced above. This close similarity in these two data series suggests the great extent to which this derivative instrument became a primary tool for speculation (e.g., by means of synthetic

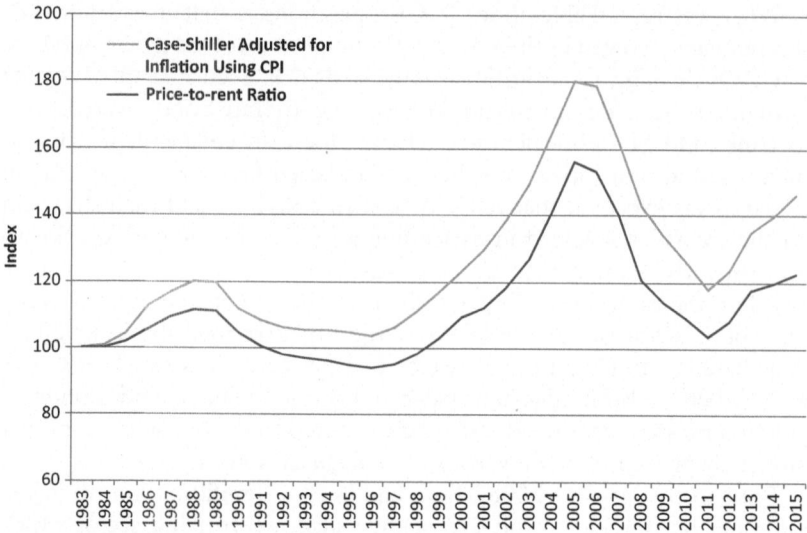

Chart 2.2 US real housing prices and house price to rent ratio for USA, 1983–2015 (*Source*: Bureau of Labor Statistics, Case-Shiller National Home Price Index)

CDOs) rather than a vehicle for insuring against a decline in the value of a mortgage bond contract.[14]

Another factor in the promotion of the housing boom was the monetary policy of the Federal Reserve. Coming out of the dot-com bubble which exploded in 1999, the Federal Reserve had reduced its short-term policy rate substantially in order to limit the impact of the loss in stock market wealth on spending and to sustain economic activity. The easy money policy of the Fed was maintained through the middle of the 2000s, which in itself acted as a spur to a run-up in housing values as the reduction in yield on stocks and bonds led investors to bid up the prices of other assets such as housing in their search for higher yields. A major question of controversy has developed over the issue of when the Federal Reserve should have begun to raise its short-term policy rate toward more normal levels in order to moderate the bubble in the housing market. According to one oft-quoted rule, based on a statistical model developed by Professor John Taylor of Stanford University, the Federal Reserve held its short-term policy rate at too low a level for too long a time.[15] The sharp

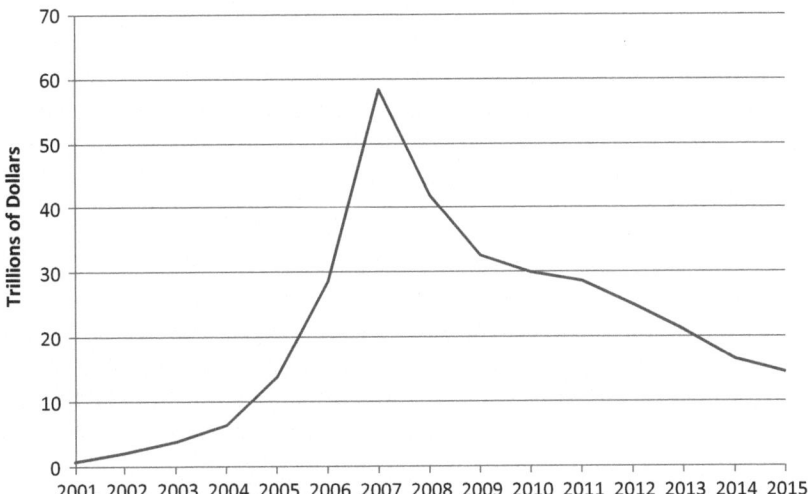

Chart 2.3 Notional value of credit default swaps (in trillions of US dollars) (*Source*: Bank for International Settlements, International Banking and Financial Statistics; International Swaps and Derivatives Association)

rise in this rate during 2006 was one factor in the collapse of the bubble in that year as the associated rise in mortgage lending rates made it more difficult to refinance mortgages for homebuyers, which served to put a brake on the bidding up of housing prices. During the housing boom, the quick rise in the equity value of homebuyers had allowed them to refinance mortgages that they had difficulty in sustaining.

From an international perspective, the fragility and high risk of the lending arrangements of the housing boom in the United States were matched by similar housing booms in Ireland, Spain and the United Kingdom. In a similar fashion to that of the Federal Reserve, the European Central Bank (ECB) during the period prior to global financial crisis pursued an easy monetary policy in which its policy rate was maintained at a very low level. In addition, large European banks became major participants in the trading and acquisition of securitized instruments associated with the boom in the United States. With the creation of the euro zone and a single financial market of its constituent member countries in 1999, banks in one country of the euro zone were allowed to do business in other countries. Cross-border bank lending also became attractive as risk premia, which had been relatively high for many borrowers in the southern tier countries of the euro zone, were sharply reduced with the creation of the single financial market. Accordingly, banks in the northern tier countries of the euro zone became active lenders to households, businesses and governments in southern countries based on the expectation that those governments would pursue a sound fiscal policy following the rules of the euro zone's Stability and Growth Pact and would not allow private creditors to default.

Looking outside the euro zone, major banks in Western Europe took an active interest in the market for securitized instruments in the United States. One common form of participation was that these banks would borrow on a short-term basis from money market mutual funds through their branches in the United States and then purchase MBS/CDOs. On a consolidated basis, these flows were treated as cross-border flows for the purpose of balance of payments accounting. However, the magnitude of these flows was largely misunderstood by analysts prior to the crisis. At that time, economists and policy-makers were mainly focused on the issue of global imbalances arising from the growing current account deficit of the United States and the expanding current account surplus of emerging market economies such as China and other countries of East Asia. The size of these imbalances was considered to be a problem, as the net capital outflows associated with the current account surplus of Asian and other emerging market economies was seen to be a factor in promoting and sustaining a housing finance bubble in the United States and some European countries. At the same time, there was concern about a sudden change in exchange rates, as governments were not allowing exchange rates to adjust in response to these imbalances or taking other monetary and fiscal measures to support the adjustment process. With the heightened focus on net capital flows between current account surplus and deficit countries, the size and implications of the gross flows between financial institutions in Europe and the United States were largely ignored. On a net basis, these inflows and outflows largely offset each other so that there was no impact on the current account position of these two regions.

Within the euro zone, however, a more typical phenomenon of financial flows between deficit and surplus countries was in evidence. While the aggregate current account position of the euro zone prior to the global financial crisis was roughly in balance, this outcome masked a sharp divergence in the competitive position of the northern and southern tier countries, which gave rise to surplus countries such as Germany and the Netherlands in the North and deficit countries such as Greece, Portugal and Spain in the South. Because of the generalized reduction in interest rates that took effect with the creation of the euro zone and the perceived reduction of credit risk of the Southern tier countries, banks in the North became active lenders to homebuyers in the South, thus sustaining a housing credit bubble in those countries and a current account deficit in the latter region.

FINANCIAL AND REAL ECONOMY LINKS IN THE TRANSITION FROM BOOM TO BUST

In order to explain the global financial crisis, one needs to understand the links between stress in the mortgage housing market and declines in economic activity on both sides of the Atlantic, which involve a number of sequential steps. The first element in this chain of linkages was the widespread circulation of securitized instruments in the form of MBS and CDOs. As noted earlier, these were attractive to banks and other financial institutions because of the broad-based market for their purchase and sale, the attractive ratings they were given and the availability of CDS to protect against the risk of their default. Once the underlying security of these instruments was placed in doubt and the perceived risk of default became more widespread, then the conditions for panic and the withdrawal of financing typical of a classic banking crisis emerged. The critical initial step in this tipping process was the end of the housing bubble and the deflation of housing prices beginning in 2006. One factor in this development was a change in expectations on the part of homebuyers and their financiers about the future course of home prices. Such a change is typical of any bubble phenomenon that has occurred in the past. In retrospect, it always becomes clear that a bubble was present in the run-up of prices for a given asset, but in real time it is difficult to predict when that turning point will occur. According to the home price data assembled by Robert Shiller cited earlier, the national index of home prices, based on a number of regional markets in the United States, rose by more than 80 per cent from January 2000 to its peak level in July 2006 and then fell by nearly the same percentage over the next five and a half years, which provides clear evidence of a bubble phenomenon. In a number of US cities, the index more than doubled in the upswing of the bubble.[16] This same pattern of home price adjustment was evident in a number of countries of the EU, and was particularly strong in the case of the United Kingdom, where average home prices more than doubled in real terms between 2000 and 2007.

It is also of interest to know what was driving the run-up in home prices. In the case of the United States, at least two factors have been identified. One is the rise of income inequality in the latter decade of the twentieth century that was creating an incentive for lower-income groups to pursue home ownership as a means of improving their relative wealth position vis-à-vis better-off groups in society. As explained later on in Chap. 6, there have been many factors at work in the rise in income inequality. One of them was the expansion in financial activity and the concentration of profits among financial traders and managers of large financial firms, which was on a rising trend in the years prior to the financial crisis. The role of income inequality in driving the housing boom was first propounded in a book by Raghuram Rajan (*Fault Lines: How Hidden Factures Still Threaten the World Economy* 2010) and further expanded in an elaborate study by Atif Mian and Amir Sufi (*House of Debt* 2014). To some extent, as noted earlier, this drive for income and wealth equality in the acquisition of homes was facilitated by the policy of Fannie Mae and Freddie Mac, at the direction of the US Congress, to encourage the expansion of sub-prime and Alt-A mortgages in order to promote home ownership on the part of the poor.

The other factor that can be identified in the housing bubble is that of speculation, which is common to all bubble phenomena. Homebuyers were active in the housing market in the expectation that their equity stake in a purchased home would increase quickly, allowing them to take on additional debt in the purchase of a larger home or the acquisition of household goods with which to furnish the home. There is some evidence that professional speculators were also active in the housing market simply for purposes of short-term financial gains, thus taking advantage of the presence of herd behavior.

One possible trigger for the change in expectations on the part of participants in the market was action taken by the Federal Reserve to reverse its easy monetary stance and raise its short-term policy rate to more normal levels. As noted earlier, one of the common criticisms of the Federal Reserve is that coming out of the dot-com bubble at the turn of the century it held its policy rate too low for too long a time, thus feeding the development of a new bubble. In any event, with the rise in long-term rates for mortgages during 2005 and 2006, the incentive for home buying was dampened. In addition, the burden of mortgage debt began to increase and the value of this debt began to rise above the value of homes for many buyers who provided little or no down payment for their purchases—which was typical for those in the sub-prime and Alt-A market. In these conditions, defaults on mortgage debt began to rise, which led to a weakened asset position for financial institutions holding such debt and doubts about the underlying safety of MBS in which low-income housing debt was embedded. With an increase in the rate of home loan defaults, creditors tightened the conditions or collateral requirements for their loans to home mortgage financial institutions and short-term financing for investors in MBS/CDOs, as well as the cost of CDS. However, with increasing doubts about the intrinsic value of these derivatives, the conditions for full-scale panic were created as the resale market for these securities dried up and the short-term funding for their investment (i.e., overnight REPOS/commercial paper) was withdrawn.

During 2007–08, the environment caused by these conditions created increasing difficulties for the "shadow" banking community, which was heavily committed to the financing of the housing bubble. The tipping point for the emergence of full-scale panic—on the part of traders in MBS/CDOs and the liability side of the "shadow" banking system—was the failure of Lehman Brothers in September 2008. Under the requirements of mark-to-market accounting, Lehman was facing mounting balance-sheet losses on its extensive holdings of mortgage-based securitized instruments as it approached the declaration of its insolvency. Prior to that point, financial market participants were not fully aware of the scale of its investment in MBS/CDOs and of the complexity of its financial relationships with other participants in the "shadow" banking system both at home and abroad. To a large extent, Lehman Brothers' true financial position—and that of other investment banks—was concealed by creative accounting practices at the end of any reporting quarter, which obscured its holdings of derivatives in order to re-assure investors or financial analysts of its financial soundness.[17]

The failure of Lehman Brothers and the unwillingness of the government to engineer a bailout of the institution led to doubts about the viability of other investment banking institutions and large commercial banks such as Citigroup, which were also heavily invested in securitized instruments through off–balance-sheet SIV/SPVs. Losses for these institutions then created problems for issuers of CDS, such as AIG, which had not set aside sufficient reserves to withstand any significant encashment of CDS against losses in the market for MBS/CDOs.

Defaults and bankruptcies in the "shadow" banking system following the failure of Lehman Brothers had negative ripple effects on other segments of the financial markets both in the United States and Europe, notwithstanding bold action on the part of the Federal Reserve and US Treasury Department to provide liquidity and equity support for financial institutions that were put at risk from these events. With full-scale panic rising in the "shadow" banking system and fears of contagion damaging the wider financial system, a generalized decline in financial-asset values took root in the last quarter of 2008 and early 2009.

At this point in the financial crisis, at least three channels of negative spillover effects spread from the financial markets to the real side of the economy. One was the decline in financial wealth, which dampened the confidence of consumers and investors in the future outlook for the economy and their willingness to maintain current spending levels. This channel could be identified with a negative "wealth effect" on spending, which has been explored in recent research by Jonathan Heathcote and Fabrizio Perri, who verified a significant impact on spending resulting from a decline of around 50 per cent in the real net worth of households with heads aged from 20 to 60 years.[18]

A second channel of negative influence from the financial crisis to the broader economy could be identified with what has been called the "financial accelerator". This phenomenon refers to the amplifying and dampening effect on spending arising from the cutback in new credit creation on the part of banks that were facing problems of insolvency or difficulties in maintaining lines of credit with other financial institutions or the broader capital markets as a normal source of funding for their lending activities. This balance sheet effect was a particularly potent force in the global financial crisis given the high degree of leverage and its fragility in the operations of the "shadow" banking system. Professor Ben Bernanke prior to his term with the Federal Reserve had established much of his academic acclaim for having established the importance of this second channel in accounting for the depth of the Great Depression.[19] It has now been shown that it played a similarly important role in bringing about the Great Recession of 2008–09. It is also important to recognize that modern financial sectors, such as the "shadow" banking system, were highly elastic and pro-cyclical in their effects on the broader economy, in the sense that they could expand quite rapidly with the benefit of high leverage to support a bubble phenomenon and could contract relatively quickly as well, with correspondingly depressive effects on the economy, as that leverage was reversed.

The third channel of negative spillover from the financial crisis to the broader economy was also shown to have played an important role in the Great Depression. This effect was identified by Professor Irving Fisher in the 1930s as the channel of "debt deflation" which referred to the negative impact on consumer spending arising from the heavy debt burden assumed by many households during the housing bubble, either directly through home purchases or indirectly through other forms of debt assumption at a time when a low interest rate environment was encouraged by the Federal Reserve for a number of years prior to the global financial crisis. When the housing bubble burst and interest rates started to rise, many households (and businesses) were faced with debts they could not sustain and began to cut back on non-debt-related spending in an effort to avoid bankruptcy. The authors of *House of Debt* cited earlier have shown that the impact of debt deflation was quite significant in the onset and duration of the Great Recession, as well as the slow pace of economy recovery since.

The negative economic consequences of the global financial crisis have been the most severe since the Great Depression. In addition to the losses in foregone output cited in Chap. 1, it is estimated that household net worth in the United States fell by US$16 trillion (or by 24 per cent) from Q3 2007 to Q1 2009. In addition, since mid-2009 real GDP has been on a recovery path that is 12 per cent weaker than the average path of previous cyclical recoveries. With the number of unemployed workers rising to 14.7 million or 12 per cent of the labor force by early 2009 (which is roughly matched by the number of underemployed and "discouraged workers" who dropped out of the labor force), it has been estimated that the cost in terms of the loss of security in the work force rose to as much as US$14 trillion.[20]

Notwithstanding some of the unique characteristics of the global financial crisis, it is clear in retrospect that it shared much in common with other financial crises that impacted emerging market economies in the 1980s and 1990s in terms of its origins, propagating mechanisms, and channels of negative impact on the real side of the economy. It is also the case that the crisis of 2008–09 shared much in common with leveraged bubbles of the past, according to research by Jorda, Schularick and Taylor (2015).[21] What is also true is that since the age of economic and financial globalization began in the late 1970s, both the frequency and impact of financial crises have increased over time. This unfortunate fact raises concerns about the inherent instability of the global financial system and the inadequacy of the international financial architecture that has been established to maintain its stability. These issues will be taken up in Chaps. 5 and 7.

Once again we have learned the fallacy of thinking that "this time is different" in the development of a housing or stock market bubble. It is also true, as will be discussed further in Chap. 7, that concerns about financial system stability need to be fully present in central bank deliberations about monetary policy.

SUMMARY AND CONCLUSION

The global financial crisis, which originated in the United States during 2007–08, was the result of multiple causes and factors originating within the "shadow", or unregulated, banking system that had grown to be as large as the traditional banking system on the eve of the crisis. As a result of the unregulated character of the "shadow" banking system, it fostered a rapid expansion in financial credit based on high leverage and low capital that are the typical features of a banking crisis. In particular, the "shadow" banking system was far more vulnerable to crisis than the traditional banking system, as it was funded typically by very short-term liquidity instruments (overnight REPOs and commercial paper) and was heavily invested in highly risky, long-term securities.

As in the case of many banking or financial crises, a bubble phenomenon had developed within the housing markets of the United States and other advanced countries in Western Europe, which was fueled by the rapid growth in credit in the form of newly developed, securitized forms of mortgage finance or mortgage-based securities (MBS) and collateralized debt obligations (CDOs). The availability of these securitized instruments allowed mortgage originators to tap into the capital markets as a means of financing home mortgages, especially those for low-income and poor households. This arrangement became the focus of fraud and abuse as mortgage originators contracted home loans without proper credit review and disclosure of the terms of the mortgage and investment banks marketed MBS and CDOs without proper disclosure of the risk and content of these derivative instruments.

The credit rating agencies (CRAs) also played an important role in fueling the development of securitization in the housing market by failing to exercise "due diligence" in the evaluation of MBS/CDOs. In many cases, the CRAs granted these securities AAA ratings on the basis of flawed statistical models that were used to assess financial risk and under pressure from the investment banks that issued and marketed them. The final piece in creating the fragile structure of household finance preceding the crisis was the expansion of credit default swaps (CDS) that had been developed originally to insure bondholders against market losses in the value of their securities and were widely marketed as protection against losses in the value of MBS and CDOs. These swaps were mainly issued by a large insurance firm (AIG) without proper reserves against losses that it would incur from significant investments it had made in MBS/CDOs and claims by the purchasers of CDS it had sold.

With the collapse of the housing bubble in 2006, there was growing concern in financial markets about the underlying value of AAA-rated MBS/CDOs and the institutions that issued them, which culminated in full-scale panic following the failure of Lehman Brothers in September 2008. Once the crisis erupted, there were clear knock-on effects from the financial turmoil that fed directly into a decline in consumer and investment spending and traditional banking operations, as is typically the case in the event of a banking crisis. These spillover effects of the crisis quickly had a negative impact on economic activity, thus bringing about the Great Recession.

The total economic and financial losses caused by the global financial crisis have been the most severe since the Great Depression of the 1930s in terms of foregone output, the loss of financial wealth and the burden of high unemployment. These losses and the slow pace of recovery in both the United States and those countries in Western Europe most exposed to housing bubbles prior to the crisis have highlighted the critical importance of financial system stability as a key objective of monetary and financial policy at the national and global levels since the crisis.

NOTES

1. Academic and official estimates suggest that the "shadow" banking system in the United States was at least as large as the traditional banking system on the eve of the financial crisis (see Daniel Sanchez "Shadow Banking and the Crisis of 2007–08" Federal Reserve Bank of Philadelphia Business Review Second Quarter 2014, pp. 7–14).

2. Two studies that review the relationship of finance and economic growth are Asli Demirguc-Kunt and Ross Levine, "Finance,

Financial Sector Policy and Long-Run Growth" Working Paper #11, World Bank Commission on Growth and Development (2008) and Group of 30 (2013), "Long-term Finance and Economic Growth" (Washington, DC).

3. This modern view of money and banking is explained in Michael Mcleay, Amar Radia and Ryland Thomas "Money Creation in the Modern Economy" Bank of England <u>Quarterly Bulletin</u> 2014 Q1, pp. 1–14.

4. See for example, Enrique Mendoza and Alberto Terrones, "An Anatomy of Credit Booms and Their Demise" NBER working paper #18379, September 2012.

5. Hyman Minsky's "financial instability" hypothesis is explained in "The Financial Instability Hypothesis" Working Paper #74, The Levy Economics Institute of Bard College, May 1992.

6. This phrase was taken from an interview of Charles "Chuck" Prince, Chairman of Citigroup, with the Financial Times on July 9, 2007: "When the music stops, in terms of liquidity, things will be complicated. But as long as the music is playing, you've got to get up and dance. We're still dancing."

7. These results can be found in Thomas Philippon, "Has the Finance Industry Become Less Efficient? On the Theory and Measurement of Financial Intermediation", Working Paper, Stern School of Business, NYU (September 2014).

8. See for example, Jean-Louis Arcand, Enrico Berkes and Ugo Panizza, "Too Much Finance?" WP/12/161, International Monetary Fund (June 2012).

9. A fuller account of the role of CDOs in the financial crisis is provided in Chap. 8 ("The CDO Machine") of *The Financial Crisis Inquiry Report* (2011) of the National Commission on the Causes of the Financial and Economic Crisis in the United States (New York: Public Affairs).

10. This rule change can be found at www.sec.gov/rules/final/34-49830.pdf (June 21, 2004).

11. AIG's operations leading up to its bailout in September 2008 are detailed by Robert McDonald and Anna Paulson "AIG in Hindsight" <u>Journal of Economic Perspectives</u> v. 29(2); pp. 181–205 (Spring 2015).

12. These data can be accessed at www.sifma.org/research/statistics.

13. Data on the outstanding value of CDS can be found on the website of the International Swaps and Derivative Associations (www.isda.org/functional-areas/research/surveys). Data for 2001–02 in Chart 2.3 are taken from the International Banking and Financial Statistics of the Bank for International Settlements (www.bis.org).

14. The use of CDS for speculative purposes was the main theme of Michael Lewis' book (*The Big Short*) and the movie of the same title.

15. An updated version of the Taylor Rule is explained in Taylor "Monetary Policy Rules and Discretion Doesn't: A Tale of Two Eras" Journal of Money, Credit and Banking v.44 (6) 2012; pp. 1017–32.

16. The Case-Shiller index of home prices can be accessed at us.priceindices.com/ index-family/real-estate/sp-case-shiller.

17. These transactions were known as "Repo 105" transactions (see www.accountingschoolguide/anatomy-of-an-accounting-scandal).

18. Jonathan Heathcote and Fabrizio Perri "Wealth and Volatility" Staff Paper #508, Federal Reserve Bank of Minneapolis July 7, 2015.

19. Ben Bernanke (1992), *Essays on the Great Depression* (Princeton, NJ: Princeton University Press).

20. These estimates are developed and explained in more detail in Tyler Atkinson, David Lutrell and Harvey Rosenblum "How Bad Was It? The Costs and Consequences of the 2007–09 Financial Crisis" Federal Reserve Bank of Atlanta Staff Paper #20 (July 2013).

21. Oscar Jorda, Moritz Schularick and Alan Taylor "Leveraged Bubbles" NBER working paper #21486 (August 2015).

CHAPTER 3

Why Did Economists Get It So Wrong?

Queen Elizabeth's query to a group of economists at the London School of Economics in November 2008 ("Why did no one notice it?"), after the global financial crisis had erupted, has been cited many times as epitomizing the public's dismay, if not anger, at policy-makers and academic economists for their failure to foresee the possibility of the crisis. Presumably, if a crisis was clearly in prospect, policy-makers would have taken steps to forestall or minimize its impact. (In some fundamental sense, it is contradictory to say that a crisis was expected, as the timing of a crisis is unpredictable or unexpected, by definition.) Nevertheless, it is appropriate to blame economists for not understanding the roots of the crisis.[1] Notwithstanding some measures by the US Federal Reserve and Treasury Department to contain the spillover effects of the sub-prime lending crisis, policy-makers and economists did not understand the dense network of financial relationships that made it possible for the failure of a financial institution such as Lehman Brothers to spread shock waves throughout the global financial system.

With the benefit of hindsight, one can point to at least three failures on the part of the economics professionals and policy-makers in their understanding of developments that were critical factors in the lead-up to the crisis. One was the failure to understand the nature of the "shadow" banking system in the United States and its rapid expansion and growth during the first decade of the current century, which can be traced to key decisions taken by policy-makers to broaden and diversify the financial system. The second failure was to ignore the rapid growth in overall credit in the financial system and its dependence on excessive leverage of financial institutions. This failure can be linked, in part, to widespread adoption of inflation targeting as the main, if not exclusive, policy objective by the central banks of the advanced countries. Finally, one can point to the failing of policy-makers to understand the dense network of cross-border financial relationships that had been building during the last quarter of the twentieth century and had expanded sharply during the decade prior to the crisis.

In order to explain how these failures came about, one must understand the intellectual climate or macro-financial framework that guided macroeconomic analysis and policy in the period leading up to the crisis. During this period, there was a remarkable coincidence of views on the part of policy-makers and leading academics regarding the lessons of experience and the appropriate design of monetary and fiscal policies to keep the economy on an even keel, without major risks arising in the financial system. One can point to three key elements, in particular, within this macro-financial framework: first, the emergence of a new macroeconomic consensus (NMC) among so-called new classical and new Keynesian economists, which was grounded in the "dynamic stochastic general equilibrium" (DSGE) modeling; second, the efficient market hypothesis (EMH) of finance and third, the Modigliani-Miller (M&M) theorem of corporate finance. Each of these key elements of the macro-financial framework that dominated mainstream academic and professional thinking prior to the crisis had been evolving and gaining popularity since the end of the third quarter of the last century and had reached an ascendency in the period just prior to the global financial crisis. One sign of the NMC was a judgment offered in 2008 just prior to the crisis by Olivier Blanchard, a professor of economics at MIT, which was the center of new Keynesian thinking, that "the state of macro is good".[2] Earlier, in a Presidential Address of the American Economics Association in 2003, Robert Lucas, the leader of the new classical school of macroeconomics based at the University of Chicago, had adopted a similar tone of optimism by declaring that the problem of depression economics had been resolved and that little time needed to be spent understanding the causes of the business cycle as the benefits of fine-tuning stabilization efforts were fairly minor in quantitative terms.[3]

The main point of the efficient market theory of finance, which has been most closely associated with the work of Professor Eugene Fama, also of the University of Chicago, was that the prices of financial assets traded in deep and liquid markets at any point in time fully reflect all available information. Thus, they are efficient in the sense that there are no differences with respect to fundamental values that can be traded away profitably by market participants, except on the basis of inside information that is not generally available to the market. In this sense, a bubble phenomenon in the stock market, as revealed prominently in the dot-com crash of the late 1990s, should not occur. Nor should there have been a run-up in asset prices for housing and the stock market prior to the global financial crisis. This theory, while not universally accepted, had an important impact on the official thinking about the benefits of seeking to expand and diversify financial markets through the development of derivatives and securitized instruments so as to make them closer to an ideal of "perfect" or complete markets, where sound investments could be financed, consumption-smoothing over time could take place and financial risks could be covered.[4]

The M&M theorem actually predates the other two pillars of the macro-financial framework just described, but it is closely related to the efficient market theory of finance. It has been the foundation for the modern thinking about corporate finance. Simply put, it propounded the idea that the value of a financial or non-financial institution was independent of the manner in which its asset holdings were financed. That is to say, the composition of a firm's liabilities as between debt and equity was irrelevant for purposes of determining the value of the firm, which was instead dependent upon its discounted flow of future earnings. Notwithstanding certain critical assumptions underlying this theory that do not apply to the real world, the basic idea of this theorem regarding the irrelevance of a firm's or bank's capital structure could have been falsely understood to justify a declining capital-asset position of financial institutions and their demand for high amounts of borrowing or leverage prior to the crisis. Each of the three propositions just identified is examined in the following sections of this chapter.

THE NEOCLASSICAL SYNTHESIS/NEW MACROECONOMIC CONSENSUS

The main questions that have been the focus of macroeconomics since the time of the Great Depression are (1) whether or not the economic system or aggregate economy is naturally self-stabilizing in the face of major disturbances or perturbations, and (2) how can it be made to operate at full employment with minimum volatility and price stability. Modern macro-economics was born in the wake of the Great Depression with the publication of Keynes' famous study, *The General Theory of Employment, Interest and Money*. Keynes' answer to the first question was decidedly negative in the light of the experience of the Great Depression, and in response to the second question he argued strongly for the role of government expenditure in expanding aggregate demand in response to a major compression in output and employment caused by a financial crisis in order to restore the economy to a position of full employment.

The debate about the self-stabilizing properties of the aggregate economy has been a perennial debate in the history of economic thought. At the time of the Great Depression, this debate was highlighted as one between Mr. Keynes and the classical economists (such as Malthus, Smith and Ricardo). The latter believed that with fully flexible prices and wages, aggregate demand would always be equal to aggregate supply (Says' Law) and that upturns and downturns in aggregate economic activity would always be self-correcting so that the economy would operate on an even keel. Keynes argued that there were times such as the Great Depression when a major collapse in private consumption and investment would occur in the wake of a financial crisis and that a fall in the level of real wages or shifts in relative prices would not be sufficient to revive economic activity. In Keynes' view, a fall in real wages, contrary to the tenets of the classical model, would simply reduce workers' income and further compress consumption demand, while investment demand would remain weak if the "animal spirits" of businesses were dampened because of the poor and uncertain prospects for economic growth. In these circumstances, the government through its budgetary expansion by means of an increase in outlays and/or a reduction in taxes could play an indispensable role in stimulating economic activity and restoring an environment that would be conducive to normal employment and business activity. Echoes of this historic debate have been evident in the policy discussions that were triggered by the emergence of the Great Recession in 2009. In this connection, it is striking to note how frequently references to Keynes and his General Theory have arisen in policy discussions in the popular media and the academic press as commentators and analysts have tried to come to grips with the fallout from the global financial crisis.

Following WW2, the debate between the Keynesian and the classical economists continued, with the former seeking to refine the underpinnings and extensions of the main analytical aspects of the General Theory, including the development of large macroeconomic statistical models that could guide policy decision-making. On the other side, the classical economists, mainly guided by the work of such luminaries as Milton Friedman of the University of Chicago, posed strong challenges to the Keynesian framework as being inconsistent with the tenets of microeconomic behavior and incorrect in its emphasis on the stabilizing role of monetary and fiscal policy.

In the late 1950s, an attempt at reconciliation between these two theoretical camps was attempted by Paul Samuelson, a dominant economic thinker at MIT, who defined the terms of a so-called neoclassical consensus in macroeconomic analysis. This consensus maintained that over the long term the aggregate economy did operate at a stable equilibrium according to the beliefs of the classical economists, but in the short-to-medium term, the tenets of the Keynesian framework applied because of rigidities or "stickiness" in the adjustment of prices and wages. Over time, it was understood that these rigidities could arise, for example, because of delays in the adjustment of retail prices in response to changes in aggregate demand (so-called menu costs) and of wage levels because of staggered contract arrangements, and because of monopolistic competition in the goods market. In these circumstances, changes in fiscal or monetary policies could have "real" effects in terms of their positive or negative impact on aggregate output and employment in the short run in response to temporary downturns in economic activity or surges in inflation, thus justifying a role for counter-cyclical fiscal and monetary policies to maintain the economy at or close to full employment with low inflation. The potential scope for monetary and fiscal policy adjustments was captured by the notion of the "Phillips Curve", which showed a roughly stable trade-off between price or wage inflation, on the one hand, and changes in employment or output, on the other. In principle, in accordance with the neoclassical synthesis, policy-makers could choose a point along this negative continuum between inflation and unemployment, and manage fiscal and monetary policies in such a way as to minimize macroeconomic volatility and stabilize the economy at close to its potential level of output with minimal inflation.[5] The origins of this neoclassical consensus could be traced to some of the early interpreters of Keynes' work, such as Sir John Hicks, and it became the standard framework for macroeconomic analysis in university textbooks for a number of decades.[6]

In the light of economic developments during the 1960s and 1970s, it became clear, however, that the stable trade-off between inflation and unemployment implicit in the Phillips Curve and the neoclassical consensus could not be exploited by short-term policy adjustments and that inflation and recession (or so-called stagflation) would result instead. Simply put, consumers would come to anticipate that when the monetary authorities pursued an expansionary policy to stimulate economic activity, they would only expect an increase in prices and would not adjust their real spending habits. In the light of this thinking, a "new classical" school of economic thinking emerged at the University of Chicago that argued that macroeconomic analysis needed to have microeconomic foundations in the sense that the theoretical behavior of consumers and firms in the aggregate needed to be grounded in timeless and stable preferences, based on the principles of utility and profit maximization and forward-looking or rational expectations.

Apart from the lessons of practical policy experience, this new classical revolution was inspired by two developments in economic analysis in the post-WW2 era. One was the increasing mathematization of economic analysis, in emulation of the physical sciences. This development, which was inspired by the work of Paul Samuelson, was defended on the grounds that economic "science" needed to develop more rigorous foundations for establishing the basis for economic theory and to foster the use of mathematical models to frame the analysis and understanding of real world economic problems and issues. The other development was the theoretical breakthrough of Kenneth Arrow and Gerard Debreu, who established in the mid-1950s a mathematical proof for the notion that subject to certain restrictive assumptions, a set of decentralized, competitive markets, in which consumers/firms would pursue utility/profit maximization in a general equilibrium framework, would bring about an efficient or optimum level of consumer welfare/satisfaction according to the principles of Pareto optimality. Pareto optimality was defined by an economic theorist (Vilfredo Pareto) of the late nineteenth century as a situation in which there can be no change in relative prices or resource allocation that would make one individual better off in terms of utility maximization without making someone else worse off. The importance of this mathematical result is symbolized by the fact that it became embodied in what has come to be known as the First and Second Fundamental Theorems of Welfare Economics.[7]

Notwithstanding the highly restrictive assumptions necessary for developing this mathematical result (as discussed below), it was considered conclusive proof for the desirability or optimality of the classical model of macroeconomics, in that an economy based on full price and wage flexibility and full market clearing would bring about a stable equilibrium consistent with full employment of its resources and an optimum level of consumer satisfaction, which can be understood as the goals of macroeconomics. On a more practical level, this result could be seen as the justification for a liberal economic policy framework in which competitive market forces should be given free rein and government intervention should be minimized to those actions that are necessary to support the development and effective operation of open, competitive markets.

The general equilibrium Arrow-Debreu model became the underpinning for macroeconomic theory and analysis over the next 50 years and the foundation for the new classical school beginning in the late 1970s. It also led to a focus on the importance of allocative efficiency in thinking about the aggregate economy, rather than on issues such as equity or income distribution. The debate over whether equity or efficiency should be seen as the overriding objective of economic policy was crystallized in a foundational book by Arthur Okun in 1965, and most mainstream economists since then have tended to favor the latter objective (i.e., efficiency) over the former, as Okun himself did.[8] The primacy of allocative efficiency was also implicit in the assumptions of modern growth theory, pioneered by Robert Solow, which focused on the long-term behavior of aggregate economy, capital accumulation and technological change.

Arrow and Debreu were clear as to the very restrictive assumptions of their mathematical model, yet these have often remained unquestioned in the implicit or explicit appeals to their model of complete markets in the work of mainstream macroeconomists, especially of the new classical school. By complete markets is meant the notion that in addition to fully flexible prices and wages implying open competitive markets and market clearing for all commodities, as well as labor, capital and financial assets, there exist a full array of futures markets to cover all conceivable risks and contingencies affecting the behavior of firms and individuals and their choices in present time. Within this system of complete markets, there are no frictions in the operations of the banking or financial system or limitations in the sharing of information between borrowers and lenders that prevent it from operating efficiently so that the needs of savers and investors are fully satisfied. This notion of perfect and complete markets was consistent with the classical idea of monetary neutrality or "money is a veil" in economic transactions, in that the financial system has no independent effect on the operations of the real economy, separate from the behavior of individuals and firms.

Notwithstanding this idealized state of a market economy, most mainstream academic economists have defended this theoretical construct and its economic effects as a benchmark against which to compare the observed results of economic behavior in the real world. One further appeal of the Arrow-Debreu model is that it is highly amenable to mathematical manipulation for purposes of developing theorems or fundamental laws of economic behavior. However, in applying these results for purposes of judging the appropriateness or desirability of observed economic outcomes, analysts have often forgotten to recognize the highly restrictive assumptions governing the results of their theoretical analysis and therefore the inherent limitations of drawing meaningful conclusions for policy or "positive" economics. It is also the case that the new classical theorists have ignored the implications of another important theoretical result that Gerard Debreu derived in collaboration with Rolf Mantel and Hugo Sonnenschein. Their theoretical work showed that there could be no basis for assuming the stability or the uniqueness of an equilibrium for the aggregate economy by extrapolating from the axiomatic results of the Arrow-Debreu model based on the postulates of rationality, a decentralized set of perfect markets and heterogeneous agents.[9]

While the new classical school of macroeconomists was extending and building on the foundations of the Arrow-Debreu model to understand business cycle phenomena and fluctuations in prices, output and unemployment, a parallel school of new Keynesian economists was looking at the effects on the behavior of the aggregate economy of altering or relaxing some of the key assumptions of the Arrow-Debreu model. In particular, what were the implications of the model for aggregate economic behavior and the role for monetary and fiscal policy when rigidities were introduced into the instantaneous adjustment of nominal prices and wages, as justified by extensive empirical research? As suggested earlier, such a change in the assumptions of the Arrow-Debreu model implied that aggregate output would respond temporarily to changes in monetary and fiscal policy if the aggregate economy was knocked off its normal path of output growth by some exogenous shock or change in technology.

Other Keynesian economists such as Joseph Stiglitz examined some of the implications for the Arrow-Debreu model of dropping the assumptions of full information sharing among market participants and perfect markets for risk management, which an analyst must do if s/he is replicating conditions of the real world. In such a world, Stiglitz clearly demonstrated that Pareto-optimum outcomes would simply not occur. Thus, there would potentially be a role for government intervention to compensate for these limitations in order to help the aggregate economy function more efficiently.[10] The results of this theoretical work were extended to other areas of the modern economy such as money and banking, where information asymmetries among lenders, borrowers and bank managers are clearly present, in order to understand the basis or causes of banking crises that have occurred in market-based capitalist systems with great regularity. The concept of asymmetric information could easily explain the need for deposit insurance, collateral requirements for borrowers and the regulation and supervision of banks. As suggested in Chap. 2, problems of asymmetric information and lack of supervision were clearly at work in the "shadow" banking system, leading up to the global financial crisis.

However, prior to the crisis, analysts were not examining the effects of asymmetric information in the "shadow" banking system. Rather, they were developing the theoretical justification for inflation targeting by central banks based on the results of so-called DSGE models. These models formed the basis for a new neoclassical or macroeconomic consensus (NMC) between the new classical and new Keynesian school of macroeconomics, which replicated the core notion of the neoclassical synthesis of the 1950s and 1960s but did so within a more sophisticated theoretical framework that was fully grounded in microeconomic principles.

Each of the words in the descriptor of DSGE models highlights a unique and essential feature of these models and the consensus. The term "dynamic" refers to the notion that these models are inter-temporal and forward-looking in nature, which means that expectations about the future play a role in determining present-day outcomes as, for example, in the role that the current and expected future path of interest rates play in determining consumption and investment. The word "stochastic" is based on the idea that each of the variables that make up the model, such as consumption, investment, employment and output is assumed to follow a pattern of fluctuation over time that contains a residual element which is random or probabilistic in nature. By this is meant that these variables are subject to shocks of one kind or another (perturbations/disturbances) that are real in nature, such as changes in technology. This feature of the model is intended to capture an essential feature of macroeconomic aggregates in real time that are subject to random disturbances over time, as distinct from a fixed linear or non-varying deterministic trend, as assumed in old Keynesian models. This definition carries the important implication that the key variables defined in the model are stationary (or trend stationary) in a statistical sense, which means that their range of variation has a normal probability distribution with a mean of zero and a fixed or finite standard deviation; thus, they follow a pattern of reversion to the mean, which implies that the effects of any shocks are transitory. It should be noted that while convenient from a mathematical point of view, the assumption of stationarity does not generally fit the behavior of macroeconomic time series in real time (see Chap. 8). Finally, the reference to "general equilibrium" means that the behavioral relationships defined in the model are inter-related and mutually consistent so that the value of key variables such as output, consumption and investment are completely inter-dependent in determining an equilibrium solution for a multi-equation model.

As in the case of the neoclassical synthesis, the NMC is based on an attempt to reconcile once again the basic tenets of new classical and new Keynesian frameworks for macroeconomic analysis. Each of these schools have adopted the DSGE modeling approach as described above, which in turn is grounded in Real Business Cycle Theory. The latter theory, which was developed in the 1980s, replaced the previous work at estimating behavioral relations for distinct parts of the Keynesian macroeconomic framework in order to explain business cycle variations with the notion that such fluctuations were mainly due to the economy's response to shifts in technology over time. In accordance with the basic principles of DSGE models, the economy's response to technology shocks over time would be governed by the aggregate equilibrium outcome of the optimal intertemporal decisions of households and firms operating under the principal of forward-looking rational expectations.

Based on these characteristics, DSGE models in their core postulate that households make optimizing decisions regarding consumption and savings based on their choice of (or "marginal rate of substitution" between) work and leisure in response to the real wage rate and a similar choice between present and future consumption based on the real interest rate. The latter variable is co-determined by the demand for investment, whereas the real wage rate is co-determined by the marginal product of labor. The model is populated by a "representative agent" operating under rational expectations, meaning that it behaves fully in accord with the optimizing assumptions of the model.

Under the new classical approach, business cycles could be explained as the equilibrium outcome of the economy in response to technology shocks in an environment characterized by fully flexible prices and wages, frictionless markets and perfect competition. In these conditions, there would be no need for stabilization or monetary policy, which in fact could be counterproductive. Thus, monetary policy was viewed as playing a neutral role in the economy, such that changes in monetary policy would have no real effects on the economy and would only bring about changes in the aggregate level of prices. Under the NMC, the neutrality of monetary policy was viewed as correct over the medium to long term, but in accordance with the new Keynesian approach in the short-to-medium term, monetary policy was viewed as non-neutral because of price and wage rigidity, as in the case of the neoclassical synthesis. Accordingly, changes in short-term nominal interest rates as a result of adjustments in monetary policy would not be matched by changes in expected inflation in the short term; instead, they would lead to changes in real interest rates with consequent effects on consumption, investment and output in accordance with the equilibrium conditions of a particular DSGE model.

In line with these features of DSGE models, the NMC also embodied a reformulation of the Phillips Curve of the previous neoclassical synthesis. Consistent with the rational expectations hypothesis (REH), expected prices were included in the formulation of the Curve rather than past prices or adaptive (or backward-looking) expectations. In addition, instead of including current or past levels of unemployment, the revised Phillips Curve included the gap between actual employment and its "natural" level. The natural rate of unemployment is not an observable statistic at any point in time but is rather a theoretical construct indicating the level of unemployment that is consistent with low inflation and maximum output at any point in time (in many discussions, the natural rate of unemployment is referred to as the NAIRU—the "non-accelerating inflation rate of unemployment"). The natural rate of unemployment is believed to vary over time, in accordance with changes in productivity, demographics and labor force behavior. One of the objectives of the central bank research activity among the advanced countries has been to provide estimates of this variable and its movements over time. Again, under the new neoclassical synthesis, the expectations-augmented Phillips Curve was seen as a guide to policy only during the short term when prices were "sticky" and the level of output differed from its "natural" level. Over the long term, an expansionary monetary policy would only lead to an increase in expected prices and inflation with no effects on output. In this respect, the Phillips Curve is converted to a straight vertical line when the rate of unemployment is at its natural level.[11]

The characteristics of DSGE models just described are desirable features from a mathematical or statistical point of view, but they imply a number of important limitations and restrictions in so far as they are intended to isolate and explain the behavior of certain key economic aggregates. One limitation relates to the so-called representative agent, which is used to account for aggregate economic behavior, which means that there is no allowance for variation in the behavior of individuals or effects on their behavior from any interaction with other agents. All consumers/investors are assumed to act in the same way so that a representative agent can be used as a symbol for aggregate behavior in the economy. Essentially, this device can be seen as a way of skirting the problems of the Debreu-Mantel-Sonnenschein theorem noted earlier. However, the notion of a representative agent is a highly unrealistic assumption to impose on the behavior of economic phenomena such as financial markets, which by their nature involve heterogeneous agents operating with different and evolving decision rules in response to their environment and anticipated changes in it. These economic phenomena are best described as an example of a complex adaptive system, which involves emergent behavior or structure that is distinct from that of its underlying agents. This approach is explored more fully in Chap. 8.

The second restriction is that the representative agent of these models is assumed to follow "rational expectations", in that his behavior is fully consistent with the inter-temporal or dynamic properties of the model and its predictions. This means that the agent is perfectly forward-looking in its behavior, which depends solely on the postulates or optimizing assumptions of the model, without interference or interaction with other agents. Finally, in line with the stochastic features of these models, the possible range of variation of each of the key variables is pre-determined by past experience in order to satisfy their stationary characteristic and the expectation of mean-reversion. Accordingly, any extreme variation in the behavior of key economic aggregates, as in a crisis situation, that is inconsistent with observed behavior in the past is ruled out. To the extent, for example, that the level of employment varies over time, this is explained in DSGE models simply as the optimal choice of a representative agent for more or less leisure or work, consistent with his preference for consumption over time and the level of the real interest rate and wage rate in the model, rather than any evidence of unemployment or imperfections in the labor market.

These characteristics would seem to limit severely the realism of DSGE models and their ability to explain in a meaningful way the behavior of key macroeconomic aggregates. In the wake of the global financial crisis, an active debate has developed focusing on precisely this issue, especially in light of the fact that DSGE models could not provide any insight into the activities in housing and financial markets that gave rise to the crisis. In one simple sense, the irrelevance of DSGE models in explaining behavior that preceded the crisis can be attributed to the assumption that, consistent with the notion of complete markets inherent in these models, the operations of a financial sector played a neutral role in real economic developments. By definition, any risk of default, illiquidity or insolvency that would create financial frictions or imbalances in financial markets, as in the period preceding the financial crisis, was assumed to be zero. Thus, financial factors and credit conditions were excluded from these models.

One of the main policy issues for which DSGE models were used was the determination of the central bank's interest rate policy in accordance with certain basic rules that would limit the use of discretionary monetary adjustments inconsistent with the basic tenets of these models. One such rule, as noted in Chap. 2, was the so-called Taylor Rule, which gained credibility in academic and policy circles because of its ability to track the general pattern of short-term interest rate adjustments over time by the US Federal Reserve. This rule was somewhat akin to the expectations-augmented Phillips Curve described above, in that it explained changes in the short-term policy rate of the Federal Reserve as the result of its response to conditions when the actual rate of inflation differed from its targeted rate and/or the level of output (employment) differed from its potential (natural) level. The magnitude of the Federal Reserve's response to deviations in the rate of inflation with respect to its inflation target was understood to be significantly greater than its response to the deviations of output or employment, given the primacy of its inflation-targeting regime. Prior to the global financial crisis, the framework of the Taylor Rule identified two important features of monetary policy. The first was the success of its inflation-targeting regime, which was evident in the experience of the Great Moderation that was discussed in the previous chapter of this book. Under the Great Moderation, the Federal Reserve was seen as successful in reducing the variability of both the rate of inflation and the output growth, which meant keeping the former close to its targeted level and the latter close to its potential. In this sense, the Federal Reserve's primary focus on inflation control was seen as bringing about the "divine coincidence" of low inflation and maximum employment during the period from the mid-1980s to the mid-2000s.[12] This experience confirmed one of the important policy implications of the NMC that pointed to the key role of the central bank in using its short-term policy interest rate in controlling inflation through a transparent inflation-targeting regime.[13]

The outbreak of the global financial crisis surely has subverted many of the postulates and axioms of the NMC, as it was powerless to explain or account for the emergence of a housing bubble, the growing leverage and fragility of the "shadow" banking system, the ensuing financial panic and crash, and its effects on the real economy leading to a sustained period of high unemployment and sluggish growth. In a basic sense, this failure can be attributed to the fact that the consensus framework completely ignored the role of a financial sector, because of the assumption of frictionless markets, and incorporated only one interest rate, that is, a short-term policy rate of the central bank that was utilized for inflation control. While the NMC envisioned a short-term role for monetary policy, this was miniscule in relation to the role that the Federal Reserve played in the wake of the Lehman Brothers' bankruptcy in terms of liquidity provision, asset purchases and capital injections. Such events were completely outside the range of stochastic variation allowed in DSGE models and the stationary behavior of the key economic aggregates they are intended to explain.

In the wake of the crisis, an active debate has developed about the validity and merits of DSGE modeling, much of it by means of commentary by academic economists and analysts participating in the "blogosphere" (e.g., John Cochrane, Paul Krugman, Paul Romer, Larry Summers). Since the crisis, there has been an explosion in the number of economist blogs that have raised important issues about the failure of macroeconomics to provide any insight into the causes of the global financial crisis and its future direction.[14] At one level, this discussion and analysis has led to adaptations of DSGE modeling to incorporate elements that were important in the lead-up to the crisis. At another level, questions have been raised about certain aspects of the methodology of academic macroeconomics that may be problematic and can be seen as having played a role in its failings in the wake of the crisis. These will be examined in more depth in Chap. 8 of this book, but some elements of this debate are useful to raise at this juncture in view of the previous discussion in this chapter of the role of DSGE models in academic macroeconomics. One concern about the methodology of modern economics, and macroeconomics in particular, that had been raised prior to the crisis and more actively since is its attachment to a reductionist or axiomatic deductive approach to model-building. Rather than developing testable hypotheses in an inductive manner based on the observation of data, from which theories can be extrapolated by trial and error, economics has proceeded from basic axioms about human behavior, based on utility and profit maximization subject to budgetary constraints. As noted before, economics has continued to be a highly mathematical field of inquiry in the sense that all economic theory is grounded and validated by a process of mathematical reasoning. This feature has been well suited to the deductive normative aspects of its inquiry and has been used to elaborate a highly detailed and sophisticated framework of analysis (while also serving in effect as a screening device for applicants to graduate training in economics and the acceptance of papers in leading economic journals). In a basic sense, the elaboration of DSGE models is a good example of this tendency and fully validates an approach to economic theory that was famously laid out by Milton Friedman in the late 1950s ("On the Methodology of Positive Economics").

In the light of the financial crisis, one can argue that the deductive-hypothetical or axiomatic approach of macroeconomics and the highly mathematical content of its theory were extremely misleading in terms of its restrictive and unrealistic assumptions, model simplicity and policy implications regarding the self-stabilizing character of national economies, the limited role for monetary and fiscal policies, and the need for only a light touch regime of bank regulation given the soundness of internal risk-control mechanisms of financial institutions.

THE EFFICIENT MARKET HYPOTHESIS OF FINANCE

Prior to the crisis, the fields of macroeconomics and finance were largely separate fields of analysis, but they were bound together by their joint adoption of the assumptions of rational expectations and complete markets. Consistent with the REH, the EMH assumes that a representative agent has access to all relevant information about states of the world bearing on the evaluation of financial assets, such that its subjective view of the probability distribution of those assets is the same as an objective one based on actual historical data that govern their likely behavior in the future, consistent with their stationary characteristics in a statistical sense. Based on these assumptions, the EMH has two components: one is that there is "no free lunch", in the sense that all relevant information for the value of a financial asset is reflected in its price, and the other is that "the price is right" in the case of assets, in that they reflect the true discounted value of future earnings.

In line with these assumptions, as noted earlier, the EMH would rule out the phenomenon of asset price bubbles, as investors should be able to determine when those prices were deviating from their fundamental value. However, it is clear that the EMH has been violated many times in the past, as for example during the dot-com bubble of the late 1990s, when the price bidding for new technology stocks reached astronomical levels and produced price-earnings ratios that could not be justified by reasonable profit expectations. In order to explain such phenomena, one has to abandon the EMH and consider the role of momentum trading and herd behavior, where interaction among heterogeneous agents have effects on market activity, which move asset prices away from their fundamental values. These ideas belong to the realm of behavioral finance, which is taken up in Chap. 8.

The award of the 2014 Nobel Prize to three scholars who have been involved in testing the EMH provides a fascinating reflection on the pros and cons of this theory. One of the three scholars, Eugene Fama of the University of Chicago, has devoted his professional career to demonstrating the power and efficacy of the EMH, whereas one of the other two, Robert Shiller of Yale University, has been one if its most active critics. In their Nobel lectures, they each provide a succinct and lucid debate on the merits and demerits of the EMH from the perspective of their empirical work.

During the global financial crisis, the development of an asset price bubble in housing, not only in the United States but also in a number of European countries such as Ireland, Spain and the United Kingdom, along with the widespread distribution of mortgage-backed securities (MBS)/collateralized debt obligations (CDOs), was clearly inconsistent with the EMH. Nevertheless, an underlying confidence in the basic assumptions of the EMH played an important role in guiding the policy and financial practice in the period leading up to the crisis. This confidence can be detected in attitudes toward the innovation of securitized financial instruments, the regulation of financial institutions and the risk evaluation procedures of financial institutions and rating agencies.

As a general matter, an implicit or explicit faith in the underlying efficiency of financial markets in accordance with the EMH created an attitude on the part of regulators and policy-makers in the period leading up to the global financial crisis that embraced some or all of the following propositions:

- The prices of financial market instruments can be understood to reflect the rational evaluation of relevant risks and rewards associated with those instruments as they reflect all available information in the market.
- These characteristics of financial instruments can be determined using mathematical and quantitative techniques developed in connection with the capital-asset pricing model.[15]
- Financial innovation as reflected in the development of new financial derivatives such as MBS/CDOs that can be traded among a widely distributed investor base serves to improve the allocative efficiency of investment and promote financial stability.
- The discipline of competitive forces, counterparty risk assessments and internal risk models of financial institutions will ensure that only those new financial products that support sound investments are sustained and that harmful risk-taking is avoided.
- In line with the above assumptions, asset "prices are right" and capital markets allocate capital efficiently in a "Pareto optimal" manner that cannot be improved upon by government intervention.

In retrospect, none of these propositions turned out to be true in the light of the housing and financial bubble that led to the global financial crisis. As recounted in Chap. 2, there was a cascade of failures throughout the whole chain of financial activity related to the housing bubble: the creation of MBS and CDOs; the performance of rating agencies; the selling of these securities by investment banks; the accounting of investment firms heavily engaged in their trading; the inability/unwillingness of stockholders/boards of directors to discipline Bank CEOs involved in purchasing these securities; the weakness of internal risk models used by financial institutions based on "value-at risk" (VAR) calculations, which assumed that future market behavior could be extrapolated from past market outcomes; and the light touch of the Securities and Exchange Commission and bank regulators who believed in the power of market discipline and the benefits of financial innovation.

THE MODIGLIANI-MILLER THEOREM

The M&M theorem has been a foundation piece of the theory of corporate finance since its first statement in 1958 by the two economists, Franco Modigliani and Merton Miller, who developed it when they were working together at Carnegie Mellon University.[16] In its simplest form, the theorem states that the value of a firm (financial or non-financial) depends upon the return on its assets and not on the manner in which it is financed, that is, on the relative shares of equity and debt chosen by the firm to acquire those assets. There has been some debate over the years as to whether the theorem, or the capital structure irrelevance assumption as it is often referred to, holds for banks and other financial institutions, but the balance of opinion is that it does. An implication of the theorem is that there is no optimal capital structure of a firm (or bank) as regards its mix of debt and equity, as changes in that mix do not affect its overall funding costs. Accordingly, if borrowing or leverage for a bank is less expensive than equity, then a reduction in the bank's funding costs arising from an increase in its leverage will be offset by an increase in the cost of equity to compensate for the additional risk it is bearing.[17] It needs to be pointed out, however, that there are some important limiting assumptions to this theorem, namely that it applies to a world of efficient markets and frictionless finance (e.g., without the distortions created by tax advantages and government subsidies for debt financing). Thus, it ties back into the world of the REH and EMH already discussed.

How does this theorem relate to the global financial crisis? In a basic sense, it can be argued that in the period leading up to the financial crisis, the attitude of the regulators was consistent with a naïve (perfect market) interpretation of the theorem. In particular, certain limitations of the M&M theorem were ignored in setting regulatory policy for banks and other financial institutions, in particular in the revision of the Basel Banking Accord in 2004 and in dealing with the shadow banking system. The regulatory changes that were made in the period prior to the financial crisis essentially led to a situation where large commercial banks and other non-bank financial institutions were essentially free to determine their own capital requirements according to their own internal risk models. In setting capital requirements for large banks, no weight was given to the potentially large social costs involved in their failure, which were not visualized in the M&M theorem. In addition, the tax deductibility of interest payments on debt and the lower debt financing costs for banks, which were deemed to benefit from an implicit government bail-out guarantee for being "too big to fail" (TBTF), led to an enormous increase in the use of leverage and debt in the financing of these institutions and a lower reliance on equity capital. In addition to these subsidies, the large banks had access to the government's financial safety net in terms of deposit insurance and the Federal Reserve's lender of last resort financing, which promoted significant "moral hazard" in their lending activities.

The combination of these arrangements created strong incentives for the banks to increase their reliance on debt over equity in their investment in CDOs and other securitized financial instruments. This development implied that for a larger balance sheet the same number of equity holders would expect a higher return on assets to cover the higher risks they assumed in a highly leveraged financial institution. Since there was a widespread belief in the safety of these derivative instruments because of their high credit ratings, high yields on these instruments resulted in high profits for the financial institution, consistent with its implied cost of capital and required return on equity. In line with the EMH, the internal risk models of financial institutions involved in the trading of financial instruments, as noted above, were based on simplistic VAR models, which were backward-looking in generating the data to determine the likelihood of default of these securities and used a standard bell-shaped curve (with thin tails) to estimate that risk, which took no account of the underlying riskiness of the separate asset groups used in their fabrication.

The original Basel Banking Accord was established in 1988 as the first international attempt to coordinate regulatory policy among the G-10 countries following a wave of bank insolvencies in the mid-1980s. (The history and evolution of this Accord is discussed in more detail in Chap. 5 that deals specifically with the international dimensions of the crisis and the defects of the international financial architecture.) This standard established a minimal capital requirement of 8 percent in relation to a bank's risk-weighted assets, with risk weights ranging from 0 to 100 percent depending upon the perceived riskiness of bank asset holdings. Holdings of government securities, AAA-rated securities and inter-bank loans, for example, carried a risk weight of 0 percent (and thus no capital requirement), whereas commercial loans to business carried a weight of 100 percent. Risk weights were aligned with those determined by credit rating agencies. Thus, there was no limit to the overall size of a bank's balance sheet and therefore no minimum capital-asset ratio. This arrangement obviously encouraged banks to use leverage in their operations and a degree of "regulatory arbitrage" in choosing their investments so as to minimize their capital requirements.

In 2004, under pressure from the large commercial banks in the United States and Europe, a revised Basel Accord was approved, which introduced a more variegated structure of risk weights to better match the risk quality of asset categories relevant for banks, again using risk weights established by the private rating agencies, which proved to be highly unreliable in the case of the new securitized instruments. However, the most significant change of the new Basel Accord, as noted above, was that in the case of the large banks, it allowed them to determine, in effect, their own capital requirements according to their internal risk models, with all the defects described above.

Together with the tax advantages for banks in using debt instead of equity in the financing of their operations, there was little appreciation within the regulatory community for the fact that by reducing, in effect, the capital requirements for banks and other financial institutions (as a result of SEC regulatory adjustments), such action only increased the fragility of these institutions and raised the risk of systemic "financial instability". This notion was based in part on a naïve faith in the power of the EMH and the self-stabilizing ability of financial markets and in part on a misunderstanding of the role of equity and capital requirements in determining the riskiness of an institution's financial activities and the potential social cost of its failure. By pleading their case for minimal capital requirements, the banks were very successful prior to the financial crisis in exploiting the government's financial safety net and its subsidies for purposes of increasing their investment in high-yield assets with high levels of debt for maximum private gain, while becoming TBTF and ignoring the potential social cost of their failure, for which they bore little burden sharing.

Again, contrary to the results of the M&M theorem under ideal assumptions, it should have been clear to government regulators that in the presence of significant financial market distortions (such as tax advantages and government subsidies for debt financing), they could not be indifferent to the mix of debt and equity in financing bank operations and that an increase in capital requirements was needed to protect the solvency of the banking system. Such an increase would have led to a reduction in the riskiness of their operations and thus the required rate of return to their equity investors.[18] In this way, it would have also greatly reduced the potential social cost of their failure in a time of financial distress so that the private incentives of the bank were more closely aligned with social welfare objectives.

Prior to the creation of the Federal Reserve and its lender of last resort mechanism, banks were mainly financed by equity investment, while today most private equity funds, mutual funds and hedge funds operate with much lower levels of leverage than banks. One prominent exception to this practice was the hedge fund (Long-Term Capital Management) that failed in 1998 because of an unyielding faith of two of its founders (Robert Merton and Myron Scholes, both Nobel laureates in economics) in a famous formula grounded in the EMH (the Black-Scholes Options Pricing Model), which they helped to develop for the valuation of derivatives. Their single-minded focus on applying this formula in financial market transactions led to enormous bets by that firm on the performance of certain financial assets backed with high levels of leverage. The negative spillovers of the failure of this firm were only contained because of the intervention of the Federal Reserve, and its coordination of the dismemberment of the firm with other financial institutions.

Much confusion has been spread through a fundamental misunderstanding of the role of capital on the balance sheet of financial institutions. In a basic sense, it plays the same role as do deposits or other liabilities in financing the asset purchases and lending operations of the institution. However, unlike other items on the liability side of the balance sheet, it exists to absorb any losses from the operations of the financial institution. Therefore, the larger the capital position of the financial firm, the safer it is. The confusion arises when analysts or financial commentators report that reserves need to be held against the value of the bank's capital or that higher capital requirements tie up idle resources of the financial firm that cannot be used for lending or investing. Both of these assertions are wrong.[19] With this misconception and a distorted view of the M&M theorem, it was easy for banks and other financial firms to make the case for lower capital requirements, especially on the basis of the claim that these firms had adequate internal risk assessment models and tools and applied strict counterparty risk analysis.

I will return to the role of capital requirements and bank regulatory reform in Chap. 7, which deals with the issue of establishing an appropriate agenda for financial reform to take account of the causes and effects of the global financial crisis.

SUMMARY AND CONCLUSION

The onset of the global financial crisis cannot be fully understood without some appreciation for the framework of thinking about the aggregate economy that was pervasive among mainstream macroeconomists and influenced the attitude of policy-makers dealing with financial markets and financial institutions.

To a large extent, most mainstream academic macroeconomists failed to examine and understand critical factors in the behavior of financial markets in the period leading up to the crisis that played a key role in its genesis. This failing was due to the strong attachment of most macroeconomists to the tenets of a new macroeconomic consensus that revived a belief in the self-equilibrating character of the aggregate economy that had been attacked by J.M. Keynes in the wake of the Great Depression. This conviction was grounded in the properties of so-called dynamic stochastic general equilibrium models, which encompassed notions of perfectly competitive and complete markets, along with inter-temporal optimization and "rational expectations" or perfect foresight on the part of economic agents. This framework also ignored the role of financial factors in aggregate economic behavior and thus the consideration of the causes, properties and consequences of financial crises.

A second strong tenet of academic macroeconomics was its attachment to the idea of the efficient market theory of finance, which was grounded in the idea that financial markets reflect the true or fundamental value of financial assets as they respond quickly and accurately to all available information in the market for those assets. Such a tenet rules out the phenomenon of asset bubbles. It was also implicit in government decisions to promote the development of financial derivatives for mortgage finance largely free of regulation, in order to expand the role of capital markets in the financing of home mortgages, in particular for low income and poor households.

A third view common among mainstream economists was that the value of a firm, financial or non-financial, was independent of the manner in which it was financed as regards the composition of debt and equity. This so-called capital structure irrelevance theorem was based on special assumptions such as the efficiency of financial markets and the absence of tax benefits or implicit government subsidies for borrowing by banks that restricted its applicability to the real world of finance. Among other things, a naïve (i.e., perfect market) interpretation of this theorem was consistent with the view of modern bank regulation preceding the crisis that capital requirements for large financial institutions could effectively be determined by these institutions on the basis of their own internal risk valuation models, which would be reinforced by counterparty risk assessments of other market participants. In effect, this distorted view of bank capital requirements led to a minimization of capital positions and an increase in leverage and borrowing by banks that allowed them to take full advantage of the government's financial safety net in order to maximize private returns to bank managers and equity holders, while ignoring the large social costs of their failure.

NOTES

1. Raghuram Rajan is widely credited for having sounded an alarm bell in 2005 in a speech at the Federal Reserve's Jackson Hole Symposium (when he was Chief Economist of the IMF), in which he pointed to the growing risks in the securitization of housing finance and the unsupervised expansion of the shadow banking system ("Has Financial Development Made the World Riskier?" NBER Working Paper #11728, November 2005).
2. This conclusion by Professor Olivier Blanchard appeared in his review of macroeconomics that was published by the NBER just prior to the outbreak of the global financial crisis ("The State of Macro", NBER Working Paper #14259, August 2008).
3. In his 2003 AEA Presidential Address, Professor Lucas said "My thesis in this lecture is that macroeconomics...has succeeded. Its central problem of depression prevention has been solved for all practical purposes, and has been solved for many decades" American Economic Review v. 93(1); pp. 1–14 (March 2003).
4. One of the sharpest critics of the efficient market theory of finance, who shared the Nobel Prize in economics with Eugene Fama, has been Professor Robert Shiller of Yale University.
5. The concept of the Phillips Curve was first applied to the United States by Paul Samuelson and Robert Solow (1960) "Analytical Aspects of Anti-inflation Policy" American Economic Review v. 50(2); pp. 177–94 (May 1960).
6. The origins of the neoclassical synthesis can be traced to the IS-LM general equilibrium framework, which was defined by Sir John Hicks in a famous 1937 paper ("Mr. Keynes and the Classics: A Suggested Interpretation" Econometrica v. 5(2); 147–59, April 1937). This was one of the first attempts to interpret Keynes' approach in the General Theory and has become the staple of undergraduate macroeconomic textbooks ever since.

7. These and other propositions of the new macroeconomic consensus are explained in non-technical terms in Kartik Arthreya (2013) *Big Ideas in Macroeconomics: A Non-Technical View* (Cambridge MA: The MIT Press).

8. Arthur Okun (1965) *Equity* vs. *Efficiency: The Big Trade-Off* (Washington DC: Brookings).

9. For a more recent examination of this theoretical proposition, see Abu Turab Rizvi (2006) "The Sonnenschein-Mantel-Debreu Results After Thirty Years" History of Political Economy v 38 (Annual Supplement); pp. 228–245.

10. An exposition of Stiglitz's thinking on these issues can be found in Joseph Stiglitz (1996) *Whither Socialism?* (Cambridge MA: The MIT Press).

11. In the conventional textbook presentation of IS-LM/AD-AS curves, the vertical Phillips Curve at the natural level of unemployment is analogous to a vertical Aggregate Supply (LRAS) curve in the long run when the level of output is at its natural or potential level.

12. The term "divine coincidence" was coined by Olivier Blanchard and Jordi Gali (2005) in "Real Wage Rigidities and the New Keynesian Model" NBER Working Paper #11806, November 2005.

13. Notwithstanding the emergence of a NMC in the decade or so prior to the global financial crisis, the new classical and new Keynesian schools of macroeconomics did not completely disappear; rather, they continued to maintain separate identities. In the popular commentary, these schools were often characterized as "freshwater" versus "saltwater" schools of macroeconomic theory. The former referred to the new classical school, which was identified with universities near the Great Lakes, prominently the University of Chicago but also the University of Minnesota and University of Rochester. The latter designation was used to identify the New Keynesian School, which was prominently identified with Harvard and MIT along the Atlantic coast of the United States and other universities such as UCLA, along the Pacific coast. The new classical school in its academic work continued to hold fast to its assumptions of full market clearing, perfect markets, and full wage and price flexibility, which in the context of DSGE models implied no stabilizing role for monetary or fiscal policy either in the short

or long term. The new Keynesian school, while adopting the methodology of the DSGE modeling, remained wedded to its assumptions of price and wage stickiness and other market frictions that validated a role for activist, stabilization policies in the short-to-medium term.

14. For one relatively recent contribution to this debate, see Paul Romer's blog (paulromer.net) of August 8, 2015: "What Went Wrong with Macro: Overview and Historical Details".

15. The capital-asset pricing model was one of the basic extensions of the EMH that attempted to explain the pricing or value of securities in terms of their expected return and riskiness in relation to market fundamentals.

16. Franco Modigliani and Merton Miller (1958), "The Cost of Capital, Corporation Finance and Theory of Investment" American Economic Review v. 48(3); pp. 261–297 (June 1958); a brief synopsis of the M&M theorems can be found in Ruben D. Cohen "An Implication of the Modigliani-Miller Capital Structuring Theorems on the Relation Between Equity and Debt" draft paper October 2004.

17. For one recent examination of this idea, see William R. Cline "Testing the Modigliani-Miller Theorem of Capital Structure Irrelevance for Banks" Petersen Institute for International Economics Working Paper 15–8 (April 2015). An earlier study by David Miles, Jing Yang and Gilberto Marcheggiano demonstrated empirically that over the long term an increase in the capital requirement of banks did not result in a significant increase in the cost of their total funding such that they charged substantially more on their loans, a result which is generally consistent with the M&M theorem ("Optimal Bank Capital" Bank of England Discussion Paper #31, April 2011).

18. This conclusion is examined in Anat Admati, Peter DiMarzo, Martin Hellwig, Peter Fleiderer (2010) "Fallacies, Irrelevant Facts and Myths in the Discussion of Bank Capital: Why Bank Equity is Not Expensive" Reprints of the Max Planck Institute for Research on Collective Goods #2010/42.

19. These assertions are examined and refuted in the paper by Anat Admati et al. cited in footnote 18.

CHAPTER 4

The Challenge for Macroeconomic Policy in the Wake of the Crisis

While the seeds for the global financial crisis were spreading during the second half of 2007 and 2008, as stress was building within the US financial system, the failure of Lehman Brothers in September of the latter year can be viewed as the tipping point for the onset of financial panic and turmoil on a global scale. This chapter first briefly reviews the size and scope of the emergency measures that were put in place in an effort to forestall a collapse of the financial system in the United States. It then examines the monetary and fiscal policy measures that were implemented to limit the effects of the crisis on aggregate economic activity and to promote recovery from what has come to be called the Great Recession, to distinguish it from the Great Depression of the 1930s. In both phases of this policy response to the financial crisis, it is fair to say that there was no clear playbook that was guiding the actions of the authorities other than a general provision of liquidity provision in the first response and a rapid easing of monetary and fiscal conditions in the second. To a large extent, government intervention was dictated by events as the crisis unfolded, and it has been highly experimental, as well as sometimes in conflict, as the shockwaves and aftereffects of the crisis have persisted. In the latter regard, it is clear that mainstream macroeconomic modeling as examined in the previous chapter has not provided any guidance on the policy response. Instead, policy-makers have instinctively relied on the general lessons that have been derived from the experience of the Great Depression as first defined by Keynes in his major treatise, as well as the experience of dealing

© The Author(s) 2017
A. Elson, *The Global Financial Crisis in Retrospect*,
DOI 10.1057/978-1-137-59750-2_4

with financial crises in emerging market economies since the onset of financial globalization.

In this connection, it is striking to note that Lawrence Summers, who was the czar of economic policy-making during the Obama administration in its first year in office, made the following observation in an interview at a conference of the Institute of New Economic Thinking in April 2011: "I would have to say that the vast edifice in both its new Keynesian variety and its new Classical variety of attempting to place micro-foundations under macroeconomics was not something that informed the policy-making process in any important way. Instead, Walter Bagehot, Hyman Minsky, and especially, Charles Kindleberger had been my guides in the crisis we just went through".[1] Similarly, Ben Bernanke, former Chair of the Federal Reserve Board, in his 2015 memoir, indicated that he was guided mainly by his understanding of the Great Depression and the policy successes and errors of that experience, as well as by the famous prescription of Walter Bagehot on the central bank's critical role as a "lender of last resort" (LOLR).

Walter Bagehot was a nineteenth-century official of the Bank of England, who defined the classic terms of the LOLR function of a central bank in the face of a financial panic and crisis. These were as follows: to lend freely on the basis of good collateral, to solvent institutions, at a penalty rate of interest. These criteria for the LOLR function of the central bank are still valid, and they essentially guided the monetary authorities of the advanced countries in their response to the global financial crisis. Summers' reference to Minsky is interesting, as he has been considered a distinctly non-mainstream economist, as noted in Chap. 2, completely divorced from the dominant macroeconomic modeling of the last 30 years, yet he understood very well the nature of asset bubbles and the role of bank credit expansion in supporting them. Similarly, Charles Kindleberger, while being an academic like Minsky, also worked outside the mainstream macroeconomic paradigm and was the first economic historian of financial panics and crashes with a celebrated book that was first published in the late 1970s and has been re-issued and updated in seven re-printings (*Manias, Panics and Crashes: A History of Financial Crises*).

What is striking in Professor Summer's statement is that the US government, and in particular the Federal Reserve System and the US Treasury, did not have any playbook for managing financial crises or recent experience to guide their policy responses. The financial crises of emerging market economies in the 1980s and 1990s were not considered relevant for an advanced economy such as the United States, even though the global financial crisis, while institutionally different from those crises, shared many of the same characteristics of the earlier crises in terms of the role of rapid credit expansion and short-term debt accumulation, the onset of panic and the role of contagion in spreading the effects of the crisis.

Through mid-September 2008, the US authorities believed that the spillover effects of the sub-prime mortgage crisis could be relatively well contained and that any impact on economic activity and unemployment would be moderate and of short duration. To a large extent, this belief was based on a very limited understanding of the fragile funding, extensive leverage and wide distribution of securitized assets within the shadow banking system and its web of cross-border linkages. It is interesting to note that since the outbreak of the crisis, a number of academic studies have demonstrated that financial crises are typically preceded by a rapid run-up in debt accumulation of the private sector, that many of these episodes are associated with housing bubbles and that the economic recoveries from these crises are typically of longer duration than other recessions unrelated to financial crises.[2] In fact, debt financed bubbles such as the one that preceded the global financial crisis are typically followed by a much slower economic recovery than is the case for equity-based bubbles such as the dot-com bubble of the late 1990s. One of the reasons for this difference is the greater damage to the financial system associated with the former category of bubbles. None of these conclusions were well understood or appreciated prior to the global financial crisis.

Against the backdrop of the Great Moderation, as described in Chap. 2, the policy challenges of dealing with the Great Recession have brought about a fundamental rethinking of the basic framework for macroeconomic policy management that prevailed prior to the financial crisis. That framework consisted of four basic tenets. First, monetary policy was understood to be the main instrument for managing macroeconomic stabilization by means of adjustments in the central bank's short-term policy rate, which in an environment of relative price stability would have predictable effects on the term structure of interest rates through a process of arbitrage, and accordingly price expectations and output in the short-to-medium term. With a primary focus on price stability through a formal or informal process of inflation targeting, the monetary authorities could adjust their short-term real policy rate to be in line with its estimated natural or equilibrium level that would bring about over time what was referred to in

Chap. 3 as the "divine coincidence" of relative price stability and a level of aggregate output close to its potential.[3] Second, because of uncertainties about the time delay and impact of discretionary fiscal measures, short-term fiscal policy was expected to support macroeconomic stabilization mainly by means of automatic stabilizers incorporated in national budgets. Accordingly, fiscal policy was expected to be focused primarily on long-term debt sustainability in order to reinforce expectations of relative price stability. Fiscal rules, such as those embodied in the Maastricht Treaty of the euro zone, were viewed as helpful for maintaining fiscal sustainability. Third, financial stability was not viewed as a central concern of monetary and fiscal policy-making and was essentially relegated to the regulatory authority in their work on micro-prudential bank supervision on a case-by-case basis. Finally, since financial bubbles were difficult to detect on an ex ante basis, it was judged best to use monetary and/or fiscal measures to deal with the effects of their collapse in order to prevent any potential threat to financial system stability. In the light of the global financial crisis, each of these four tenets has had to be re-examined and re-defined.

The primary emphasis on the role of monetary policy in macroeconomic stabilization prior to the global financial crisis had in effect been validated by the experience of the Great Moderation discussed in Chap. 2. The potency of monetary policy was also captured by the so-called Taylor Rule, which showed that the observed changes in the Federal Reserve's (the Fed's) short-term ("federal funds") policy rate during the period of the Great Moderation could be well replicated by a simple statistical formula. As noted earlier, this formula specified a reaction function by which the Fed's policy rate would be adjusted above or below a long-term average level in real terms of 2 percent by a factor of 1.5 for any deviation of inflation from its assumed targeted level of 2 percent and by a factor of 0.5 for any deviation in the growth of real GDP from its potential rate of 2 percent.[4]

The Nature of the Emergency Response

The variety, size and scope of governmental interventions in the United States that were introduced beginning in mid-2007 to deal with a growing financial crisis were quite significant and unmatched by any period of financial stress in the post-WW2 period. The fact that the chairman of the Fed at the time (Ben Bernanke) was a scholar of the Great Depression was quite fortuitous, in the sense that he understood the powerful depressing effects that a financial crisis could have on aggregate economic activity and the need for a LOLR to prevent the collapse of the financial system. In this regard, it is important to recognize that according to a large number of metrics such as stock market activity, personal financial wealth, trade, employment and output during the first 12 to 18 months of the crisis marked from the beginning of 2008, the United States and the euro area were on a similar or worse downward trajectory than during a comparable period of the Great Depression.[5] The fact that these metrics began to bottom out after that time period, rather than continuing to decline, can be attributed to the timing and impact of monetary and fiscal measures that were adopted with sufficient political support.

Initially, the US government's response was managed by means of interventions in specific cases where a large financial institution was faced with a liquidity, as distinct from a solvency, crisis. While conceptually it is possible to distinguish between these two cases, in a crisis it may not be so clear. In a liquidity crisis, a financial institution may be holding sound investments backed by good collateral but faces difficulty in selling or disposing of some of its assets when confronted with a sudden withdrawal of deposits or other short-term funding. Access to temporary funding from the central bank is appropriate and necessary in such a case. In a solvency crisis, a financial institution is carrying assets of low quality against which inadequate provisions have been made to cover losses or for which insufficient or weak collateral has been posted. With a withdrawal of funding because of a loss of confidence on the part of the institution's creditors, a write-down of capital and potential bankruptcy proceedings may be necessary. In a generalized crisis, however, the distinction between these two cases may become fuzzy as the loss of market liquidity may affect not only the ability to dispose of certain assets but also their market value, say, because of a deterioration in the financial situation of the institution that issued them and/or an unwillingness of other investors to maintain them in their portfolios. This discussion highlights, once again, the inherent fragility of banks and financial intermediation, which was noted in Chap. 2, arising from the maturity mismatch of a financial institution's short-term liabilities and its medium- and long-term assets. When a financial firm engages in a mix of domestic and foreign borrowing and investing, then a currency and maturity mismatch may be involved, thus compounding its potential vulnerability to financial turmoil and contagion.

The beginning of the crisis in the United States and European Union can be marked from the middle of 2007, with the rise in delinquencies in the sub-prime mortgage market following a downturn in housing prices and losses for institutions, such as Countrywide Financial Corporation that had been heavily engaged in that market. In August 2007, BNP Paribas, the largest bank in France, had suspended its trading in mortgage-backed securities (MBS) because of a lack of liquidity and had closed three of its funds invested in these securities; similar liquidity problems overwhelmed the Northern Rock bank in the United Kingdom at about the same time. By the end of that year, the US economy was already entering into a recession.

Initially during the latter part of 2007, the Federal Reserve Board was mainly focused on its interest rate policy, with reductions in its federal funds rate from 5.25 percent to 4.25 percent in two steps in September and December of that year. In December 2007, it also established what was to be the first of a number of special credit facilities (the Term Auction Facility or TAF) for lending to broker dealers (such as investment banks) facing liquidity needs in the repurchase agreement (REPO) market, for which good collateral in the form of treasury securities needed to be posted. During the early part of 2008, the Fed took actions to reduce the federal funds rate and the rate on its regular lending (its primary credit rate) in four stages to levels of 2 and 2.5 percent, respectively, by the end of April 2008. In March 2008, the Fed created the second of its special lending/liquidity programs (the Term Securities Lending Facility or TSLF) to lend up to an amount of US$200 billion of government securities in exchange for a variety of public and private assets of commercial banks (including MBS), as well as the Primary Dealer Credit Facility (PDCF) for lending to primary dealers against investment grade securities. These three facilities (the TAF, TSLF and PDCF) were unusual in the sense that they were intended not for commercial banks but rather for investment banks, which in normal circumstances do not borrow directly from the Fed as do commercial banks with deposits insured by the Federal Deposit Insurance Corporation (FDIC).[6]

Then in April 2008, Bear Stearns, an investment bank, was facing a loss in value in its MBS investments because of a withdrawal of willing buyers for those securities. In order to avoid a collapse of that firm, the Fed intervened with a special loan of US$30 billion under the TSLF to an off-balance-sheet entity (Maiden Lane LLC I) which, in turn, purchased an equivalent amount of collateralized securities from Bear Stearns to enable its acquisition by JP Morgan. In this case, the Fed's loan was justified as a measure to prevent a threat to financial system stability under the "emergency and exigent circumstances" referred to in section 13(3) of the Federal Reserve Act and on the judgment that the assets of the rescued institution were protected by good collateral. Later in the year, this same judgment and financial intervention were withheld in the case of Lehman Brothers, even though it became a clear trigger of financial system instability. Much debate has taken place as to whether these two cases should have been handled in the same manner; in the light of events, an argument can certainly be made in the affirmative.[7] However, at the time, the government authorities were trying to send a signal that there was a limit to the extent to which the Fed and Treasury would engage in bailing out operations. The failure of Lehman Brothers became the catalyst for the full force of the global financial crisis as investors suddenly became aware of Lehman's extensive holdings of MBS, its links to a number of other domestic and foreign financial institutions, and the absence of any appropriate framework under bankruptcy law to handle the insolvency of a large financial institution, both nationally and internationally.

The failure of Lehman Brothers came soon after the government decided that it was necessary to take under conservatorship Fannie Mae and Freddie Mac. These two government-sponsored enterprises (GSEs) were heavily involved in the securitization of sub-prime and Alt A home mortgages and were facing increasing difficulties in securing funding for their asset allocations. As noted in Chap. 2, Fannie and Freddie, while being privately run, were established to provide government guarantees for home mortgages in order to encourage home ownership. They also had initiated the creation of MBS prior to development of the housing bubble. While the debt they raised in the private markets was not guaranteed by the US government, these GSEs were widely perceived to carry an implicit guarantee, which was reflected in the lower borrowing costs that they could command. By the peak of the crisis in 2008, the two GSEs had guaranteed US$5.3 trillion, or roughly half of home mortgages. However, in the years 2004–06, they had also invested significantly in the so-called private-label MBS originated by other lenders in order to boost their earnings. With the disruption and collapse of the market for these securities, the GSEs were facing increasing difficulties in rolling over their funding requirements. As a result, in order to prevent their failure, the government announced in early September 2008 that they would be transferred to the formal regulatory status of conservatorship, thus making explicit the government guarantee of their borrowing requirements that market participants had expected while submitting them to supervisory control until such time as they were deemed to be viable under private management.[8]

It is noteworthy that prior to the failure of Lehman Brothers in mid-September 2008, in the last meeting of the Fed's policy-making committee (the Federal Open Market Committee or FOMC) in early August, there was very little discussion among its members, according to the published *minutes* of its deliberations, of impending financial risks and negative spillovers from financial weaknesses in the "shadow" banking sector. The term "systemic risk" was barely mentioned in remarks by Chairman Bernanke and was generally ignored as it was considered to be a term that was difficult to explain and to measure. The only Governor who raised the possibility of growing financial distress was Frederick Mishkin, an academic economist who was retiring from the Board after that meeting. Instead, following the guidance notes prepared for the committee by the Federal Reserve staff as contained in the standard beige-and-blue books that each member receives prior to the meetings of the FOMC, the participants focused primarily on the outlook for inflation and output growth and whether its short-term policy rate (the Federal Funds rate) should have been maintained at 2 percent or increased by 25 basis points. In its meeting of early August, the committee decided once again to leave the rate unchanged as it viewed the downside risks to output growth and upside risks to inflation as about evenly balanced. In the light of events, a debate has been generated as to whether the passive monetary policy stance at that time in the face of underlying weakness in the economy represented an unintended tightening of policy instead.[9]

Notwithstanding the variety of interest rate and credit operations that the Federal Reserve Board had taken since September 2007, the Board was convinced until the failure of Lehman Brothers in mid-September 2008 that the difficulties in the housing market could be contained and that it could limit the risk of recession through an easing of monetary conditions. According to the *minutes* of the FOMC, one cannot detect any widespread concern over the growing turmoil in the financial markets, which is quite remarkable in retrospect. To a large extent, this posture can be explained, according to one recent study, by the nature of the information provided to and deliberated upon by the FOMC, as the decision-making body of the Board, which is heavily focused on macroeconomic conditions bearing on inflation and unemployment risks.[10] Rarely, if ever, were representatives from the bank regulatory side of the Fed's operations asked to speak or comment on potential financial risks in the economy. Nor is there much opportunity for members of the FOMC, because of its relatively large size, to dialogue with each other on important issues or to pursue a line of questioning with senior Fed staff attending their meetings on the projections and proposals provided to the committee.[11]

The failure of Lehman Brothers became the trigger for widespread panic in the financial markets. In the face of this crisis, the US government took dramatic action on a broad front and displayed a remarkable degree of cooperation among the Federal Reserve (both at the Board level and through the Federal Reserve Bank of New York), the US Treasury and the FDIC. Consistent with Bagehot's rule, the Fed and other central banks of the advanced countries extended credit as lenders of last resort during the 2007–09 crisis period equivalent of around US$4 trillion, which implied, on average, a doubling of their respective balance sheets and much more in individual cases.[12] Over the course of the last three months of 2008, the FOMC lowered the federal funds rate to a level between 0 and 0.25 percent while expanding greatly its liquidity provision through existing and new facilities (AMLF, CPFF, MMIMF and TALF). In addition, in coordination with the US Treasury, the Fed authorized on the day after the failure of Lehman Brothers an exceptional credit of US$85 billion to American International Group on the grounds of its systemic importance, as well as subsequently in November, two additional lines of credit through separate off-balance-sheet vehicles (Maiden Lane II and III) of US$22.5 billion and US$30 billion, respectively, to purchase some of its collateralized debt obligations (CDOs) and MBS. In addition, in line with its LOLR function, the Fed gradually expanded its swap lines of credit with initially four central banks in advanced countries (the Bank of England, European Central Bank, Bank of Japan, and Swiss National Bank) and then to central banks of ten other advanced and emerging market economies to support the repayment of foreign lines of credit by commercial banks in these countries to banks in the United States. Total drawings under these swap lines of credit reached a peak amount of US$600 billion by February 2009.

Meanwhile, within a week of Lehman's failure, the Treasury Department used US$50 billion from its Exchange Stabilization Fund to establish a temporary guarantee of all investments in money market mutual funds, which was followed in early October by action on the part of the FDIC to increase the threshold of its deposit insurance in FDIC-insured banks to US$250,000. The US Treasury also secured Congressional approval in early October 2008 for the creation of a US$700 billion Temporary Asset Relief Program (TARP), which was used to make temporary equity investments in solvent banks facing capital deficiencies, as well as lines of credit for two of the largest automobile manufacturers, Chrysler and General Motors. The total amount of emergency assistance under these facilities amounted to US$430 billion, most of which was repaid by the end of 2015, according to data reported by the US Treasury Department. The US government received an amount roughly similar to its disbursements in repayments, sales, dividends, interest and other income, offsetting a loss or write-offs of around US$35 billion.[13]

Notwithstanding the success of the TARP investments, it is striking to note that at the time the program was approved by Congress, the Federal Reserve and Treasury Department were still not clear as to how these funds were to be allocated, that is, whether they would be used to purchase impaired assets of banks (in line with the name of the program) or to make temporary equity purchases in banks in order to bolster their capital position. Following internal debate, the latter route was chosen. As events transpired, it is clear that without this rapid and substantial infusion of liquidity and capital injections to banks and other financial institutions, the economic impact of the financial crisis would have been far worse than in fact it was.[14]

Notwithstanding the rapidity and boldness of these official actions in the wake of the Lehman failure, they were not enough to forestall widespread panic in financial markets. This panic had all the features of a traditional bank panic involving the withdrawal of private bank deposits of various maturities in response to significant losses in the value of a bank's loans or investments because of poor risk management, a major economic downturn or some other exogenous event. The difference in 2008 of course was that the conditions of panic originated in the "shadow" banking system (outside the traditional bank sector), where liabilities were largely composed of overnight REPOs or commercial paper that were collateralized by an institution's investments in MBS/CDOs whose value was largely unknown in the wake of the Lehman failure. That failure also provoked panic because of great uncertainty not only about the value of these securitized instruments developed during the housing boom but also about the number and size of bank and non-bank institutions that had invested in them or were linked to financial institutions that had heavily invested in those instruments through special lines of credit.

These conditions of panic and fear had an immediate effect on economic activity, as consumers and investors sharply adjusted down their expectations of future economic conditions and reduced their spending in response to a variety of negative signals from financial markets. Equity markets (i.e., the S&P 500 index) fell by 40 percent during the two-month period from mid-September (a few days after the Lehman bankruptcy) to mid-November 2008, while real GDP fell by 2.2 percent in the fourth quarter of 2008, following a more modest decline of 0.5 percent in the previous quarter. Because of the extensive cross-border financial linkages across the Atlantic, economic and financial developments within the European Union were broadly similar.

In this crisis, as in other financial crises, one can trace a sequence of effects running from a collapse in asset prices associated with the end of the housing bubble leading to a downturn in housing activity and then to turmoil in the financial markets, which in turn had major second-round effects on the real economy. The sequence as applied to the global financial crisis began in a segment of the real economy involving the collapse of the housing bubble in 2006–07, which had negative consequences for homeowners whose home values fell below the amount of their home mortgages, as well as negative spillover effects on selected financial institutions owing to the suspension of trading in CDOs/MBS or a collapse in the prices for these securities. The breakdown in the market for these securities occurred as "shadow" banking institutions, facing major liquidity requirements to meet the demands of their lenders, tried to dispose of their holdings in CDOs/MBS but found few willing buyers except at "fire sale" prices. This development then led to a widespread withdrawal of short-term funding for "shadow" banking institutions invested in these securities, with further second-round effects on the real economy as widespread fear of major financial distress set in. Financial panic would also have been fed by a process of contagion as the withdrawal of funding from one financial institution in difficulty raised concerns about other similarly placed institutions or fears about other institutions that may have been linked through short-term lines of credit. Citibank became a victim of this kind of market reaction as with the general withdrawal of liquidity it was forced to close its off-balance-sheet special investment vehicles and bring onto its balance sheet the impaired assets in the form of CDOs/MBS that these entities had purchased. This maneuver raised doubts about the capital adequacy of Citibank, and in response to investor fears it became one of the first institutions to call on the TARP for an equity infusion amounting to US$50 billion, the largest of any financial institution.

One of the actions taken by the new Obama administration in early 2009 to complement the TARP that helped to quell the financial panic was the announcement in early February that "stress tests" for the largest banks would be conducted by the major regulatory agencies for the 19 largest commercial banks with assets exceeding US$100 billion, which accounted for two-thirds of banking system assets and one-half of bank loans. These tests were intended to show the extent to which the major banks were at risk of insolvency because of a lack of adequate capital to withstand a further extreme financial event. In May 2009, the results of the stress tests were made public, showing that 10 of the 19 banks needed to bolster their capital position, which they were required to do before the end of that year, either by means of raising additional equity through private placements or by drawing on the TARP.[15]

THE MONETARY AND FISCAL POLICY RESPONSE TO LIMIT THE ECONOMIC EFFECTS OF THE CRISIS

With the outbreak of the financial crisis in the last quarter of 2008, the monetary and fiscal authorities reacted with a series of measures, as outlined above, to contain the economic impact of the financial crisis and to promote macroeconomic recovery. These measures were primarily focused on the financial system, based on the judgment that a widespread collapse of financial institutions would have had a major and long-lasting impact on economic activity. Some attention was given to relieving the burden of household debt on consumers, but this was more limited and less vigorously pursued.[16] The burden of debt on consumers and certain financial institutions would prove to be a serious hurdle in promoting economic recovery because of the problem of so-called debt deflation, which was discussed in Chap. 2. With the decline in housing values, the net worth of consumers declined, and consumers facing a sudden shift in their debt position either defaulted on their loans or cut back on other expenditure in order to lower their mortgage indebtedness. In either case, the shift from a continued rise in home values to a decline in home equity removed a source of financing for durable and other consumer purchases and forced a cutback in these kinds of outlays. The phenomenon of "debt deflation" was also a factor determining the behavior of banks, as they dealt with the problem of loan delinquency or non-performing loans to households and businesses. In the face of a decline in asset returns or a write-down in the value of their loans, banks would have been required to cut back on new lending in order to meet their minimum capital requirements and reduce their debt financing as well.

Looking beyond the response of the Fed in fulfilling its role as a LOLR to prevent a complete collapse of the financial system, central bank authorities in the United States and other advanced countries were faced with the challenge of what further monetary policy adjustments they could make once the "zero lower bound" of short-term policy rates had been reached. In the United States this limit was reached at the end of December 2008 when the Fed decided to have the federal funds rate fluctuate within the narrow range of 0–0.25 percent. The fact that this target range for the Fed's short-term policy rate was maintained through the end of 2015 is strong evidence of the difficulties faced by the Federal Reserve authorities in using "unconventional monetary policies" to promote a sustained economic recovery from the recession caused by the global financial crisis. The Bank of England, the Bank of Japan and the European Central Bank also faced similar challenges at the end of 2008.[17]

The existence of the zero lower bound for the Fed's short-term policy rate presented the FOMC with an asymmetric and unprecedented policy challenge. If economic recovery proved to be relatively rapid as it had been in the previous post-WW2 recessions, then the Fed could return to its normal practice of adjusting its short-term policy rate through open-market operations to achieve its macroeconomic objectives. However, as long as the effects of the recession persisted, the Fed was forced to rely on unconventional monetary policy actions not involving the direct use of its short-term policy rate in order to promote its objectives. The zero lower bound had first been confronted by the Bank of Japan after it was faced with the challenge of promoting economic recovery in that country following the collapse of a housing and stock market bubble in the late 1980s. That episode, as well as the aftermath of the global financial crisis, presented an example of what Keynes had defined in the 1930s as a "liquidity trap" for central bankers. With interest rates effectively at their zero lower bound, private agents would be indifferent as to whether they would hold cash or short-term government securities, and thus the central bank was powerless to promote spending through a reduction in interest rates on the assumption that it would not lower the yield on its financial assistance into negative territory. In these conditions, Keynes argued that an increase in aggregate demand through an expansion in fiscal policy would be needed in order to compensate for the reduction in household and business expenditure and promote economic recovery and an eventual increase in interest rates.[18]

To a significant extent, the policy challenge of "a liquidity trap" and the potentially positive role of fiscal stimulus in boosting economic activity were well understood by Chairman Bernanke and the new economic team that was formed by President Obama following his election in November 2008. In relatively quick order, his administration was able to win Congressional approval of the American Recovery and Reinvestment Act, which was signed into law on February 17, 2009, soon after the initiation of stress tests for the major banks. This program involved a variety of tax reductions, aid to state and local governments, and discretionary spending amounting to US$787 billion, or around 5 percent of GDP. This was a significant achievement, coming as it did only a little more than four months after the approval of the TARP for a roughly similar amount. Notwithstanding the good timing of the fiscal stimulus, there were proposals at the time within his economic team for an even larger amount, which in the light of the slow and long duration of the recovery were probably justified.

The policy challenge of the zero lower bound for the Fed was in part alleviated by the decision that was taken in October 2008 to initiate the payment of interest on the commercial banks' excess reserves held at the Federal Reserve. This change in Fed procedures had been made with the approval of the US Congress to give it an additional tool in the conduct of monetary policy. However, it would also of necessity involve a change in the manner in which the Fed would raise or lower its short-term policy rate in the future. One rationale for the decision to pay interest on bank reserves was to eliminate an implied cost or tax on financial intermediation or the holding of non-interest-bearing currency and deposits in commercial banks. The other rationale for the payment of interest on reserves was that it was thought that this change would allow the Fed to target its rate for overnight reserves, which determines its federal funds or short-term policy rate, in a more precise way. In practice, however, the federal funds rate has fluctuated between the lower bound for its targeted level and the Fed's interest rate on excess reserves, which is why from the end of 2008 the FOMC has set a range of 0.25 basis points for the fluctuation of its policy rate.[19]

The two main instruments of the unconventional monetary policy that the Fed introduced in response to the Great Recession and the dilemma of the zero lower bound were "forward guidance" and large-scale asset purchases (LSAP) or "quantitative easing" (QE), as it has come to be known. Along with the introduction of these new monetary policy tools, the Fed has established a number of innovations in its communication practices in order to improve its transparency and interactions with financial markets. At the time these two new instruments of unconventional monetary policy were introduced, it was clearly anticipated that the recovery would be much quicker than in fact it has been, so that the Fed could return to its normal policy arrangement based on periodic adjustments in its overnight federal funds rate through the practice of open-market operations. The fact that this expectation has not turned out to be correct has meant that the Fed has been dealing with a highly unusual and unprecedented policy challenge, which with the passage of time has complicated the timing and duration of monetary policy normalization. The long duration of the Great Recession and slow pace of economic recovery in the United States since the middle of the 2009 when it reached its low point is testimony to the uncertain economic effects of the unconventional monetary policy, notwithstanding its impact on lowering the term structure of interest rates and raising the prices of financial assets, more generally. To a large extent, the weakness of this transmission mechanism of monetary policy has reflected the uncertain environment for new private investment, the persistent impact of "debt deflation" and the lack of a supporting role from fiscal policy, as discussed later on in this chapter. Recent research has also shown that the persistence of the Great Recession has lowered the level of "potential output" that had prevailed prior to the crisis and may have been the prelude to a period of "secular stagnation".[20]

Under its LSAP program, the Fed targeted the purchase of long-term assets such as medium- to long-term treasury securities and MBS guaranteed by the two GSEs, with a view to reducing the yield on these securities and through a market process of arbitrage the yields on other long-term instruments such as home mortgages and corporate bonds in order to encourage home purchases or re-financing and new business investment. The program was also expected to induce a decline in the yield of other financial asset groups such as equities, through an increase in their valuation. In the event, this program endured far longer than anyone at the Fed anticipated, that is, through October 2014, and was executed through three separate operations of asset purchases, as well as one (called "Operation Twist") involving the simultaneous purchase of longer-term treasury securities and sale of shorter-term ones, also with the effect of lowering the yields on long-term securities. The fact that the LSAP program lasted so long is testimony to the enduring effects of the financial crisis on economic activity in contrast with the normal course of business cycles.

The Fed's program of LSAP or QE in effect began well before the end of 2008 as the Fed increased its various asset purchase programs to provide liquidity to financial markets, including the purchase in November of US$600 billion of MBS guaranteed by the GSEs and the opening of swap lines of credit to foreign central banks. By early February 2009, these actions had led to a doubling of the size of the Fed's balance sheet (to around US$1.5 trillion) compared with its pre-crisis level. Then in early March 2009, the Fed announced what was to become the first of the three programs of LSAPs of around US$1.1 trillion, involving an expansion of US$850 billion in the purchase of MBS from the GSEs and a purchase of government securities of US$300 billion from other financial institutions. The simple announcement of this program lowered the yield on 10-year government debt from 3 percent to 2.5 percent. This program of asset purchases was to extend through March 2010, after which it was expected that the economic recovery would be well entrenched and policy normalization could begin. In retrospect, it is clear that the macroeconomic forecasts of the Federal Reserve staff (as well as consensus forecasts of business economists more generally) were far too

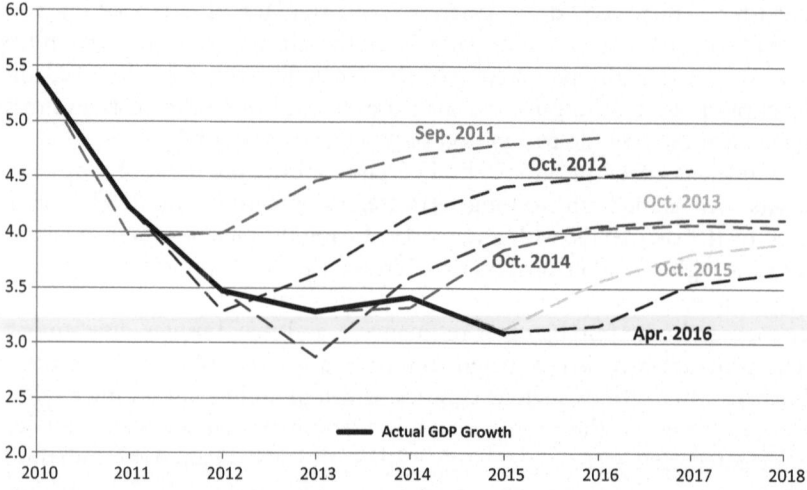

Chart 4.1 IMF WEO projections for World GDP in constant prices (Source: IMF World Economic Outlook Database)

optimistic as regards the timing and pace of economic recovery from the recession, which officially ended in June 2009. (Chart 4.1 shows how the actual pace of recovery of the global economy has been significantly below the IMF projections made in 2011 and in each of the five subsequent years.)

During 2010, as economic activity continued to remain subdued, the Federal Reserve Board began to discuss the possibility of a second round of LSAP, or QE2, as a means of continuing to purchase long-term treasury securities with a view to reducing their yield and that of other comparable securities and other debt instruments in an effort to spur investment and consumer durable spending. There was far less unanimity among the FOMC members as to whether such action was justified, and a number of members began to voice concerns over the potentially inflationary impact of the Fed's QE program. This concern was also expressed later in the year by a group of prominent conservative economists and commentators in a letter published in the Wall Street Journal on November 15, soon after the FOMC agreed to pursue a second program of LSAP ("An Open Letter to Ben Bernanke"). This program of QE2 set a target of the Fed's purchase of US$600 billion of treasury securities through June 2011 (or US$75 billion per month).

With continuing concerns about the pace of economic recovery, the FOMC then decided in September 2011 to supplement its QE program with a maturity extension program, or "Operation Twist" as it came to be known in the financial press. Under this program, the Fed initiated purchase on a monthly basis of long-term government securities in the range of 6–30 years to reach a cumulative amount of US$400 billion, which was to be offset by the sale of short-to-medium government securities from its portfolio of an equivalent amount in the range of zero to three years. While this swap operation was intended not to have an impact on the total supply of government securities in financial markets, it was expected to have an effect similar to the QE program on the supply and yields on long-term government securities and other financial assets of a similar maturity. This program was terminated in December 2012.

During the two phases of QE and "Operation Twist", the FOMC observed a steady but slow pace of reduction in the rate of unemployment, from its peak of 10 percent in February 2009, along with a subdued rate of growth in "core" inflation (i.e., total CPI excluding food and energy) and labor income. In these circumstances, Chairman Bernanke and other members of the FOMC debated in 2012 whether further stimulus from monetary policy was warranted, and agreed to a final program of LSAP (or QE3) in September 2012. This program was on an open-ended basis when it was announced and involved the purchase of long-term Agency-guaranteed MBS of US$40 billion a month. In December 2012, this LSAP program was supplemented by the purchase of US$45 billion of longer-term government securities, thus continuing the pace of monthly purchases that had been maintained under "Operation Twist" but without the effect of sterilization. In January 2014, the Fed started to taper the amount of its monthly purchases, and the program was terminated in October 2014. In quantitative terms, QE3 was the largest of the three LSAP programs, as the balance sheet of the Fed increased from around US$2.8 trillion to US$4.5 trillion over the course of two years.

One operational problem that arose in the implementation of QE was that there was little or no coordination with the public debt operations of the US Treasury. Any overt consultation between the two institutions would have been considered a potential threat to the operational independence of the Fed. Nevertheless, studies have shown that during the lifetime of the Fed's QE programs (2008–14) long-term purchases of government securities by the Fed were partially offset by the Treasury Department's placement of long-term bonds as it tried to take advantage of the relatively low interest rate environment to increase the duration of its debt. The net effect of these two programs was that the quantitative impact of the Fed's QE program was reduced by around one-third.[21]

The basis on which each of the LSAPs was established in terms of their size and duration was never made public, but they were intended to be substantial enough to have an impact on the supply of the affected bonds in the market. Measured in relation to GDP, the Fed's balance sheet expanded from around 5.5 percent in 2008 to a maximum of 25 percent by mid-2014, by means of which the central bank purchased around 60 percent of all Treasury securities issued during that time period and an unprecedented 80 percent in 2014.[22] Apart from the size and duration of QE, it is unclear how the FOMC determined the choice of long-term securities to purchase under its LSAP, whether it be MBS or government securities. To the extent that the Fed engaged in sizeable purchases of MBS, as it did under QE1 and QE2, one could argue that the FOMC was engaging in a type of targeted credit allocation program to encourage housing sector activity, both at the construction and retail sale stages.

On the basis of the three programs of QE and Operation Twist, the Fed's holdings of long-term treasuries and agency-guaranteed MBS expanded by around US$4 trillion from early 2009 through the end of 2014. These data suggest a significant expansion in monetary stimulus, as the main counterpart of these purchases was an increase in reserve money (i.e., currency issue and bank reserves) reflecting the growth in liquidity associated with the LSAP. Chart 4.2 shows the increases in the balance sheet of the Federal Reserve as a result of this program, which was largely mirrored by similar activity of the Bank of England, the ECB and the Bank of Japan, although the mix of asset purchases and credit easing varied in each case.

It is interesting to note that the growth of M2 and M3 in the United States has not kept pace with the growth of base money, with the result that the money multiplier (i.e., the ratio of M2 or M3 to base money) has declined sharply since the onset of the financial crisis. Such an outcome has completely altered the standard textbook model of the money multiplier (as discussed in Chap. 2) that had been developed to explain a fairly pre-

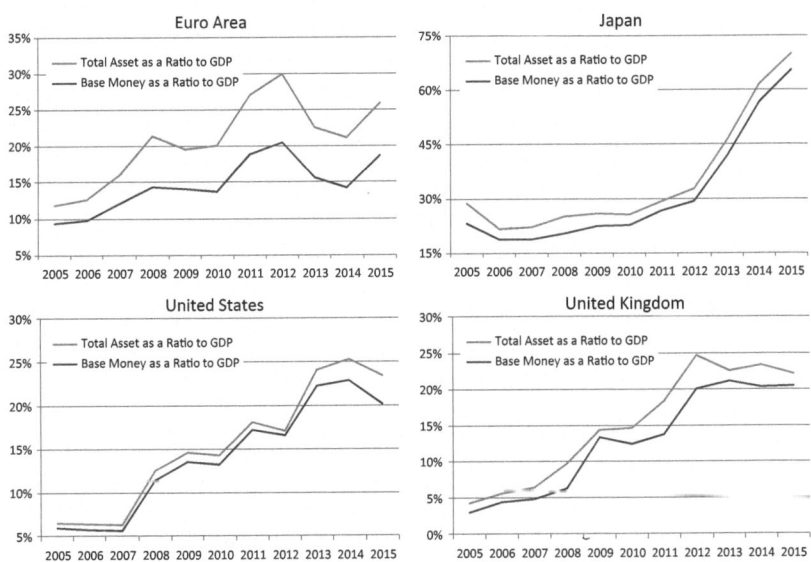

Chart 4.2 Central bank total assets and base money as a ratio to GDP (Source: IMF International Financial Statistics)

dictable relationship between base money and the stock of money (M2 or M3) in the period prior to the financial crisis. The multiplier itself was relatively stable and was determined by two other ratios: the currency-deposit ratio, which was determined by preferences of the general public, and the reserve-deposit ratio, which was determined by banks. In an era when no interest was paid on excess reserves held by banks (i.e., prior to October 2008), banks sought to maintain their excess reserves, or reserves in excess of Federal Reserve requirements, at a minimum level. Both the reserve-deposit and currency-deposit ratios were fairly stable over time and predictable, and thus the money multiplier itself was relatively constant over time. Accordingly, in the monetarist tradition of Milton Friedman and the Chicago School of economics, the Fed was seen as capable of determining the growth of the money supply, and thus the rate of inflation, through its control of base money. This presentation has been at the core of economics textbooks for decades. However, this is no longer the case under the current regime of the Federal Reserve. For some time, even prior to 2008, the Fed has shifted away from an emphasis on the money supply as an anchor for monetary policy toward a focus on the federal funds rate as a means of controlling inflation (by means of the demand for credit) and open-market operations as a tool for controlling that rate. The policy focus on a low rate of inflation of around 2 percent had been implicit in the FOMC deliberations for many years prior to the global financial crisis and became explicit with the release of a policy statement of the Fed in January 2012. This announcement was one of the many adjustments in the Fed's transparency and communication policy that were introduced by the Federal Reserve under Chairman Bernanke.

Another innovation was the policy of "forward guidance", which was initiated in the Fed's FOMC meeting in December 2008 with a view to communicating to the markets the FOMC's expectations for economic activity and the likely course of its short-term policy rate. Forward guidance had been used in previous FOMC statements, but on an irregular basis. For a number of years prior to the global financial crisis, statements had been issued following each FOMC meeting that contained a brief one- or two-paragraph view of the current economic situation and outlook along with a signal of the concerns or conditions that would guide policy rate adjustments in the future. Beginning in December 2008, with the zero lower bound in effect, the committee began to make more explicit its expectations for the future path of its policy rate.[23]

Forward guidance was expected to influence future interest rates in a manner similar to actual adjustments of the federal funds rate. The primary purpose of forward guidance was to influence financial market expectations of the future path of short-term interest rates that would, in turn, influence long-term interest rates, especially if the guidance provided by the FOMC was different from financial market forecasts. As noted earlier, changes in long-term rates would affect those pertaining to auto loans and mortgages for consumers, as well as business purchases of plant and equipment. More specifically, forward guidance can affect both components of long-term interest rates: first, the component that reflects the expected future path of short-term interest rates and second, the term premium related to the extra risk of holding a long-term financial instrument in a world of interest rate uncertainty. If the Fed's guidance suggests that an accommodative stance will last longer than expected by the public, then both components of long-term interest may fall.

How forward guidance affects actual private spending behavior, however, depends upon whether it is perceived to be a policy commitment on the part of the FOMC or simply a forecast of the future path of short-term interest rates. In the former case, the expectations channel linked to long-term interest rates is likely to be stronger than in the latter case, with more durable effects on private sector spending. In the latter case, forward guidance may only validate private sector expectations, or if it suggests a weaker outlook than expected by the public, it might even dampen consumer and business sentiment with unintended, negative effects on spending. The impact of forward guidance may also be difficult to disentangle from the effects of QE. The Fed's announcement and implementation of an LSAP program may be viewed as its fulfillment of forward guidance, and therefore both components of the Fed's policy may be at work in influencing the course of long-term interest rates.

Beginning in December 2008, the FOMC issued its first statement for the future course of short-term policy rates in fairly general language as follows: "The Committee anticipates that weak economic conditions are likely to warrant exceptionally low levels of the federal funds rate for some time." In March 2009, the committee issued a similar statement, with the substitution of the phrase "for an extended period" for the phrase "for some time". According to a study by two Federal Reserve economists, each of these statements resulted in a decrease in market expectations of future rates, as reflected in the price of federal funds futures contracts.[24] Notably, each of these meetings was accompanied by first the launch and then the intensification of QE1. Beginning in August 2011, the FOMC shifted the timeline of its forward guidance from an indefinite to a more date-specific basis. Following the FOMC meeting of August 9, 2011, for example, the committee issued a statement in which the last four words of the phrase "economic conditions are likely to warrant exceptionally low levels of the federal funds rate for an extended period", which had been used in statements prior to that date, was changed to "at least through 2013". Once again it was possible, according to the study just cited, to detect a decline in the market expectations of the future funds rate. One month after this meeting, as noted earlier, the FOMC initiated its maturity extension program. On the basis of these estimates, one can conclude that financial market participants viewed each of these innovations in forward guidance as a credible signal, if not commitment, of the Fed's future policy intent.

A further change was introduced in the FOMC approach to forward guidance in December 2012 when for the first time the committee linked its forecast for the stance of monetary policy to specific economic conditions. Accordingly, the statement on December 12, 2012, indicated that the "exceptionally low range for the federal funds rate (i.e., near zero) will be appropriate at least as long as the unemployment rate remains above 6 ½ per cent, inflation between one and two years ahead is projected to be no more than a half percentage point above the Committee's 2 per cent longer term goal, and longer-term inflation expectations continue to be well-anchored". In addition, the FOMC statement conveyed that monetary policy was expected to be "highly accommodative" for a "considerable time" after the end of the LSAP program. Following that meeting, labor market conditions improved and the unemployment rate fell more quickly than had been expected by both Fed and private market economists. Thus, the threshold of a 6.5 percent rate of unemployment was reached more quickly than was anticipated in the FOMC's December 2012 meeting. As a result, in its March 2014 statement, the FOMC altered once again its targeted reference point for forward guidance from a quantitative to qualitative basis by indicating that the duration of exceptionally low policy rates would depend on a "wide range of information" in the area of "labor market conditions". This change initiated a period until the present time in which the FOMC has emphasized the "data dependent" nature of its policy rate decisions.

It is important to note that the innovations in the use of forward guidance by the FOMC since the outbreak of the financial crisis have also been accompanied by other changes in the transparency and communication policy of the Fed. In February 2009, the FOMC began the practice of releasing on a quarterly basis the range of committee members' individual projections for inflation, unemployment and growth for the medium term (three years out). Then in early April 2011, the chairman initiated the practice of holding a press conference on the occasion of these releases. This action was followed by the formal adoption, as noted earlier, of a 2 percent inflation target, which was announced in a statement on longer run goals and policy strategy on January 12, 2012. In this same spirit, the FOMC released a statement on September 17, 2014, on "policy normalization principles and plans" to provide some guidance to the public on the conditions that would guide the adjustment of the federal funds rate to a more normal level and the reduction in the size of the Fed's balance sheet.

While the adjustments described above in the forward guidance offered by the FOMC suggest its experimental nature, one can also question the basis on which the committee was giving preference to its twin statutory objectives of maximum employment and low inflation in its policy deliberations. Even though the committee had adopted an explicit target of 2 percent for the rate of inflation over the medium to long term, the timetable for accommodative monetary policy seemed to have been conditioned mainly on labor market conditions. This focus represented a major shift in the perspective of the FOMC compared with that of the period leading up to the outbreak of the global financial crisis when, in mid-September 2008 for example, the main concern of the committee in its statements was the risk of rising inflation. By contrast, the fact that the FOMC began its process of interest rate normalization in December 2015, even though the rate of inflation was well below the Fed's target of 2 percent, has led to some criticism that the Fed's action was pre-mature if not unclear as to what the basis for its decision was. This critique has given rise to many calls, including from the US Congress, for the FOMC to adopt a formal model, such as one based on the "Taylor Rule" discussed earlier, at least for purposes of providing a quantitative reference point for the FOMC to use while making its decision about the actual level of that rate to be set for purposes of defining the stance of monetary policy.[25] However, adopting such a rule would be an important shift away from the operational independence that the Fed now enjoys in pursuing a specific target for stable inflation of around 2 percent and maximum employment, while being subject to ex post accountability for the achievement of these goals. Under the Taylor rule's approach, there is likely to be an erosion of central bank independence with closer Congressional scrutiny of each monetary policy decision of the FOMC.

ASSESSING THE IMPACT OF THE GOVERNMENT'S POLICY TO PROMOTE ECONOMIC RECOVERY

Now that the Fed's experimentation with unconventional monetary policy has been concluded, it is fair to ask what was the impact of its use of forward guidance and QE on the pace of economic recovery. As a first step in answering this question, it is useful to try to measure the extent to which monetary policy was expansionary or contractionary since the outbreak of the crisis. In normal times, for purposes of making this judgment, one could compare the actual federal funds rate adjusted for inflation with some measure of a "neutral" rate, which is deemed to be consistent with stable inflation and full employment consistent with actual output at or near its potential level. If the actual policy rate is above the neutral rate, then the stance of monetary policy can be judged to be contractionary, in the sense that output is likely to be well below its potential level. Conversely, if the actual policy rate is below the estimated neutral rate, then monetary policy is likely to be unduly expansionary, in the sense that inflation may exceed its targeted level. The concept of the neutral rate of interest appears to have been first discussed by the FOMC at its meeting of October 27–28, 2015.[26]

The neutral rate of interest is not an observable or measurable statistic, however, and needs to be estimated on the basis of data that can be observed. Prior to the financial crisis, the neutral rate was estimated to be around 2 percent—that is, a nominal rate of 4 percent less an expected or targeted rate of inflation of around 2 percent. However, since the outbreak of the financial crisis, the neutral rate is estimated to have declined sharply to a maximum negative level of around 5 percent in mid-2009, with a gradual recovery since then, albeit still being in negative territory, according to various models used by the Fed (Yellen 2015). With the actual federal funds rate at the zero lower bound since the end of 2008, it too has been at negative levels of around 1 percent, taking measured inflation into account. By this comparison, the stance of monetary policy has been highly contractionary. However, such a comparison fails to take account of any impact of the Fed's unconventional monetary policy. In order to quantify this gap, studies have been carried out that have attempted to calculate what the trajectory of a "shadow" policy rate for the Fed would have looked like if the federal funds rate were not limited by the zero lower bound. This path can then be compared with an estimated path of the neutral policy rate to show how well aligned the shadow rate has been

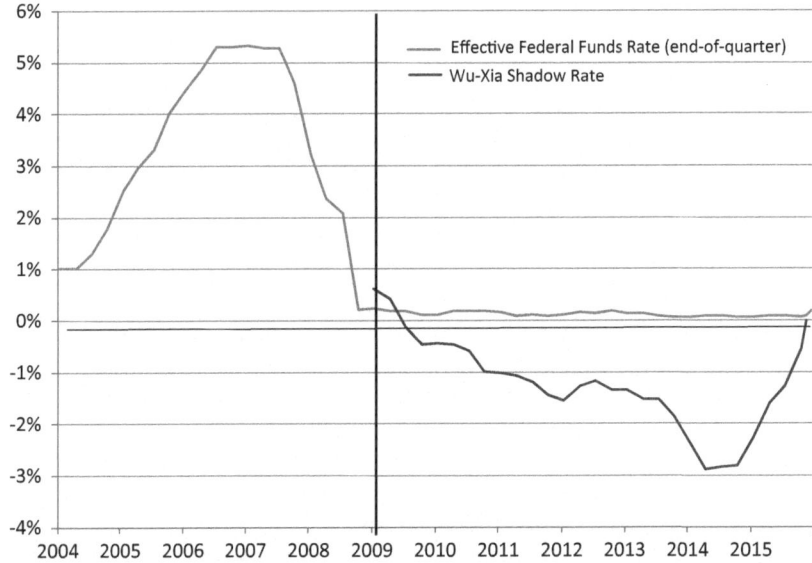

Chart 4.3 Actual and "shadow" federal reserve policy rates (in percent) (Source: Estimates of the Shadow Federal Funds Rate by Jing Cynthia Wu and Fan Dora Xia, available at the Federal Reserve Bank of Atlanta (www.frbatlanta.org/cqer/research/shadow_rate))

with such a rate, and whether or not the stance of the FOMC was relatively expansionary or contractionary by the degree to which the shadow rate, adjusted for inflation, was above or below the neutral rate. As shown in Chart 4.3, the results of one of these studies show that the shadow policy rate has fallen steadily during the period of QE to minus 3 percent in nominal terms by mid-2014 (or roughly 4–4.5 percent in real terms); at that point in time, the shadow policy rate would have been lower than the neutral policy rate estimated by the Fed, thus suggesting that the stance of monetary policy had become highly accommodative. By the end of 2015, it has been estimated that both the shadow policy rate and the neutral rate were approaching the zero lower bound.[27]

What determines the neutral rate of interest and why has it declined so sharply since the outbreak of the crisis? In normal times, the neutral rate of interest could be expected to rise or fall in line with the expected growth in the labor force, labor productivity and investors' risk perception. A reduced rate of growth in the labor force and labor productivity would imply a minimal growth in total output and thus a low level of the neutral rate of interest. By the same token, a higher risk premium for investment, due for example to great uncertainty in the economic outlook, would require a lower neutral or risk-free rate of interest to encourage the same level of investment as in the past. The neutral rate also reflects the degree to which consumers have a preference to consume today rather than tomorrow. A high household preference for consumption today would tend to raise the neutral rate of interest, so as to encourage an increase in savings for consumption in the future.

The sharp fall in the neutral rate of interest since the outbreak of the crisis reflects a number of negative shocks related to many of the factors just noted. If one thinks of the neutral rate of interest as the equilibrating device between savings and investment, clearly there has been a downward shift in investment demand since the outbreak of the crisis, which has been accompanied by a decline in the neutral rate. With an uncertain economic outlook, investment demand has continued to be weak, consistent with the notion that there has been an increase in investors' risk perception. There have also been outward shifts in the supply of savings reflecting an increase in inequality, as well as trends suggesting an increase in global savings. Finally, one can point to a slowdown in the growth of the labor force associated with a decline in labor force participation rates and an aging population. These trends have been matched by a decline in labor productivity.[28]

A number of analysts have argued that the neutral rate or real rate of interest has been trending downward for a period of time beginning well before the financial crisis. This fact, along with the slow pace of economic recovery, has raised concerns that the economy may be facing a period of "secular stagnation", noted earlier, similar to that experienced by Japan in its nearly two-decade period of weak economic growth. Such a prospect would suggest that the neutral or equilibrium rate of interest will not return to levels typical of the pre-crisis period. Indeed, in its deliberations, the FOMC has suggested that the process of interest rate normalization can be expected to be a slow and gradual one. In their published projections, FOMC members have also tended to predict that the federal funds rate will not return to levels that had been observed in the period prior to the crisis.

Given the slow pace of recovery from the crisis and the significantly expansionary stance of monetary policy as reflected in measures of the shadow federal funds rate, it is fair to ask what has been its quantitative effect in macroeconomic terms. Rather than try to isolate the effects of the Fed's forward guidance and QE, most studies have tended to look at their combined effects. One recent study by the Fed's research department has estimated that the Fed's unconventional monetary policy contributed 1.5 percentage points to the decline in the unemployment rate since mid-2009 and 0.5 percentage points to the rate of inflation. These are significant but not dramatic effects, especially given the magnitude of the policy response by the Federal Reserve.[29] The same study also suggested that the policy impact of the FOMC decisions might have been larger had there been a greater impulse at the beginning of the crisis period than toward the end, contrary to what in fact occurred. Such a conclusion, however, suggests that there exists more clarity as to what have been the channels by which the policy intentions of forward guidance and QE have been transmitted to the broader economy. For example, it is not clear to what extent the impact of QE on inflation and unemployment came about as a result of the effect on spending of a decline in medium- and long-term interest rates or of an increase in wealth associated with a rise in asset prices or through some other channel.

Notwithstanding these positive effects of the Fed's LSAP, some concerns have been raised about the negative effects of this program on increasing financial risks in the financial system through the creation of such an abnormally low interest rate environment. In this environment, investors have been inclined to take on increasingly risky investments in a search for higher yields in their investment portfolio, such as high yield "junk" bond mutual funds or exchange-traded funds. In late 2015, as FOMC officials were sending clearer signals of their intent to begin a process of interest rate normalization, these kind of investment vehicles came under increasing pressure and a number of them had to be closed. Another concern could be the impact of QE on the prices of assets other than bonds directly affected by the program, such as stocks, real estate, land and commodities. Has there been any mispricing of these assets that has distorted investment patterns?

The emergence of these risks raises questions as to whether the Fed was pursuing due diligence in so far as its responsibility for financial system stability was concerned. In the wake of the crisis, the Fed was given an explicit mandate under the Dodd-Frank Bill of 2010 to oversee financial system stability along with a newly created, inter-agency council called the Financial Stability Oversight Council under the chairmanship of the

Secretary of the Treasury. Apart from its oversight responsibilities, the challenge for the Fed going forward is how it might utilize specific macro-prudential tools to address system-wide risks associated with a new bubble phenomenon, for example, as distinct from its micro-prudential responsibility that it exercises through individual bank examinations and supervision. These issues are discussed in Chap. 7.

In light of the empirical findings on the impact of the Fed's unconventional monetary policy and the undershooting of its inflation target through the end of 2015, it is fair to ask whether there was any other policy initiative that the monetary authorities could have tried in order to spur a more rapid pace of economic recovery. One suggestion that has been made was to experiment with the device of so-called helicopter money. This term conveys the notion, which can be attributed to Milton Friedman, that the US Treasury Department would engage in a one-time lump sum transfer of cash, for example, to every taxpayer or citizen, of a certain amount to be financed by a non-debt creating loan of the Federal Reserve. Such an amount would be seen as "manna from heaven" or helicopter money by its recipients and would presumably generate successive rounds of spending. Adair Turner has presented a particularly strong case for this type of fiscal-monetary stimulus, although it is recognized that this proposal represents more a theoretical proposition than a practical policy solution to the slow pace of economic recovery.[30]

Another issue of debate in judging the impact of the Fed's unconventional monetary policy is whether or not it has had negative spillover effects on emerging market economies. Here the evidence suggests that emerging market economies have become more sensitive to capital flows induced by monetary policy conditions in the US economy and expectations of changes in those conditions. During the period of highly accommodative monetary policy and successive rounds of QE, capital flows to emerging market economies have been quite buoyant. This aspect of financial globalization has raised challenges for exchange rate and monetary policy management in these countries to avoid an overheating of their economies. In some cases, capital controls have been introduced to discourage capital inflows. Concerns of competitive devaluation (or "currency wars") and "beggar-thy-neighbor" policies have also been raised. When Fed officials began to discuss the possibility of a reduction in the volume of monthly bond purchases under QE3 in the middle of 2013, signals of this kind created additional volatility in capital flows ("taper tantrum") and a reversal of capital flows, which were intensified as the Fed moved closer to its date of starting a process of interest rate normalization in December 2015. Fed officials have tended to downplay concerns about the negative spillover effects of their actions by arguing that there has been extensive consultation among central bank authorities of G20 countries through various international fora and that as long as the policy intent of the Fed is focused on improving economic conditions in the US economy, such an outcome has to be, on balance, a net positive benefit for the global economy.[31] Following his retirement from the Fed, Ben Bernanke used the occasion of the annual Mundell-Fleming Lecture at the IMF in early November 2015 to argue that the negative spillover effects of the Fed's QE policy via a depreciation of the dollar on US exports were largely offset by the positive effects of an increase in global demand and US imports arising from an expansionary policy.[32] The issue of international policy coordination is discussed further in Chap. 7.

Clearly, one of the implications of the empirical studies on the economic effects of unconventional monetary policy is that the Fed was facing significant "headwinds" in its effort to promote economic recovery. One of these was the dampened risk appetite on the part of private investors owing to the uncertain economic outlook, as noted above. Another has been the appreciation of the US dollar, especially since the middle of 2014, which has acted as a brake on export growth. With policy interest rates at or somewhat below the zero lower bound in the United States and Western Europe, the announcement of policy changes or intentions had dramatic effects on the dollar-euro exchange rate as a result of shifts in the expectations of financial market participants well before policy implementation began. These effects were particularly strong during the second half of 2014 as the ECB was signaling its intent to move to a more expansionary monetary stance while the Fed was signaling its intent to move in the opposite direction; as a result, the euro depreciated by around 20 percent against the dollar.

Still another factor dampening the impact of the Fed's relaxed monetary stance was the shift to a contractionary fiscal stance, which occurred during the early period of economic recovery. Notwithstanding the political consensus that was developed in early 2009 to support a significant fiscal stimulus package, this consensus was quickly eroded as signs of an economic and financial turn-around began to be visible after the middle of that year. What is striking about this experience in fiscal policy-making is the degree to which there has been a complete absence of any political or academic consensus on a counter-cyclical role for fiscal policy, unlike the case for monetary policy. At one level, doubts about fiscal policy have reflected concerns about the size of government spending and the level of the public debt; such concerns were fostered by a view that fiscal retrenchment could be stimulative for the economy in situations where the size of the public debt was judged to be too high. At another level, there has been a vigorous debate about the economic impact of fiscal expansion and the size of government multipliers. In the United States, concerns about the size of government spending and the public debt have been a major source of debate between the two major political parties, which has for all intents and purposes prevented the use of discretionary or temporary fiscal measures as a means of counter-cyclical macroeconomic policy. With the increase in federal spending for extraordinary measures such as the TARP, the early 2009 fiscal stimulus bill and the effects of the economic recession on tax revenues, the overall central government deficit in the United States rose from the equivalent of 3 percent of GDP in 2008 to around 10 percent in 2009 (according to data of the Congressional Budget Office), while the government debt held by the public increased from 39 percent to 52 percent, measured on the same basis.

In these conditions and with signs of an incipient economic recovery in 2010, political pressures for fiscal retrenchment grew sharply in the US Congress, with little appreciation for how the size and timing of a shift in fiscal policy could represent an important drag on the economic recovery. This shift was reinforced by the effect of balanced budget requirements at the state and local government levels, which at least during 2009 had been overridden by special transfers from the central government as part of its fiscal stimulus package. Accordingly, at the general government level, following a near doubling of the overall deficit to around 13 percent of GDP in 2009, the overall government deficit was reduced by one-half over the next four years, with most of the reduction front-loaded in 2010–11. According to calculations of the Brookings Institution, the impact of these changes in fiscal policy on the growth in real GDP shifted from a positive impulse of around 2 percentage points during 2009–10 to a negative one of an estimated 1 percentage point during 2012–14.[33]

Much of the misconception about the potential counter-cyclical role of fiscal policy relates to the size of fiscal multipliers. Keynes in the *General Theory* was the first economist to focus on the notion of a fiscal multiplier, especially at a time of weakened aggregate demand such as during the Great Depression, in raising national income by an amount larger than the increase in government spending. Since his time, there has been a great debate about the size of fiscal multipliers, and until recently, especially in the age of new Keynesian dynamic stochastic general equilibrium (DSGE) models, they were viewed as relatively small and certainly less than one. At a conceptual level, one challenge to Keynes' idea of a significant fiscal multiplier has come from the new classical school of economists, who have argued the case of "Ricardian Equivalence". This notion, which is grounded in the notion of rational expectations, argues that any increase in government spending, whether financed by an increase in taxes or borrowing, will not have any expansionary effect on national output as private agents will reduce their spending by an equivalent amount in order to pay now or at some time in the future the taxes that are needed to pay for that spending. By this logic, fiscal multipliers should be zero.

However, empirical studies have shown that fiscal multipliers can be positive and larger than one, especially at a time of aggregate demand contraction such as during the Great Depressions and Great Recession. For example, one study by Auerbach and Gorodnichenko (2015) has concluded that fiscal multipliers can be as high as 1.5–2 (i.e., one dollar of government spending can raise aggregate output by US$1.50–$2) and tend to be higher in economic recessions than in expansions.[34] The significance of fiscal multipliers has also been confirmed in the European context in relation to the impact of fiscal consolidation or retrenchment programs within the euro zone, and in particular in the case of Greece (which is discussed further in Chap. 5).[35]

In view of the weak recovery and the likely significant size of the fiscal multiplier, a number of economists have argued that an increase in government expenditure on infrastructure projects could contribute in an important way to the economic recovery without increasing the debt-to-GDP ratio for the United States because of the low rates of interest available to the government for its financing needs.[36] In this regard, it is noteworthy that the Federal Government spending on investment fell to its lowest level in relation to GDP in 2014 and a full percentage point below the average of 1.5 percent registered for the 1970–2010 period.[37]

THE FUTURE OF MONETARY POLICY

In order to start the process of interest rate normalization, the Fed faced a new challenge of how it would manage upward adjustments in the federal funds rate at the end of 2015. Given the enormous expansion in the reserve deposits of banks at the Federal Reserve, the traditional practice of open-market operations could no longer be used. In these conditions, the Fed has made use of two new procedures to bring about increases in the federal funds rate. One is an upward adjustment in the level of the interest rate it offers on banks' excess reserves that is expected to set a ceiling for the level of the federal funds rate. Following the decision of the FOMC on December 17, 2015 to raise its target for the federal funds rate from a range of 0–0.25 percent to one of 0.25–0.5 percent, the rate on banks' excess reserves was raised from 0.25 percent to 0.50 percent. In order to reinforce the effect of this adjustment, the Fed has begun "reverse REPO" operations with non-bank financial institutions, such as money market funds, to negotiate the sale of some of its holdings of short-term treasury bills through overnight REPOs at a rate within the new target range for the federal funds rate. These transactions have had the effect of withdrawing liquidity from short-term money markets and raising the cost of funds in those markets to match those charged in the inter-bank market.

To begin the process of interest rate regularization, the Fed suggested after its last meeting in December 2015 that it would make four 0.25-point increases in the federal funds rate during 2016, but this projection was subsequently relaxed in the light of economic developments. The initial set of projected adjustments in the Fed's policy rate reflected the median of the forecasts made by each member of the FOMC which spanned a significant range. In the future, it would be clearer if the FOMC agreed on one path of projected interest rate adjustments, subject to revision at subsequent meetings, to provide a clearer signal of the Fed's intentions for monetary policy, instead of publishing a "dot plot" of 14 different projections.

Once the Fed has raised its short-term policy rate to more "normal" levels, it will begin the process of reducing the size of its balance sheet, first by not rolling over its investments in long-term securities when they come to maturity and then by selling other holdings at a measured pace. The plan of selling the Fed's holdings of government securities during a period when interest rates are likely to be higher than they are now and have been for a number of years raises the distinct prospect of losses for the Fed. Potentially this process of normalization could threaten the Fed's solvency and shift its position from that of being a significant source of interest income and revenue to the US Treasury to one of being a contributor to the government's budget deficit, apart from any special transfers the Fed might require to restore its equity position.

During this process of interest rate normalization, the Fed has had to manage the somewhat delicate process of keeping commercial bank reserve deposits at their extraordinary levels. In the absence of Federal Reserve requirements mandating such high levels of commercial bank reserves, banks have always had the freedom to convert those balances into other earning assets in the form of loans to consumers and businesses. With a required reserve ratio of 10 percent, each dollar of excess reserves could support a loan of ten dollars. According to one analysis, the current equilibrium of large excess reserves of the banks depends upon an implicit understanding that each bank will maintain a high level of excess reserves as long as it believes that other banks will do the same. This situation could obviously change, especially were there to be a significant improvement in business activity. In the event of a sudden surge in bank lending activity, the Fed would be faced with a new challenge of how to forestall a significant jump in the rate of inflation. In these circumstances, the Fed would need to start selling portions of its large portfolio of government securities in order to absorb some of the excess reserves of the banks or increase the required reserve ratio of the banks. These events would represent a major departure from the policy scenario which the Fed has recently been pursuing and would potentially introduce a destabilizing shock into the financial system.[38]

SUMMARY AND CONCLUSION

The policy responses to the financial crisis, first in terms of emergency measures to deal with the outbreak of full-scale panic and the threat of economic collapse and then in terms of policy actions to promote economic recovery, were unusual in that there was no clear playbook or guidance from contemporary macroeconomic thinking to frame the measures that were actually adopted by the fiscal and monetary authorities. Instead, they relied on the basic lessons of the experience of the Great Depression as regards the need for extraordinary actions by the central bank and the government. Beginning at the end of 2007, the Fed played an effective role as an LOLR both at the domestic and international levels to prevent a collapse of the financial system and sharply reduced its short-term policy rate to limit the downturn in economic activity. Soon after the failure of Lehman Brothers in September 2008, the US government complemented the Fed by introducing a strong program of bank capital repair and fiscal stimulus. Similar measures were adopted in the other advanced countries most affected by the financial crisis.

Facing the dual challenge of a "liquidity trap" and zero lower bound on its policy lending rate at the beginning of 2009, the Fed quickly shifted to unconventional monetary policies in the form of "forward guidance" and "quantitative easing (QE)" in order to stimulate economic recovery. Contrary to the Fed's normal focus on short-term interest rates, the latter policies were aimed directly at reducing long-term interest rates as a means of promoting home purchases or re-financing the purchase of consumer durables and business investment. What was not well appreciated initially by the authorities was the slow and prolonged pace of economic recovery, which typically follows a financial crisis and the need for a strong program of stimulus early in the cycle or more rounds of monetary and fiscal expansion than initially assumed.

By most metrics, the Fed and US Treasury injected significant monetary and fiscal stimulus into the economy during 2009–10, but this coordination was weakened in subsequent years with a shift to fiscal consolidation or budget deficit reduction. This reversal of fiscal policy resulted in a significant drag on economic activity through 2014. During this time period, there were also conflicts between the Fed's purchase of long-term government securities in the financial markets and the US Treasury's debt management program aimed at lengthening the term structure of its public debt. Most studies suggest that the Fed's unconventional monetary policy programs had some limited effect on raising the rate of inflation and lowering unemployment, but the channels through which these effects were transmitted to the economy are not clear.

At a time when short-term policy rates have been at their zero lower bound or even below as in the case of Western Europe, the experience of dealing with the effects of the crisis has demonstrated that large increases in central bank base money arising from "QE" are not inflationary, that fiscal expansion does not raise interest rates and that fiscal multipliers are greater than unity. Each of these conclusions contradicted economic doctrine widely held prior to the crisis, in particular as regards the impact of fiscal policy.

Notwithstanding the sustained impulse of monetary expansion that was initiated in the wake of the crisis, economic recovery has remained weak. One reason for this development is related to the long-term impact of the crisis on potential output as a result of lost labor skills resulting from long-term unemployment, deferred investment in a climate of economic uncertainty and a decline in the capital stock. These effects of the crisis are captured by the term "hysteresis". The negative aftereffects of the crisis and the difficulty of promoting full economic recovery has also raised concerns among many economists that the United States and other advanced economies may be facing a period of "secular stagnation" because of a decline in labor force growth and participation, along with a long-term slowdown in the growth of labor productivity.

The Fed and other major central banks face a number of unprecedented challenges going forward in attempting to normalize their monetary policy program and reduce the size of their balance sheets, which have expanded substantially in relation to GDP especially in the case of the Federal Reserve and Bank of England. This process of normalization is likely to play out over several years and will need to be managed carefully in order not to destabilize the financial system or result in significant capital losses for the central banks involved. The sustained low level of central bank policy rates, which have been reduced below zero in the case of a number of central banks in Western Europe, may have stimulated increasingly risky behavior on the part of investors in search of higher yields while creating difficulties for banks and other financial institutions because of the tightening of their interest rate margins.

Notes

1. These remarks were made in an interview with Martin Wolf at a Bretton Woods Conference of the Institute for New Economic Thinking on April 9, 2011, which can be found on YouTube.com.

2. Since the beginning of the crisis, two studies of the historical record that examine these issues have been carried out by Oscar Jorda, Moritz Schularick and Alan Taylor "Financial Crises, Credit Booms and External Imbalances: 140 Years of Lessons" NBER Working Paper 16569 (Dec. 2010) and "Leveraged Bubbles" NBER Working Paper 21486 (Aug. 2015). A more elaborate account of the nature of economic recoveries from financial crises is presented in Carmen Reinhart and Ken Rogoff (2009) *This Time is Different* (Princeton, NJ: Princeton University Press).

3. The term "divine coincidence" can be attributed to academic writing by Olivier Blanchard and Jordi Gali "Real Wage Rigidities and the New Keynesian Model" NBER Working Paper 11806 (Nov. 2005).

4. The "Taylor Rule" is attributed to Professor John Taylor of Stanford University and was first elaborated in Taylor "Discretion vs. Policy Rules in Practice" Carnegie-Mellon Conference Series in Public Policy (1993).

5. Jason Furman has provided a number of charts providing comparative macroeconomic data on the aftermath of the Great Depression in the United States and the Global Financial Crisis for the United States and the European Union ("It Could Have Happened Here: The Policy Response that Helped Prevent a Second Great Depression" Remarks at Macroeconomic Advisors' 25th Annual Washington Policy Seminar on Sept. 9, 2015, which is available at the website of the White House Council of Economic Advisors www.whitehouse.gov/administration/eop/cea).

6. Ben Bernanke (2015) provides a good first-hand account of the Federal Reserve's policy actions during the period immediately preceding and following the outbreak of the crisis in late 2008 (Ben Bernanke *The Courage to Act: A Memoir of a Crisis and its Aftermath* (New York: W.W. Norton)).

7. Alan Blinder provides a sober analysis of why the Federal Reserve's treatment of Bear Stearns and Lehman Brothers should not have been different. However, with the benefit of hindsight, things may appear differently than they did at the height of crisis ("What Did We Learn from the Financial Crisis, the Great Recession and the Pathetic Recovery" Working Paper #243 Griswold Center for Economic Policy Studies Nov. 2014).

8. According to some analysts (Wallison 2015), Fannie Mae and Freddie Mac bear primary responsibility for fomenting the crisis because of their heavy involvement in the development, spread and acquisition of MBS. While these institutions certainly played a role in the onset of the crisis, other factors must also be considered, such as the role of the rating agencies, weak financial supervision by bank regulators and the SEC, and the absence of oversight of derivative trading; see Peter Wallison (2015) *Hidden in Plain Sight: What Really Caused the World's Worst Financial Crisis and Why It Could Happen Again* (New York: Encounter Books).

9. For one contribution to this debate, see Robert Hetzel "Monetary Policy in the 2008–09 Recession" <u>Economic Quarterly</u> Federal Reserve Bank of Richmond v. 95 (2); pp. 201–33, Spring 2009.

10. This commentary is based on a study by Stephen Golub, Ayse Kaya, and Michael Reay entitled "What Were They Thinking? The Federal Reserve in the Run-up to the Crisis" Review of International Political Economy, vol. 22(4), pp. 657–692 (2015).

11. Under the Chairmanship of Ben Bernanke, FOMC members were encouraged to speak out on a variety of issues relevant to the Fed's work, including FOMC policy decisions. This practice has contributed to greater transparency regarding the Federal Reserve's role in the economy.

12. These estimates of the impact of lender of last resort financing is taken from Qianying Chen, Marco Lombardi, Alex Ross and Feng Zhu "Global Impact of US and Euro Area Unconventional Monetary Policies: A Comparison", a paper presented at the 16th Jacques Polak Annual Research Conference of the IMF, Nov. 5–6, 2015.

13. The official record of investments and repayments under the TARP can be found in the fiscal year Agency Financial Reports – TARP of the Office of Financial Stability of the US Treasury Department, which are available at www.treasury.gov/initiative/financial-stability/reports.

14. According to one model-based set of estimates (Blinder and Zandi (2015), in the absence of the government's emergency financial measures in late 2008 and early 2009, the decline in real GDP for the US economy would have been 14 percent instead of 4 percent, the unemployment rate would have peaked at 16 percent instead of 10 percent and the recession would have persisted for three years, or more than twice as long as it did in fact (Alan Blinder and Mark Zandi "The Financial Crisis: Lessons for the Future" Report of the Center for Budget and Policy Priorities, October 15, 2015, available at www. cbpp.org).

15. The new Secretary of the Treasury under President Obama, Tim Geithner, was the leading proponent of stress tests and bank recapitalization as an alternative to outright nationalization of the banks that was strongly advocated by some officials in the administration or members of Congress. For an analysis of the stress test operation, see Marcelo Fernandez, Deniz Egan and Marcelo Pinheiro "March Madness in Wall Street: What Does the Market Learn from Stress Tests?" IMF Working Paper/15/271 (Dec. 2015); Timothy Geithner (2015) *Stress Test: Reflections on Financial Crises*

(New York: Broadway Books); and Gary Gorton "Stress for Success: A Review of Timothy Geithner's Financial Crisis Memoir" Journal of Economic Literature v. 53(4); pp. 975–95, Dec. 2015.

16. This thesis is fully explored by Atif Mian and Amir Sufi (2015) *House of Debt* (Chicago: University of Chicago Press) and is also examined by Bernanke (2015) op. cit. in his comments on the failed restructuring programs of the Federal Housing Authority.

17. Technically, the ECB did not reach the zero lower bound for its main lending rate until the end of 2015, following a reduction to 1 percent in mid-2009 and an aborted attempt to raise it in mid-2011.

18. For an updated version of Keynes' concept of the liquidity trap, see Paul Krugman (1998) "It's Baaack: Japan's Slump and the Return of the Liquidity Trap", Brookings Papers on Economic Activity 1998 (1); pp. 137–205.

19. The determination of the federal funds rate before and after the decision to pay interest on the excess reserves of commercial banks at the Federal Reserve is explored in Stephen Williamson "Monetary Policy Normalization in the US" Federal Reserve Bank of St. Louis Review v. 97(2); pp. 87–108 (2015).

20. The impact of sustained recessions on lowering "potential" output, a phenomenon referred to as "hysteresis", has recently been well documented in studies by Olivier Blanchard, Eugenio Cerutti and Lawrence Summers "Inflation and Activity – Two Explorations and Their Monetary Policy Implications" IMF Working Paper/15/230 (Nov. 2015) and Robert Martin, Teyanna Munyan and Beth Anne Wilson "Potential Output and Recessions: Are We Fooling Ourselves" International Finance Discussion Papers #1145 (Sept. 2015). Professor Lawrence Summers of Harvard has been a leading proponent of the thesis of "secular stagnation", which argues that as a result of a number of long-run changes in the economy, such as a decline in productivity growth and in the growth of the labor force due to demographic changes, the United States and other advanced countries may be facing an indefinite period of lower economic growth than in the past. The views of Professor Summers and others is presented in Coen Teulings and

Richard Baldwin (2014) *Secular Stagnation – Facts, Causes and Cures* (CEPR 2014), an eBook available at www.VoxEu.org.

21. The conflict between the Federal Reserve's LSAP and the Treasury Department's public debt policy is explored in Robin Greenwood, Samuel Hanson, Joshua Rudolph and Lawrence Summers "Government Debt Management at the Zero Lower Bound" Working Paper #5 of the Brookings Institution's Hutchins Center on Fiscal and Monetary Studies (Sept. 30, 2014).

22. The data on the Fed's purchases of government securities are taken from a speech by J. Christopher Giancarlo, a member of the Commodity Futures Trading Commission, to the Harvard Law School on December 1, 2015, which is available at www.cftc.gov.

23. For a retrospective view on "forward guidance", see Ben Bernanke "Communications and Monetary Policy" Herbert Stein Memorial Lecture (National Economists Club), November 19, 2013. The discussion in this part of the chapter also reflects views presented in A. Lee Smith and Thealexa Becker "Has Forward Guidance Been Effective?" Federal Reserve Bank of Kansas City <u>Economic Review</u> v. 100 (3); pp. 57–78 (Quarter 3, 2015).

24. Smith and Becker (2015), op. cit.

25. The Fed Oversight Reform and Modernization (FORM) Act, which was passed by the US House of Representatives on November 19, 2015, would require the Fed to establish a mathematical formula, or "directive policy rule" to determine how the FOMC should adjust the stance of monetary policy at each of its meetings. For a critique of the bill presented by Fed Chair Janet Yellen prior to its passage, see her Ryan-Pelosi letter of November 16, which is available at www.federalreserve.gov.

26. For an early public statement by the Federal Reserve on the neutral rate of interest, see Janet Yellen "The Economic Outlook and Monetary Policy" Remarks at Economic Club of Washington DC on December 2, 2015, which is available at www.federalreserve. gov. A more extended, analytical examination of the neutral rate can be found in James Hamilton, Ethan Harris, Jan Hatzins, and Kenneth West "The Equilibrium Real Funds Rate: Past, Present and Future", a paper presented at the US Monetary Policy Forum in New York City (February 27, 2015).

27. The data for the "shadow" federal funds rate can be located at the Center for Quantitative Economic Research at the Federal Reserve Bank of Atlanta (www.federalreservebankatlanta.org/cqer/research/shadow-rate). The methodology for calculating the "shadow" rate is explained in Jing Cynthia Wu and Fan Dora Xia "Measuring the Macroeconomic Impact of Monetary Policy at the Zero Lower Bound", forthcoming in <u>Journal of Money, Credit, and Banking</u>, which can also be accessed at website cited above.

28. Lukasz Rachel and Thomas Smith in "Secular Drivers of the Global Real Interest Rate" Bank of England Staff Working Paper #571 (Dec. 2015) present an illuminating analysis of the various factors that can account for the secular decline in the equilibrium real rate of interest in the US and other advanced countries.

29. Eric Engen, Thomas Laubach and David Reifschneider "The Macroeconomic Effects of the Federal Reserve's Unconventional Monetary Policies" Federal Reserve Discussion Series Working Paper #2015-005 (January 2015).

30. The case for "helicopter money" has been forcefully argued by Adair Turner (2015) *Between Debt and the Devil: Money, Credit and Fixing Global Finance* (Princeton, NJ: Princeton University Press).

31. The issue of spillover effects from the Fed's QE programs is examined in Qianying Chen, Andrew Filardo, Dong He and Feng Zhu "Financial Crisis, US Unconventional Monetary Policy and International Spillovers" IMF Working Paper/15/85 (April 2015).

32. Ben Bernanke, "Federal Reserve Policy in an International Context" Mundell-Fleming Lecture presented at the 16th Jacques Polak Annual Research Conference November 5–6, 2015, which is available at www.imf.org

33. These calculations are based on the fiscal impact measure of the Hutchins Center on Fiscal and Monetary Policy, which can be found at www.brookings.edu/research/interactives/2014/fiscal-barometer.

34. These estimates are presented Alan Auerbach and Yuriy Gorodnichenko "How Powerful are Fiscal Multipliers in Recessions?" <u>NBER Reporter</u> 2015 (2); pp. 21–24. A separate issue is whether the multiplier associated with tax adjustments is different from that for expenditure changes; for example, there is some empirical evidence showing that the fiscal stimulus of tax cuts may be stronger than that of expenditure increases, whereas expen-

diture cuts may be more significant than tax increases in reducing fiscal deficits and the debt-to-GDP ratio during fiscal consolidations; see Alberto Alesina and Sylvia Ardagna "Large Changes in Fiscal Policy: Taxes versus Spending" in Jeffrey Brown (editor) *Tax Policy and the Economy* (Chicago: University of Chicago Press) 2010; pp. 35–68.

35. An analysis of the implied fiscal multipliers in fiscal consolidation programs in the euro zone is presented in Olivier Blanchard and Daniel Leigh "Growth Forecast Errors and Fiscal Multipliers" IMF Working Paper/13/01 (January 2013).

36. This case was most effectively presented in a paper by Brad DeLong and Lawrence Summers (2012), "Fiscal Policy in a Depressed Economy" Brookings Papers on Economic Activity 2012 (2); pp. 233–297 and Lawrence Ball, Brad DeLong, and Lawrence Summers (2104) "Fiscal Policy and Full Employment" Center on Budget and Policy Priorities (Washington, DC), April 2, 2014.

37. These data are taken from the blog, "Money, Banking and Financial Markets", January 4, 2016 (www.moneyandbanking.com).

38. The issue of banks' excess reserves and potential bank credit growth is examined in Christopher Whelan "Should We Worry About Excess Reserves?" Economic Policy Paper of the Federal Reserve Bank of Minneapolis (December 2015).

CHAPTER 5

The Role of the International Financial Architecture Prior to and Since the Global Financial Crisis

Given the international dimensions of the financial crisis, it is important to consider the defects in the global financial order or international financial architecture (IFA) that contributed to the onset of the crisis and how it has responded since. During the post-WW2 era, the Bretton Woods Institutions, and the International Monetary Fund (IMF) in particular, have been at the core of the IFA that governments established to oversee and promote global financial stability. With the growth and expansion of economic and financial globalization, the IFA has needed to be reformed over time, but the outbreak of the global financial crisis in late 2008 provided clear evidence of the defects in that system and the need for further reform.

In the remainder of this chapter, I discuss briefly the main elements of the IFA and how it has evolved over time. Then I examine in more detail the particular problems in the functioning of the IFA that contributed to the onset of the crisis. This discussion is followed by an examination of the main reforms of the IFA that governments have initiated and the contributions that the IFA has made to the resolution of the crisis. Finally, I consider the role of the IMF in the crisis of the euro zone, and in Greece in particular, within the context of the so-called Troika (the European Commission (EC), European Central Bank (ECB) and the IMF).

© The Author(s) 2017
A. Elson, *The Global Financial Crisis in Retrospect*,
DOI 10.1057/978-1-137-59750-2_5

WHAT IS THE INTERNATIONAL FINANCIAL ARCHITECTURE (IFA)?

The global financial order or IFA comprises the "rules of the game" or standards and codes that countries are expected to observe in their international financial relations and the cooperative institutional arrangements that governments have established to oversee and promote stability of the international monetary and financial system.[1] The international monetary system refers to the arrangements for the payment and transfer of funds from one currency to another to support trade in goods, services and financial assets. It centrally involves the exchange rate arrangements among members and the rules on exchange transactions and currency controls. The international financial system includes the international monetary system, as well as the flows in capital across countries and the changes in the asset and liability positions of private and public agents. The IMF was established in 1944 to be the central institution of the international monetary system for the oversight of its members' exchange rate arrangements and macroeconomic policies, to foster inter-governmental cooperation in international monetary relations and, along with other international organizations, to promote international financial stability.

Initially, the post-war international monetary order was organized on the basis of a gold-exchange standard, which was intended to be a more flexible version of the gold standard that had existed for many decades prior to WW1 but could not be managed effectively in the period between WW1 and WW2. Under the gold-exchange standard or Bretton Woods system established after WW2, the dollar was tied to gold at a fixed price of US$35 per ounce and all other currencies were tied to the dollar at exchange rates that were to be monitored and adjusted, if needed, with the supervision and approval of the IMF. The IMF was also available to provide financial assistance to countries in making the transition from one exchange rate peg to another or moving toward a regime of full current account convertibility, which was a principal objective of IMF membership. This system worked well for a time to support the resurgence of global trade in the aftermath of WW2 but had to be abandoned in 1972 as the United States failed to maintain a stable rate of inflation and was unable to honor its commitment to surrender gold in exchange for excess dollar liabilities accumulated by other countries.

In the wake of this breakdown, the members of the IMF agreed to move to a more decentralized system of exchange arrangements, in which each country was free to determine the nature of the exchange rate system it would operate (whether fixed or floating) and the IMF was charged with exercising surveillance over that system and the supporting macro-economic policies to make it viable. Under the Bretton Woods system, trade in goods and services grew to dominate international monetary transactions, while capital flows were generally subject to control and limitation during an era when domestic banking transactions were subject to tight regulation. However, international banking transactions had been expanding in offshore markets (such as the euro-dollar market), and from the mid-1970s these and other capital flows began to dominate international monetary transactions (as discussed in Chap. 1), thus opening the era of financial globalization as the advanced countries relaxed limitations and controls on capital flows.

As capital account convertibility became widespread among advanced countries and some emerging market economies during the 1980s and 1990s, the members of the IMF debated toward the end of that period whether capital account convertibility should also be established as a goal of IMF membership. But this proposal was formally rejected in 1998 because of the resistance from many emerging and developed countries in the IMF. These countries were worried about the volatility of international capital flows and the difficulty of managing international capital flows at a time when they were still pursuing reforms in exchange rate management, domestic monetary policy and banking regulation. There was also great concern at the time among these countries regarding their vulnerability to financial crises and the frequency of these events, which raised doubts among the emerging market economies about the benefits and virtues of full capital account liberalization.

The emerging market financial crises, which reached a peak of virulence in East Asia in the late 1990s, led to a second reform of the IMF and what had come to be known as the IFA. The latter reform was intended to strengthen the arrangements for promoting the stability of the global financial system and for protecting countries in their transition toward capital account liberalization. While not a formal objective of IMF membership, as in the case of current account convertibility, the official view within the IMF was that capital account liberalization was still a desirable goal for developing and emerging market economies in terms of the benefits of foreign direct investment, access to foreign project financing and consumption smoothing during temporary periods of commodity price swings. What had to be clarified were the pre-requisites and prior reform stages that countries needed to complete in pursuit of this objective. Some of these were embodied in a series of international standards and codes, which were developed to define the appropriate institutional and disclosure requirements to support statistical and financial reporting, and fiscal and monetary policy decision-making, as well as the arrangements to encourage the development of capital market institutions and banking and financial market regulation. Many of the latter codes were defined by international committees or organizations, such as the Basel Committee on Banking Supervision, which had been established by the advanced countries (organized via the G10) since the 1980s and convened from time to time at the facilities of the Bank for International Settlements (BIS) in Basel, Switzerland. In 1999, these various fora were loosely organized under an umbrella organization called the Financial Stability Forum (FSF), which among other things was given responsibility for focusing the work of these committees and organizations on the oversight of the global financial stability and for coordinating with the IMF in presenting their views to the semi-annual meetings of its International Monetary and Financial Committee (IMFC). The IMFC is the political directorate of finance ministers and central bank governors that examines key developments in the global economic and financial system and approves the work program of the IMF. The FSF also organized institutional reviews in coordination with the IMF and the World Bank of the progress countries, both advanced and emerging markets, were making in bringing their internal operating procedures in conformity with the international standards and codes through the preparation of Reports on the Observance of Standards and Codes (ROSCs) and the Financial Sector Assessment Program (FSAP). Along with the FSF, a new informal G20 committee of leading advanced and emerging market countries was formed to monitor developments in the global economic and financial system and efforts to improve the IFA. Political governance of the IFA still remained under the de facto control of the G7 (Canada, France, Germany, Italy, Japan, the United Kingdom and United States).

Within the IMF, efforts were made to strengthen its macroeconomic surveillance activities and increase its financial resources while establishing a new precautionary lending facility to provide a contingent line of credit for emerging market countries that could be vulnerable to sudden, destabilizing shifts in capital flows. A new Sovereign Debt Restructuring Mechanism (SDRM) operating under the umbrella of the IMF was also considered in the early 2000s as a means of promoting early resolution of the external debt sustainability problems for countries that could not be addressed solely by means of macroeconomic adjustment programs. Because of the resistance of the US government and some other advanced countries reflecting the concerns of private creditors, a much less ambitious approach on debt restructuring was adopted, which introduced new clauses in debt contracts to allow for collective action by a majority of creditors to establish new terms for sovereign debt in arrears even if some other creditors objected.

THE ROLE OF THE IFA IN THE LEAD-UP TO THE GLOBAL FINANCIAL CRISIS

In the period leading up to the global financial crisis, it was generally assumed among policy-makers in the advanced countries that efforts to improve the IFA needed to be focused primarily on the developing and emerging market economies as they moved toward capital account liberalization. Financial crises were assumed to be a problem mainly for these countries, which needed to be addressed by the IFA as regards both its crisis-prevention and crisis-management dimensions. The advanced countries generally guided the process and pace of IFA reform and, in many instances, used their practices and policies as benchmarks for "best practice" guidelines in many of the standards and codes that were developed.

At the same time, as major participants in the institutional framework of the IFA, the advanced countries were mainly responsible for the defects of the IFA in addressing problems that were brewing in the lead-up to the crisis. These can be classified into four principal domains: international policy coordination, the oversight of global financial stability, international financial regulation and the international lender of last resort (ILOLR) mechanism. In each of these operational dimensions of the IFA, there were major shortcomings that contributed to the outbreak of the financial crisis, which are briefly discussed in the paragraphs that follow.

International Policy Coordination

One of the objectives of the IFA is to provide a mechanism or forum to promote international policy coordination or cooperation to deal with emerging threats to macroeconomic stability at the regional or global level. The issue in this domain is why the IFA, and the IMF in particular as the principal international organization charged with responsibility for exercising surveillance over its members' macroeconomic policies and financial risks, was unable to bring about a coordinated adjustment of policies to deal with growing financial imbalances associated with the housing bubbles in a number of advanced countries. In the period prior to the crisis, it was generally recognized that there was a major expansion in global liquidity (or "savings glut") associated with growing imbalances in the flow of capital from surplus countries in East Asia to the advanced countries that supported a decline in real interest rates and an unconstrained increase in financial leverage and innovative finance linked to housing bubbles. This growth in liquidity within the advanced countries associated with the growing problem of global imbalances prior to the financial crisis can be identified with a surge in financing that supported housing bubbles not only in the United States but also in the United Kingdom, Ireland, Portugal and Spain. In the case of the United States, this phenomenon played out, as detailed in Chaps. 2 and 4, within the "shadow" banking system and with the growth in new securitized financial instruments. In the European Union, and euro zone in particular, this phenomenon was revealed in the flow of banking credits from northern tier countries to southern tier countries following the inauguration of the euro zone and the sharp drop in risk premia associated with borrowing by the southern tier countries. Soon after the launch of a common currency and monetary policy, coupled with agreed rules on fiscal behavior, credit risks across the euro zone were perceived to have reached a common convergence point that gave rise to a sharp growth in bank credits from the current account surplus countries of the northern tier of the euro zone to the deficit countries of the southern tier.

In this environment of growing global and regional imbalances, the IMF's surveillance operations at the country and global levels ideally should have been able to identify emerging financial risks and vulnerabilities and to advise countries on the needed policy adjustments to deal with them. One of the objectives of the IMF's macroeconomic surveillance operations is to promote orderly adjustment programs for countries facing domestic or external financial imbalances and to facilitate international policy collaboration to bring about joint adjustment efforts or to deal with the spillover effects of these efforts. The IMF's influence on countries is greatest when a country is seeking its financial assistance, as in these circumstances the IMF can seek to establish policy conditions attached to the disbursement of such assistance. At other times, when the IMF has identified a macroeconomic problem requiring policy adjustment, it is up to the member country to demonstrate a willingness to cooperate with the IMF in finding a solution to the problem.

The IMF's macroeconomic surveillance of member countries is carried out by means of its annual Article IV consultation exercise, which results in an examination and discussion of a staff report for each country, typically once a year, at its Executive Board comprising representatives of all the IMF membership. Since the late 1990s, these exercises also included for many advanced and emerging market countries an FSAP report, if voluntarily undertaken by the member country. At the global level, the IMF's surveillance function was carried out through two semi-annual exercises focused on its World Economic Outlook (WEO) report and Global Financial Stability Report (GFSR). Beginning in the mid-2000s, the IMF began to experiment with a new multilateral surveillance exercise, which was focused directly on the issue of global imbalances and involved the United States, the euro zone, China, Japan and Saudi Arabia.

In an internal review of the IMF's surveillance activities in the lead-up to the financial crisis conducted by the IMF's Independent Evaluation Office (IEO) in 2011, that office identified a number of shortcomings in the IMF's country and global efforts. At the national level, the IEO concluded that the IMF failed to "warn countries at the center of the crisis, nor the membership at large, of the vulnerabilities and risks that eventually brought about the crisis" and that it "gave too little consideration to deteriorating financial sector balance sheets, financial regulatory issues, to the possible links between monetary policy and global imbalances, and to the credit boom and emerging asset bubbles".[2] On the basis of these conclusions, it is clear in retrospect that the IMF in its bilateral surveillance of the major countries with systemic financial importance was too sanguine in its assessment of potential financial risks and gave too much credence to the authorities' views about the benefits of financial innovation, the resilience of financial systems and the soundness of financial regulation and supervision.

In the case of the United States, it is worth noting that its bilateral consultation procedure did not encompass an FSAP report during the period of the housing bubble as it did for many other advanced countries. This is simply because at that time the FSAP exercise was voluntary and the United States did not agree to undertake one. Whether an FSAP exercise would have identified the problems associated with the surge in housing finance that led to the crisis in the United States will never be known; however, it is likely that such an exercise would have called attention to the absence of a proper regulatory framework for the "shadow" banking system.

In mid-2006, the IMF Managing Director at the time initiated a new multilateral consultation procedure in an effort to focus greater attention on what was perceived to be a growing problem of global imbalances in the current account positions among the countries noted earlier. The IMF staff as the technical secretariat for this exercise prepared an analysis of each country's contribution to this problem and possible policy adjustments each country could make to deal with it. The representatives of each participating country, however, only took note of the IMF proposals and essentially re-affirmed policy commitments they had already made at the national level, without indicating a willingness to pursue further policy adjustments. In their review, the IMF Executive Board and the IMFC essentially ratified these responses and failed to call for any follow-up action. Accordingly, the consultation procedure was suspended at just about the time that the first signals of the global financial crisis in the United States were being registered. This exercise was a good example of the unwillingness of major countries in the IMF to use the institution as a forum for achieving policy coordination.[3]

Among the advanced countries operating within the G7 grouping, there have been isolated instances of macroeconomic policy coordination that reached a high point during the period 1978–87. These were high-ranking policy meetings at the finance minister level, which crystallized agreements at a Bonn Summit in 1978, to pursue macroeconomic stimulus in response to the 1974–75 global recession, followed by two agreements to deal with adjustment of the US dollar (the Plaza Accord of 1985 and Tokyo Accord of 1987).[4] These were ad hoc policy agreements growing out of an informal club of the leading advanced countries that may not have any analogue at the multilateral level, notwithstanding the merits of one, owing to the focused objective of the meeting, the small number of participants, and their similar economic stature. Only more recently, in the immediate aftermath of the global financial crisis, has the G20 forum been utilized for such a purpose, as detailed in the next section of this chapter.

Oversight of Global Financial Stability

In the second dimension of the IFA's responsibility dealing with the oversight of global financial stability, one can also identify shortcomings in the period leading up to the global financial crisis. In this dimension of the IFA, the IMF again plays an important role, but one which it shared with two other organizations, the BIS and the FSF. The BIS has provided technical support for a number of specialized committees, such as the Basel Committee for Banking Supervision and the Committee on the Global

Financial System (CGFS), which had been established by the G10 countries (of Western Europe and North America) to monitor developments in these areas.[5] The FSF, as noted earlier, was set up in 1999 to provide a coordinating mechanism for these and other committees of the G10 with the work of the IMF and World Bank.

In the years immediately preceding the outbreak of the financial crisis, the CGFS undertook studies on two topics directly related to the crisis, namely the role of credit ratings in structured finance (CGFS 2005) and the role of housing finance in global financial markets (CGFS 2006).[6] However, in both reports the committee came to a relatively benign assessment of the risks associated with the securitization of mortgage finance and generally endorsed the expanded role of capital market funding of household financial products. It also did not find any conflict of interest in the role of the credit rating agencies in their evaluation of these securitized instruments. More generally, it highlighted the role of reputational credibility across institutions and financial agents in sustaining the integrity and soundness of the transactions and operations in these activities. In retrospect, this was obviously a flawed assessment of developments under way in the "shadow" banking system but one that was in accord with the views of the US monetary authorities at the time.

For a number of years, the staff of the BIS has provided an important independent assessment of the developments in the global economic and financial system, which is crystallized in the organization's annual reports. In the years prior to the crisis, these reports were calling attention to the risks associated with the persistence of global imbalances and the underpricing of risks in the expansion of derivatives and securitized finance. However, as a selective club of central bank organizations (including of course the governors of the G10 central banks), the BIS does not have a clear mandate for the oversight of global financial stability. Thus, while its reports can provide a basis for discussion and debate, they are not intended to guide policy action on the part of BIS member governments.

The FSF had a potentially important role in the period leading up to the financial crisis as it had a mandate from the G7 countries to coordinate the work of a number of specialized committees in Basel, the BIS and the IMF in their joint work on global financial surveillance. Accordingly, it was the Chairman of the FSF, rather than the Managing Director of the IMF, who was authorized to address issues of global financial stability at the semi-annual meetings of the IMFC. The IMF's views on global financial stability emerged from its work on its semi-annual GFSRs, but these did not receive any input from the FSF. The primary focus of the FSF in the years prior to the crisis was on reforms in the area of international financial regulation (see next section of this chapter) and the ongoing program of international standards and codes.

The GFSRs of the IMF represented its primary output in the oversight of global financial stability. Prior to 2007, the GFSRs were focused to a significant extent on the problems of the emerging market economies in addressing vulnerabilities that gave rise to the financial crises of the 1990s, as a primary concern of the IMF. However, they also called attention to the potential negative spillovers of growing global imbalances and the risks associated with the rapid growth of household financial debt in the US economy. Unfortunately, these concerns were not translated into a call for clear policy action, neither at the level of the Executive Board of the IMF nor within the IMFC. In part, this outcome reflects the consensus style of deliberation in these councils and a reluctance to engage in serious criticism of individual member countries, especially in the case of the advanced countries. This lack of a strong independent voice in the institutional arrangements of the IFA was one weakness that was highlighted in the Turner Review of the UK Financial Supervisory Authority in its early 2009 evaluation of the factors leading up to the financial crisis.[7]

In the area of global financial oversight, one has ultimately to find fault with the surveillance carried out by the G7 central bank governors and finance ministers, which prior to the financial crisis represented the political steering committee for the IFA. In the communiqués of their meetings prior to the financial crisis, concerns about global imbalances were being raised but not about the financial conditions in the advanced countries that gave rise to the crisis, notwithstanding warnings from some of the work coming out of the BIS and IMF. This lack of focus obviously reflected benign views within the G7 on the benefits of capital market development and the expansion of derivative trading.

International Financial Regulation

The primary focus of attention of the IFA in this domain has been for a number of years the development and enforcement of minimum capital standards for commercial banks. This work began in the 1980s with the formation of the Basel Committee on Banking Supervision and was formalized in 1988 with the first Basel Capital Accord (Basel I). This accord established minimum capital requirements for commercial banks within the G10 countries, which over time have become a global banking standard. The basic approach of the first Basel Accord was to establish a minimum capital requirement of 8 percent in relation to a bank's assets, which was differentiated according to risk weightings of selected categories of those assets ranging from zero to 100 percent. Holdings of sovereign debt or marketable securities carrying an AAA rating of a credit rating agency received a risk weighting of zero and therefore no capital requirement, while loans to businesses and households typically carried a 100 percent weighting and therefore the full 8 percent capital requirement.

While an important step in harmonizing bank regulation across countries, over time the Basel I Accord was seen as defective. One concern was that the capital requirement had a pro-cyclical bias in its effect on bank lending activity, especially in conjunction with "fair-value" or mark-to-market accounting rules, which tended to magnify or reinforce the normal cycles of economic activity. During the upswing of a credit cycle, when the valuation of bank assets as sources of collateral and earnings increased, the capital position of banks would improve and they would have an incentive to take on more leverage to increase their loans and investments. During a subsequent downturn, as asset valuation was reduced and loan impairment rose resulting in charges against capital, banks would have to restrain new lending, thus reinforcing a weakening in economic activity. Another defect of direct relevance to the surge in housing finance was that the capital standard encouraged banks to shift investments in mortgage-backed securities (MBS) and collateralized debt obligations (CDOs) to off-balance-sheet entities (special investment/purpose vehicles) where they would be subject to very low capital charges. This limitation in the Basel Capital Accord clearly encouraged the expansion of the "shadow" banking system.

In the late 1990s and early 2000s, work began on the development of a revised banking standard, which was intended to establish, among other things, a more refined breakdown of risk weightings for purposes of determining capital requirements for all but the largest banks. This revision (Basel II) was finalized in 2004 and was being implemented in Western Europe and North America as the pre-conditions for the global financial crisis were coming to a head. It was broadly reflected within a revised EU Capital Accord in 2007 and was in the process of being incorporated in the regulation of the top 15 or so internationally active banks in the United States. For these banks, the revised accord represented, in effect, a significant relaxation of the capital requirements that had been in place. Instead of a uniform risk weight-adjusted capital requirement, the new accord introduced a new three-pillar approach, which in the light of the financial crisis has been shown to have been severely flawed. The first pillar established that each of the large commercial banks would determine their capital requirements on the basis of their own internal risk models and assessment programs. The second pillar required that these models and assessment methods be subject to supervisory review. The third pillar required that the banks increase the public disclosure of their financial positions and risk exposures in order to allow greater private market scrutiny of their activities as a disciplining force on their operations. As noted in Chap. 2, this new approach turned out to be significantly flawed in practice as bank risk assessment models were inadequate to cover the full range of risks that banks could be exposed to, while bank supervision was too mild in its scope and penetration. In addition, the information that banks released to the markets was incomplete and misleading in many cases. In the wake of the financial crisis, it was agreed that a radically different approach needed to be developed under a Basel III Accord, which is discussed in the next section of this chapter.

The International Lender of Last Resort (ILOLR) Mechanism

In this domain of the IFA, the IMF had a potentially important role to play as the rough counterpart at the international level of a central bank in its function as a lender of last resort at the national level. However, in practice, the IMF is strictly limited in the amount of financial resources that it can provide to its membership, and except in the case of natural disasters, these resources are extended on a phased basis, subject to the fulfillment of certain policy conditions agreed with the member country. Thus, the IMF cannot "lend freely at a penalty rate of interest on the basis of good collateral", as a national central bank can. Nevertheless, during the 1980s and 1990s, the IMF was usually called upon by countries experiencing financial crises, simply because it was the institution best situated to provide financial assistance and macroeconomic policy advice on a relatively quick timetable. This arrangement has reflected a certain asymmetry in how the ILOLR mechanism has functioned for the advanced countries and other developing and emerging market economies. For the former group, ad hoc, unconditional swap lines of credit have been established outside the operation of the IMF, as and when the need arose, to deal with liquidity problems, with the Federal Reserve playing a key role in its provision of dollar liquidity. For most other countries, the IMF has been for all intents and purposes the ILOLR, but with limits and conditions on its financial assistance.

In the wake of the Asian financial crises of the late 1990s, it was agreed in 1999 to establish within the IMF a new Contingent Credit Line (CCL) to provide a more rapid disbursement facility for countries facing "sudden stops" in capital flows and speculative currency attacks. Under the CCL, a country would be pre-qualified for access on the basis of a favorable assessment resulting from the IMF's annual Article IV consultation or macroeconomic assessment exercise and its subscription to the Fund's standard for data dissemination. However, in view of the fact that no country sought access to the facility, it was terminated in 2003. Essentially, there were two problems with its operation. One was that the amount of financial assistance that could initially be drawn down at the time of activating a request was relatively limited, and further access was made subject to mutual agreement between the IMF and the country seeking assistance on a policy program to deal with the conditions motivating the request. This limitation created doubts among potential borrowers as to whether adequate financial assistance would be provided under the facility at the time of activating a request. The other concern with the CCL was that an announcement of eligibility to use the facility might be considered to be a signal of potential problems that financial market participants were not aware of.

More generally, in the wake of the emerging market financial crises of the 1990s, many of the middle-income countries participating in the international capital markets considered that conditional access to IMF resources was too onerous and that it carried a stigma in terms of the negative signal it sent to potential private lenders. Accordingly, beginning in the early 2000s, one can observe a process of extensive foreign reserve accumulation on the part of these countries that represented a form of self-insurance. This trend continued throughout the period leading up to global financial crisis and represented one of the factors contributing to the global savings glut and global imbalances noted earlier. Foreign reserve accumulation was particularly strong among countries in East and Southeast Asia and Latin America, which had been heavy borrowers from the IMF in previous decades. As such, this trend of self-insurance reflected a failing on the part of the IFA to provide an adequate ILOLR mechanism.

THE ROLE OF THE IFA IN THE WAKE OF THE GLOBAL FINANCIAL CRISIS

Given the global dimensions of the financial crisis of 2007–09, the IFA played an important role in coordinating a response. Through mid-2010, the response of the IFA in its crisis-management role can be judged to have been generally positive. In addition, in view of the defects in the IFA discussed above, which contributed to the onset of the global financial crisis, a number of reforms were introduced to improve its crisis-prevention capabilities. The first important response of the United States, the United Kingdom and the euro zone was to summon the G20 to replace the G7 as the coordinating political body for the IFA. This was formalized in the first meeting of the G20 at the leaders' level in Washington, DC, in November 2008, which was followed up by meetings in London (April 2009) and Pittsburgh (September 2009). The agenda of the G20 was focused essentially on three aspects of crisis response: the first was the mobilization of financing for liquidity support for countries directly affected by the financial crisis; the second was the coordination of a policy response; and the third was initiating the process of IFA reform to prepare for a post-crisis global financial order. Each of these is briefly discussed in the rest of this section. Then in the final section of the chapter, the role of the IMF as crisis lender to countries in the euro zone, and Greece in particular, is examined.

The IFA and Crisis Financing

Consistent with the two-tier structure of the ILOLR described earlier, actions were taken to expand on an unprecedented scale the size and scope of the Federal Reserve international swap network and the financing arrangements mobilized through the IMF for other countries. As noted in Chap. 4, the Fed began to set up its swap line network in December 2007 with the opening of lines of credit for the ECB and the Swiss National Bank. In September 2008, the network was expanded with the opening of credit lines for the central banks of Australia, Canada, Denmark, England, Japan, Norway and Sweden. Shortly thereafter, in October 2008, a swap line was opened with New Zealand and then in November 2008 for the first time with the central banks of Brazil, Korea, Mexico and Singapore; the latter four ended up being precautionary as no dollars were requested under these lines of credit. By September 2008, the limit for the swap lines had been raised to US$620 billion, but in November it was decided that drawdowns by the Bank of England, the ECB, the Bank of Japan and Swiss National Bank would be exempted from any limit because of the high demand for dollar liquidity in those countries. By February 2009, the total amount drawn under all these swap lines reached a peak of US$600 billion.

In the case of the IMF, a number of initiatives were taken to allow it to play a vital second line of defense for countries seeking financial assistance in the wake of the global financial crisis. First, between September 2008 and July 2009, lines of credit under the normal "stand-by arrangements" of the IMF were approved for 12 countries, mainly in Eastern and Western Europe (Armenia, Belarus, Bosnia & Herzegovina, Georgia, Hungary, Iceland, Latvia, Romania, Serbia and Ukraine), as well as Pakistan and Mongolia. In addition, three arrangements that were cautionary in nature were established for Costa Rica, El Salvador and Guatemala, under which no drawings were made. In many cases, normal limits for borrowing were relaxed and parallel credits were arranged with the European Union and/or the World Bank. As a result, the total financing available under these programs amounted to around US$143 billion.[8] In addition to these financing arrangements, further efforts were made to create an emergency liquidity line for emerging market countries in a strong macroeconomic position that was unsuccessful with the establishment of the CCL in 1999. In March 2009, the Flexible Credit Line was created, which allowed total access in individual cases to reach ten times a country's quota or financial subscription in the Fund (far in excess of normal borrowing limits) and for a period of up to three years. Under these conditions, three countries (Colombia, Mexico and Poland) came forward in April and May 2009 to request assistance for a total amount of US$80 billion. Consistent with the precautionary nature of these credit lines, no disbursements were made. The total amount of Fund resources made available under these 18 arrangements (around US$223 billion) was an unprecedented commitment of IMF financing at a single point in time (mid-2009).

In view of the potentially large demand for Fund resources, the G20 leaders in April 2009 agreed to triple the available resources of the IMF to around US$750 billion by means of an augmentation of special lines of credit that a number of advanced countries had made available for the Fund to draw on for its lending operations under the so-called New Agreements to Borrow, which were raised to a limit of US$500 billion. As a result of these augmentations, the IMF was able to expand its lending on a major scale in the aftermath of the crisis. During the period from late 2008 to the end of 2013, the Fund approved lending arrangements for a cumulative amount of US$400 billion to 38 countries affected by the crisis.

At the same time, the leaders authorized a special allocation of Special Drawing Rights (SDRs) by the Fund equivalent to around US$250 billion, which was made available to all countries in amounts proportional to their quotas. SDRs were initially created in 1969 to become a supplement to other reserve currencies in the international monetary system (dollars, euros, pounds and yen), but prior to 2009 there had only been two allocations amounting to around US$35 billion. Thus, they constituted only a relatively small part of foreign reserve assets in the system, contrary to the expectations at the time they were created.[9]

The actions described above taken by the Federal Reserve and the G20 through the IMF represented a bold attempt to enhance the ILOLR mechanism of the IFA in order to quell the panic phase of the global financial crisis that erupted in September 2008. Although these adaptations were ad hoc and experimental in nature, they undoubtedly were important in limiting the potential damage that the crisis could have thrust upon the global economic and financial system. The complete absence of any similar set of arrangements in the 1930s is one important reason why the economic collapse of the Great Depression was as large as it was.

Setting the Policy Agenda

The second essential role the G20 played in response to the global financial crisis was to forge agreement on a set of appropriate policy actions to be implemented at the national level, which would be coordinated in an effective manner. These actions essentially involved a substantial easing of monetary policy, official support for the financial sector, and a strong fiscal stimulus. The work of the G20 in the wake of the crisis in the area of international policy coordination represented a major change in the role of the IFA in this domain compared with the pre-crisis experience and was highlighted in the communiqué of the Leaders' Summit in September 2009 when they declared that the G20 was "the premier forum for international policy cooperation." During the 2008–10 period when this cooperation was at its highest, the IMF for all intents and purposes was assigned the role of technical secretariat for the G20. The IMF took the lead in determining the size of the fiscal effort that would be appropriate to sustain the global economy in the wake of the crisis and in quantifying the magnitude of the financial sector losses in the most affected countries that would need to be addressed through public and private capital injections. The IMF also prepared periodic updates on the state of the global economic and financial system for G20 meetings as well as reports on the implementation of policies by G20 countries in the three areas noted above.

On the policy front, the G20 called for early action by the central banks of the advanced countries to provide liquidity support to financial institutions facing a withdrawal of funding or difficulties in liquidating assets. At the same time, policy interest rates were reduced to very low levels and programs of quantitative easing were initiated to provide monetary stimulus at a time of substantial economic retrenchment. The Federal Reserve, Bank of England and Bank of Japan were particularly aggressive in this area, whereas the ECB was somewhat slower to react. Through June 2009, the total amount of liquidity support among the central banks of the advanced countries amounted to US$2.7 trillion, or an average of nearly 7 percent of each country's GDP.[10]

Along with liquidity support, the G20 endorsed early action to provide support to the financial sectors of the most affected countries through a broad-based program of deposit guarantees, asset purchases, loan guarantees and capital injections. Through mid-2009, the quantitative impact of these actions was quite substantial, with an amount of US$7.7 trillion having been committed, or the equivalent of around 25 percent of GDP for the G20 countries.[11]

In the fiscal area, the G20 in its first meeting in November 2008 played an important role in calling for programs of substantial fiscal stimulus and endorsed the call of the IMF Managing Director for a coordinated fiscal stimulus equivalent to 2 percent of GDP (not counting the effect of automatic stabilizers). The European Union was initially hesitant in this area, in large part because of the resistance of Germany, but with the urging of the EC, it too agreed to a program of fiscal relaxation. For 2009, estimates of the IMF suggest that for the G20 as a whole, government fiscal positions deteriorated by around 6 percent of GDP, on a weighted average basis, with respect to the pre-crisis level of 2007. Of this amount, 2 percentage points can be attributed to the discretionary action of fiscal stimulus on the part of governments to deal with the crisis while the remainder reflected the impact of automatic stabilizers triggered by the crisis.[12]

One important initiative of the G20 in following up on members' policy commitments was a process of "peer review" or Mutual Assessment Program (MAP), which the leaders agreed to in the Pittsburgh Summit of September 2009. This process was agreed at both the finance ministers' and leaders' levels in the context of a "Framework for Strong Sustainable and Balanced Growth", which was intended to identify and coordinate adjustments in aggregate demand and supply on the part of G20 member countries that could be expected to restore global economic growth to its pre-crisis trajectory. The IMF was called upon to play a key role in the MAP in that it was expected to evaluate the economic recovery programs that G20 countries developed for their global impact and consistency and propose any adjustments for governments to consider in their summits in Toronto (June 2010) and Seoul (November 2010). The MAP of the G20 was a clear improvement over the failed attempt at a multilateral consultation process within the IMF prior to the outbreak of the financial crisis, which was discussed earlier. The information sharing, the transparency on policy goals and programs, and the active interchange of views within the G20 represented an unprecedented effort at institutionalizing a mechanism for international policy cooperation, if not coordination, in the macroeconomic field that had not existed beforehand at either the ministerial or leaders' level. Generally, under the MAP, a positive effort was made in assessing the impact of government's policy commitments and monitoring their implementation, but there was little evidence of a change in a government's policy program resulting from the MAP. The process that came closest to this aspect of "peer review" was one of "comply or explain" in which participants were expected to report on the degree to which their policy programs fulfilled prior commitments and to provide an explanation for any shortfalls or deviations. With the passage of time, however, one problem that has interfered with the MAP and the G20's focus on IFA reform has been that its agenda has become much more diffuse, with national and international agencies pressing to have the G20's agenda expanded to cover a number of other issues of international concern. As a result, in the Leaders' Summit in Turkey (November 2015), for example, a dense communiqué of 12 pages (single-spaced) was issued, to which was attached over 100 annexes, reports and supplementary materials on a variety of topics relevant to the wide-ranging Summit deliberations.[13]

From a substantive policy perspective, the main problem arising from the MAP was that, acting on the IMF's advice, the G20 advocated in 2010 a shift from fiscal stimulus to fiscal consolidation in 2010–11, which turned out to be premature in view of the weak recovery of the global economy. This advice received particularly strong support from EU governments, which were concerned about the significant build-up in government debt and solvency risks arising from their initial response to the financial crisis. At the same time, the IMF and G20 continued to advocate substantial monetary easing as the most effective policy to support economic recovery. In retrospect, it can be argued that a coordinated monetary and fiscal expansion would have been much more effective in promoting economic recovery, especially given the potentially large fiscal multipliers at a time of suppressed aggregate demand owing to a large private debt overhang and the relatively limited incremental demand for credit in response to lower interest rates. As a result of the fiscal consolidation effort supported by the MAP, it is estimated that the overall general government balance in relation to potential GDP for the OECD countries shifted from an average deficit of around 3 percent in 2009 to near balance in 2010 and a surplus of 1 percent in 2011, thus reversing most of the fiscal stimulus introduced in 2009.[14]

Initiating the Process of IFA Reform

The main focus of the G20 in the area of IFA reform was to make institutional changes in order to improve its capabilities in the oversight of financial system stability and international regulation. The first area mainly involved strengthening the surveillance operations of the IMF, while the second involved reforming the Basel capital standards, among other things. In regard to both of these objectives, an important institutional change was the conversion in April 2009 of the FSF to a Financial Stability Board (FSB). With the creation of the FSB, its membership was expanded to include all the G20 members and its responsibilities in coordinating the activities of the various committees associated with the BIS were strengthened. Essentially, the IMF and the FSB have become the twin pillars of the IFA, with the IMF having a principal role in the international adjustment mechanism and international policy coordination and the FSB with oversight for international financial regulation and other infrastructural aspects of the IFA such as international accounting rules, the organization of securities markets and the control of money laundering; the FSB and IMF both share responsibility for the oversight of financial system stability. This new arrangement for systemic stability oversight under the IFA was confirmed by the G20's request to have the FSB and IMF collaborate in the preparation of a joint semi-annual assessment of global financial stability risks (or "Early Warning Exercise") for both the G20 finance ministers/central bank governors and the IMFC, drawing on their separate specializations under the IFA.

The main focus of reform for the IMF in the wake of the global financial crisis was to strengthen its surveillance operations in an effort to deal with some of the problems that had been identified in the lead-up to the crisis noted earlier. At the country level, one change that was made in 2010 was to have an FSAP exercise and an accompanying Financial System Stability Assessment (FSSA) conducted on a mandatory basis for each of the 25 systemically important financial center countries, once every five years. While this was an important change, as prior to the financial crisis the FSAP was a voluntary exercise, one can certainly question whether the FSSA should not be conducted on a more frequent cycle at least for the most important financial centers such as the United Kingdom and the United States. Another innovation that has been made in the IMF surveillance exercises was to initiate so-called Spillover Reports for a number of advanced countries in order to assess the economic effects on other countries of policy adjustments made in those countries. Also, as a complement to its semi-annual WEO and GFSR exercises, the IMF initiated in 2009 a new Fiscal Monitor Report in order to assess the current outlook and medium-term sustainability for the public finances of the main advanced and emerging market economies.

In the area of financial regulation, the G20 working through the FSB initiated a broad reform agenda involving a strengthening of the Basel capital standard, shifting the trading of derivatives from a non-transparent OTC basis to central clearinghouses, establishing guidelines for the resolution or liquidation of large complex financial institutions (i.e., "too-big-to-fail" banks) and extending supervision and regulation to shadow banking institutions such as money market funds and any non-bank financial institution that is deemed to be systemically important. The FSB has been actively involved in coordinating the work of the various Basel-based agencies in implementing these reforms and in monitoring compliance by the G20 countries.

In the case of the United States, most of the reforms mentioned above were embraced in the Dodd-Frank Wall Street Reform and Consumer Protection Act that was signed into law in July 2010. That bill also established a new macro-prudential supervisory responsibility for the Federal Reserve to focus on issues of financial system stability in addition to its bank-specific or micro-prudential regulatory function and the macro-economic focus of its monetary policy operations. This new dimension of financial supervision was also reinforced by the creation of a Financial Stability Oversight Council that is chaired by the US Secretary of the Treasury and comprises representatives of all the supervisory agencies of the US government. One of the challenges for the Fed and other central banks in recent years in fulfilling their mandate for macro-prudential or systemic stability oversight is determining how the traditional interest rate tool of monetary policy should or should not be used, and when and which macro-prudential tools (e.g., loan-to-value and debt-to-income limits for mortgages) should be employed. Generally, the Fed has adopted the approach that monetary policy should continue to be focused on its twin mandated objectives of low and stable inflation and full employment and that systemic financial oversight is best exercised through enhanced supervision of systemically important financial institutions, for example by means of annual stress tests.[15]

Perhaps the most detailed regulatory reform spearheaded by the G20 in the light of the financial crisis has been the revision of the Basel Capital Standard (Basel III). While the basic framework of the three-pillar approach of Basel II was maintained, a number of new features were added. These included an overall leverage or capital-asset ratio of at least 3 percent, a liquidity coverage ratio and net stable funding ratio, in addition to important changes to the basic capital requirements for banks. For example, the basic definition of "core" capital was strengthened to include equity investment and retained earnings, and the minimum requirement for this component was raised from an actual average of around 1 percent prior to the crisis to 7 percent. In addition, a counter-cyclical capital buffer was added along with a capital surcharge for large complex financial institutions. While there has been much debate as to whether these changes go far enough (see Chap. 7), it is clear that they represent an improvement with respect to the regime (Basel II) that was being implemented just prior to the global financial crisis.

IMF INVOLVEMENT IN THE EURO ZONE CRISIS

The euro zone crisis that erupted in full force in 2010 represented the second phase of the global financial crisis. Prior to the outbreak of the crisis in September 2008, a number of EU countries, such as the United Kingdom, Ireland, Portugal and Spain, had been experiencing credit booms and housing bubbles similar to those of the United States. This pattern of financial market behavior was another symptom of the global savings glut that had reduced long-term interest rates and increased financial flows between emerging market economies and the advanced economies. While the external current account for the euro zone as a whole was roughly in balance, as noted in Chap. 2, which implied that net capital inflows between it and the rest of the world were close to zero, there were large imbalances within the zone. Essentially, the northern tier countries of Germany, Netherlands and Belgium were large net exporters of capital, while the countries on the periphery such as Greece, Ireland, Portugal and Spain were large importers. These imbalances within the euro area were similar to the global imbalances between emerging market and advanced countries, which were fueling credit booms in the latter countries more generally. As noted earlier, these imbalances within the euro zone were facilitated by the large reduction in risk premia for loans and sovereign debt spreads for the latter group of countries and the widespread faith in the Stability and Growth Pact (SGP) for maintaining fiscal sustainability within the euro zone.[16] In practice, however, the SGP had many design flaws and was very weakly enforced and observed, even in the case of the core euro zone countries (France and Germany).

Initially, following the outbreak of the global financial crisis, the euro zone suffered many of the same aftereffects as those suffered by the United States, given the large entanglement of its banks in the acquisition of new securitized instruments/derivatives (MBS, CDOs and CDS) and the financing of housing bubbles in the four countries cited above. In addition to solvency concerns for a number of individual banks in the northern tier countries, there was a "sudden stop" in bank credit flows from the surplus countries to deficit countries within the euro area in the wake of the financial crisis, which created more systemic concerns in the latter group. Except in the case of Greece and Portugal, the problem of bank debt was one of private sector debt, which was most extreme in the case of Ireland. In that case, prior to the crisis, bank debt had risen by a factor of more than four times from 2001 to 2007 and was equivalent to nearly 800 percent of GDP in the latter year.[17]

Essentially, the global financial crisis confronted the euro zone with two problems. One was how to handle bank debt problems in the deficit countries where there was no central euro zone facility for bailouts, as the ECB was proscribed from assuming that role. This problem first played out in the case of Ireland. In 2009, when its largest banks faced threats of insolvency because of mortgage credits that could not be repaid after the bursting of a housing bubble, the government decided that it had to provide a blanket guarantee of their deposits and liabilities given their systemic importance, which ultimately lead to a substantial increase in government debt (of around 35 percent of GDP). The second problem was one of macroeconomic adjustment for the deficit countries that had experienced much higher inflation than the surplus countries prior to the crisis and had lost external competitiveness as a result. With a withdrawal of external financing, the problem for those countries was how they would be able to restore competitiveness and a viable balance of payments position when they were part of a currency union and could not benefit from a devaluation of their own currency.

The trigger for the euro zone crisis was the revelation by a new government in Greece in October 2009 that prior governments had misreported fiscal data to the EC for purposes of the SGP for a number of years and that its debt problems were much larger than had previously been reported. As a result, according to the new government, the budget deficit was expected to rise to the equivalent of 12.5 percent of GDP in 2009, or more than three times the projections of the previous government, while its debt-to-GDP ratio was expected to reach 130 percent. In the light of these revelations, it is clear that Greece had been in flagrant violation of the Maastricht criteria embodied in the SGP calling for a fiscal deficit of 3 percent of GDP and a public debt ratio of 60 percent of GDP for a number of years if not since its entry into the euro zone.

With the euro zone already in recession because of the fallout from the global financial crisis, government finances in the periphery countries were under pressure because of the effects of automatic stabilizers in lowering revenues and increasing expenditure for social safety net programs. As a consequence, countries with high public debt burdens, such as Greece, Ireland and Portugal, were facing the prospect of perverse debt dynamics because of an increase in sovereign debt spreads owing to higher risk premia. Thus, they would need to borrow additional funds simply to cover the debt service on existing debt, which could quickly give rise to an unsustainable debt situation. The prospect of a default scenario was made more likely by actions on the part of the credit rating agencies in downgrading the ratings on their bonds in late 2009 and early 2010. The debt problems for these governments also had the potential of creating problems for banks within the euro zone that were heavily invested in the sovereign debt of its members because of the AAA ratings it had received prior to the crisis. Within countries such as Ireland, this "doom loop", as it has been called, operated in reverse, as the debt assumed by the government in guaranteeing the solvency of its major banks, coupled with the impact of the economic contraction caused by the financial crisis on government finances, created serious concerns in financial markets about the government's fiscal sustainability.

In the wake of the global financial crisis, the euro area was very poorly prepared in terms of crisis-management institutions to deal with the asymmetric shocks caused by the financial crisis within the zone. There was no central fiscal authority to pool the resources of deficit and surplus countries, which would allow for cross-border risk sharing and resource transfers to countries experiencing the impact of a sharp economic downturn. Nor was there any stabilization mechanism attached to the euro area that would allow explicit lending to governments in need of funding to deal with a debt crisis. The only central institution underpinning the monetary union was the ECB, which had the power to expand liquidity in response to changes in macroeconomic conditions, but it was proscribed from lending to member governments or national central banks for bailout purposes. Its emergency lending facility, which it operated through member central banks of the zone, was intended to function as a standard LOLR mechanism for banks with good collateral facing a liquidity shortfall.

As a partial remedy for this institutional gap, the governments of the euro zone agreed to establish a European Financial Stability Facility (EFSF) in May 2010, which was authorized to borrow funds in the international capital markets up to a limit of 440 billion euros, with the guarantees of its constituent member governments, to finance stabilization loans to euro zone governments. This facility was replaced in October 2012 lender of last resort permanent European Stability Mechanism (with a total lending capacity of 500 billion euros), in which euro zone governments made equity contributions.

In these conditions, the IMF was seen as a potentially important external creditor, which had already become active in stabilization loans to countries of Eastern and Central Europe in late 2008 with the outbreak of the financial crisis. At first, there was reluctance on the part of euro zone leaders to involve the IMF on the notion that they were expected to deal with any economic or financial difficulties without the assistance of outside institutions. However, in view of the IMF's financial resources and its experience designing stabilization programs, it was decided to have it work in partnership with the ECB and the EC, acting on behalf of the

EFSF, under what came to be known as "the Troika". This was an unprecedented arrangement for the Fund and raised questions about its governance, especially in view of the junior status it was given by its European partners. In line with a long-standing tradition, the IMF was headed at the time of the financial crisis by a European, Dominique Straus-Kahn, a former finance minister from France, who was eager to have the IMF involved in the problems of the euro zone, even if its independence was somewhat compromised. In addition, members of the EU have had a disproportionate weight in Board representation and voting power in the Fund, which only began to be reduced in a reform of IMF governance that was approved in late 2010. (This reform, however, only became effective in early 2016 because of extensive delays by the US Congress in approving it.) In retrospect, it would have been preferable for the IMF to have operated in parallel but independently of the ECB and EC, as it has done in many other programs of financial assistance, for example with the US Treasury Department, the World Bank and regional development banks.

Greece became the first euro zone country to enter into a macroeconomic adjustment program supported by financial arrangements with the Troika in May 2010, followed by Ireland in November 2010, Portugal in May 2011, a second arrangement with Greece in 2012, and Cyprus in 2013.[18] Spain, the other country of the periphery that was facing private debt and bank solvency problems as a result of the financial crisis, decided to manage its own adjustment program without outside assistance. The IMF programs with Greece, Ireland and Portugal were some of the largest financial arrangements in IMF history not only in absolute amounts but also in relation to the country's quota in the Fund and the size of its GDP. What was also unusual in these programs is that the IMF invoked a special exemption from an operational requirement established in 2002 that financial arrangements involving exceptional access to IMF resources well in excess of normal borrowing limits needed to have a certification from its management and staff that the country's external debt was sustainable with a high degree of probability. However, without formal discussion, an exemption from this requirement was first sought in the case of Greece on the grounds that there was a high risk of contagion and systemic spillovers from the Greek crisis for other governments and banking sectors in the euro zone. This systemic exemption has been highly criticized not only for the ad hoc way in which it was requested but also because of the undue influence of European governments in the decision-making of the IMF. The need for debt restructuring in the adjustment program for Greece had been discussed within the IMF, but this possibility was ruled out by the ECB on the grounds that it would have inflicted significant losses on banks within the euro zone that held Greek sovereign debt.[19]

Each of the programs supported by the IMF for the euro zone countries focused on three objectives: a reduction in the country's external current account deficit, an improvement in the government's fiscal position and debt sustainability and the repair of financial institution balance sheets.[20] The results of the programs revealed some common patterns. In each of the euro area programs, the reduction in the external current account deficit turned out to be larger than projected, but the debt-to-GDP ratio remained higher than programmed because of a weaker level of output. As planned, the current account adjustment was achieved by an improvement in the government finances and a depreciation in the real effective exchange rate. Because of the common currency arrangement for these countries, a real depreciation had to be achieved by an "internal devaluation" involving a decline in the ratio of the domestic price index in relation to that of their major trading partners. Historically, this pattern of exchange rate adjustment has proven to be very difficult to achieve without a change in the nominal value of the currency that, for example, other countries in Europe outside the euro zone, such as Iceland, were able to rely upon in their recovery from crisis.

During the program period 2010–14, the rate of internal devaluation based on changes in the consumer price index achieved in the four euro area programs ranged from a high of 5.5 percent for Greece to a low of 1.75 percent for Portugal. According to IMF estimates, using relative unit labor costs, the real effective exchange rate devaluation was much greater, ranging from 8 percent in the case of Portugal to 15 percent for Greece.[21] This discrepancy in the two measures of internal devaluation can be explained by the fact that labor market reforms in the adjustment programs for these countries were generally achieved in advance of product market reforms and the supply response of new businesses was weaker than projected because barriers to entry were removed more slowly than expected with the result that consumer prices were slower to adjust than unit labor costs.

It should be noted that the adjustment programs for the euro zone countries were made more difficult by the fact that there was no arrangement within the zone for surplus countries or countries with lower-than-average inflation to pursue an expansionary fiscal policy in a counter-cyclical fashion, which would have eased the deflationary burden on the countries in the periphery. To a large extent, this defect was inherent in the fiscal limits of the SGP, which were uniform for all countries regardless of their cyclical position. This austerity-only policy of the euro area reflected in particular the attitudes of the ECB and the German government and represented one of the main factors inhibiting a stronger economic recovery for Europe in the wake of the financial crisis.[22]

On the fiscal side of the adjustment programs, the cyclically-adjusted primary government balance in the euro area programs improved by around 5.5 percent of GDP over a three-year period, broadly in line with program targets. This outcome, however, implied that the actual improvement in the primary balance was larger than the number just cited because of the lower-than-projected level of output that resulted from these programs. Studies by the IMF have shown that the fiscal multipliers during the three years from the start of each of the programs were significantly larger than assumed in the programs. As a result, the growth forecast errors, that is, the difference between actual outcomes and program projections, were found to be more negative in programs that included a larger fiscal adjustment.[23] Simply put, fiscal austerity in the euro area adjustment programs was amplified by large fiscal multipliers. Other studies have shown that fiscal multipliers can be equally large on the upside, especially in situations where there is weak aggregate demand and the zero lower bound on interest rates is in effect, thus confirming Keynes' original hypothesis developed at the time of the Great Depression.[24]

The program with Greece has been the most difficult and contentious of the adjustment efforts supported by the Troika. In part, this was due to the fact that the original program excluded any debt restructuring, as noted earlier, even though the public debt ratio for Greece at 145 percent of GDP was much higher than for the other three countries. As a result, the internal adjustment effort was programmed to be much larger than in the other three cases. The adjustment program also included a number of structural conditions to deal with institutional defects in public sector operations and weaknesses in the business environment of Greece. This plan created implementation problems for the government, and as a result it was unable to complete some of the program reviews and qualify for full disbursement of the financial package assembled by the Troika. Accordingly, a new program that included a roughly 50 percent reduction in the face value of Greek public debt was negotiated in March 2012. By then, euro area governments were beginning to experience some decline in the spreads for their sovereign debt, but this reduction became much more significant following the commitment made by Mario Draghi, the President of the ECB, in a speech at the end of July 2012 "to do whatever it takes to preserve the euro". This speech was followed in early August 2012 by the announcement of the ECB's Outright Monetary Transactions program, under which the ECB would engage in the direct purchase of euro area sovereign bonds in the secondary market to support their prices by buying them in potentially unlimited quantities on the condition of economic and fiscal reform efforts by the government concerned, as for example under programs agreed with the Troika.

One other factor that affected the outturn under euro area programs that needs to be recognized is the degree of political commitment exhibited by the government and other political bodies to the adjustment program negotiated with external creditors. This commitment was probably the strongest in the case of Ireland and weakest in the case of Greece. The program with Ireland is notable in that the Irish government was already well advanced in a fiscal adjustment program before an agreement with the Troika was completed in November 2010. The government was also clear with its creditors as to what it could realistically deliver in terms of policy measures and in assessing the quantitative impact of its fiscal adjustment effort. There was also a strong degree of public trust in what the government was trying to achieve and a recognition among the major stakeholders in the country that a program supported by the Troika offered the best chance of recovery.[25]

These same qualifications cannot be made about the adjustment programs with Greece. In that case, a uniform degree of commitment to the program was clearly lacking in the national parliament, with many factions viewing the program conditionality as an imposition from the outside. As time has passed, there has been a significant weakening of trust between the government of Greece and its European creditors, as the latter group has continued to insist on internal adjustment measures that have become increasingly more difficult to implement without further debt restructuring. As a result, in the first two adjustment programs with the Troika, the degree of compliance with program targets and conditions was very uneven, with slippages not only with respect to quantitative fiscal targets but also in regard the structural reforms in areas such as tax administration, the pension system and collective bargaining arrangements. As a result, Greece was only able to complete 5 of the 12 reviews included in its second program with the Troika. Thus, a third adjustment program was negotiated in mid-2015. At this point, the IMF decided to operate independently of the Troika, in particular to be able to press for further debt restructuring as a basis for its continued involvement.[26] As of early 2016, the program with Greece needed to be revised (once again) because of non-compliance with program targets; nevertheless, the European members of the Troika continued to insist on fiscal targets (without debt restructuring) that the IMF claimed were unattainable.

Among other things, this experience has shown the important role that an SDRM could play within the IFA (and the euro zone as well), which is taken up in Chap. 7. More generally, the crisis of the euro zone has revealed major structural flaws in its design as regards its inability to function as a banking union, a fiscal union and a political union in support of its common currency.[27]

Summary and Conclusion

In view of the global dimensions of the crisis, it is important to consider the role of the IFA in the lead-up to the crisis and since. The IFA represents the cooperative arrangements that governments have put in place to safeguard global financial stability by means of its crisis-prevention and crisis-management capabilities. Since the end of WW2, the IMF has been at the center of the IFA because of its global and country macroeconomic assessment exercises and its ILOLR financing. Since the 1980s, its work has been supplemented by a number of specialized committees and organizations that have focused on certain infrastructural aspects of the global financial system, such as financial regulation, accounting and the organization of securities markets. In the decade preceding the crisis, these activities were overseen by the FSF.

Prior to the crisis, there were clear deficiencies in the activities of the IFA in four areas: the oversight of global financial stability, international policy coordination, international financial regulation and LOLR financing. In its oversight function, the work of the IMF and FSF was not well coordinated in assessing risks to the global financial system, in part because both organizations were heavily focused on dealing with vulnerabilities of the emerging market economies in the wake of a series of financial crises in the 1990s. International policy coordination was handled on an ad hoc and limited basis among the G7 countries, but these countries were not willing to use the IMF as a forum for such purposes as revealed in the failed multilateral consultation exercise during 2006–07. International financial regulation had been mainly oriented to the establishment of minimum capital requirements for commercial banks in the advanced countries, but these requirements were in the process of being significantly relaxed for the major banks just prior to the crisis. This change, together with regimes of "light touch" supervision, reflected an attitude in the major financial centers that financial markets and institutions were largely self-regulating. The ILOLR mechanism operated on an asymmetric basis for advanced countries and the rest of the IMF membership. The former group enjoyed essentially unconditional access to emergency funding under an ad hoc network of central bank swaps, whereas other countries had to rely on limited access financing from the IMF subject to policy conditions. Prior to the crisis, many emerging market countries had begun a process of self-insurance through the accumulation of substantial foreign reserves in response to the stigma and limitations they associated with borrowing from the IMF. This action contributed to a global savings glut and the problem of global imbalances that supported the development of housing bubbles and credit booms in a number of advanced countries.

Since the outbreak of the crisis, the G20 has replaced the G7 as the political directorate for the IFA and acted quickly to mount a response in three areas: the mobilization of exceptional financing for the IMF, the coordination of fiscal and monetary policy adjustments among its membership to support global economy and the commencement of reforms to the IFA. In the first area, the G20 tripled the resources of the IMF to around US$750 billion, while the Federal Reserve expanded its swap network to 14 countries with financing of US$600 billion. In addition, an allocation of SDRs amounting to US$250 billion was distributed among IMF member countries. In the second area, the G20 forged agreement among the advanced countries on a program of fiscal stimulus equivalent to 2 percent of GDP, along with a program of monetary easing and support for their financial sectors through asset purchases and equity injections. The IFA reforms have focused on strengthening IMF surveillance and its coordination with the FSF (now FSB), improving the Basel Capital Accord through stronger capital requirements, shifting OTC derivative transactions to central clearinghouses and establishing resolution mechanisms for large and complex ("too-big-to-fail") financial institutions.

The IMF has also played an important role together with the EC and the ECB in supporting adjustment programs for four countries of the euro zone that experienced a series of debt crises during the second phase of the global financial crisis beginning in 2010. The programs with Cyprus,

Ireland and Portugal were generally successful in supporting fiscal stabilization and economic recovery, notwithstanding the constraints on monetary and exchange rate policies inherent in the euro zone financial architecture. The program with Greece, however, has suffered from protracted difficulties since 2010, reflecting defects in program design and implementation and insufficient debt relief.

Notes

1. A more elaborate and detailed discussion of the IFA can be found in Anthony Elson (2011) *Governing Global Finance: The Evolution and Reform of the International Financial Architecture* (New York: Palgrave Macmillan).
2. IMF Independent Evaluation Office (2011) "IMF Performance in the Run-up to the Financial and Economic Crisis: IMF Surveillance in 2004–07" (IMF-IEO 2011), p. 7.
3. A detailed critique of the IMF multilateral consultation procedure can be found in Paul Blustein "A Flop and A Debacle: Inside the IMF's Global Rebalancing Acts" Center for International Governance Innovation (CIGI) Paper #4 (June 22, 2012).
4. These agreements are examined in Jeffrey Frankel "International Coordination", a paper presented at the Asia Economic Policy Conference organized by the Federal Reserve Bank of San Francisco, Nov. 19–20, 2015. A more elaborate assessment of the Plaza Accord of September 1985 can be found in C. Fred Bergsten and Russell Greene (eds.) *International Monetary Cooperation: The Plaza Agreement after 30 Years* (Washington DC: Peterson Institute of International Economics) April 2016.
5. The G10 actually comprises 11 countries, that is, the G7 countries and Belgium, the Netherlands, Sweden and Switzerland.
6. These reports of the CGFS are "The Role of Ratings in Structured Finance: Issues and Implications" CGFS Report #23 (January 2005) and "Housing Finance in the Global Financial Market" CGFS Report #26 (January 2006) both of which are available at www.bis.org/cgfs
7. The Turner Review, which was one of the first assessments of the failure of global banking regulation and the international financial architecture in the lead-up to the financial crisis, together with an outline of regulatory reform, was produced under the direction of

Adair Turner, then chairman of the Financial Services Authority (FSA) of the UK (FSA "The Turner Review: A Regulatory Response to the Global Banking Crisis", March 2009).

8. These early post-crisis IMF arrangements are reviewed in IMF (2009), "Review of Crisis Programs" IMF Policy Paper (September 14, 2009).

9. As an international reserve asset, SDRs can be exchanged by member countries of the IMF with a need for international liquidity for the usable or convertible currencies (i.e., dollars, euros, pounds and yen) held by other countries. An allocation of SDRs does not increase the total amount of liquidity in the international monetary system but rather allows it to be redirected toward countries with a need for foreign exchange to meet their foreign payment obligations. On November 30, 2015, the IMF decided to include the Chinese renminbi (yuan) along with the other four currencies mentioned above as part of the basket of major currencies used for purposes of determining the value of the SDR, with effect from October 1, 2016. In addition to explanatory material about the SDR on the website of the IMF, one can find a useful discussion of the SDR in Maurice Obstfeld "The SDR as an International Reserve Asset: What Future?" Rapid Response Report #11/0885 International Growth Centre (London School of Economics), March 2011.

10. These figures are cited in Stijn Claessens, Geoffrey Underhill, Deniz Igan and Luc Laeven, "Lessons and Policy Implications from the Global Financial Crisis" IMF Working Paper #10/24 (February 2010).

11. The actions taken by the advanced countries to support their financial sectors in the wake of the crisis are discussed in Claessens et al. (2010).

12. These data are taken from IMF "The State of Public Finances Cross-Country Fiscal Monitor: November 2009" IMF Staff Position Note #09/225 (November 3, 2009).

13. As just one particular example, one can point to the Report of the G20 Climate Finance Study Group, which has been conducting an ongoing exercise since 2012 in identifying ways in which G20 countries, among other things, have been developing financial instruments to support climate finance and stimulate climate-friendly private investment consistent with the UN Framework Convention on Climate Change. This is a large, open-ended com-

mitment on a major global issue that requires the sustained attention of the G20 Leaders and Finance Ministers, along with many other problems requiring global cooperation.

14. These data are taken from a report of the IEO of the IMF, reviewing the response of the IMF to the financial crisis during the 2008–13 period (IMF-IEO "Evaluation of the IMF Response to the Financial and Economic Crisis" October 27, 2014).

15. One study that examines the trade-offs involved in the use of monetary policy for systemic stability objectives can be found in IMF "Monetary Policy and Financial Stability" IMF Policy Paper, August 28, 2015.

16. For a succinct and well-reasoned analysis of the factors leading up to the euro zone crisis, see Richard Baldwin et al. (2015) "Rebooting the Euro Zone" Center For Economic Policy Research, Policy Insight #85 (November 2015).

17. These data are taken from Baldwin et al. (2015).

18. The IMF financial and adjustment programs with Greece, Ireland and Portugal during 2010–11 were evaluated by the Independent Evaluation Office of the IMF in a report issued on July 28, 2016 ("The IMF and the Crises in Greece, Ireland and Portugal: An Evaluation by the Independent Evaluation Office"), which can be accessed at www.ieo-imf.org.

19. The issue of debt restructuring in the 2010 adjustment package for Greece and the background to the "systemic exemption" for the IMF financial arrangement is discussed in Paul Blustein "Laid Low: the IMF, the Euro Zone and the First Rescue of Greece" CIGI Paper #61 (April 2015).

20. This section draws on material provided in an internal IMF evaluation of its financial arrangements with all countries affected by the global financial crisis during the period 2008–14 (IMF "Crisis Program Review" IMF Policy Paper, November 9, 2015).

21. These figures are drawn from Figure 18 on page 28 of the IMF report cited in footnote 20.

22. These issues are explored in a paper by Ashoka Mody "Living (Dangerously) Without a Fiscal Union" Bruegel Working Paper 2015/03 (March 2015).

23. This statistical result was established in a paper by Blanchard and Leigh (2013), which was cited in Chap. 4, and was corroborated by the IMF study cited in footnote 20 (IMF 2015).

24. These studies are examined in an article by Auerbach and Gorodnichenko (2015), cited in Chap. 4.
25. These points were made by Patrick Honohan, just prior to his resignation as Governor of the Central Bank of Ireland, in a speech at the London School of Economics on November 17, 2015 "Debt and Austerity: Post-Crisis Lessons From Ireland".
26. A brief, but incisive, analysis of the state of play between Greece and the IMF was presented by Olivier Blanchard, the former Economic Counselor of the IMF, in the IMF blog (iMFdirect) "Greece – Past Critiques and The Path Forward", July 9, 2015.
27. Progress has been made since 2012 in the creation of a banking union but not in the other two dimensions needed for a successful economic and monetary union (EMU). These issues are examined in the context of a long-term plan for implementation in a special report of the European Commission "The Five Presidents' Report: Completing Europe's Economic and Monetary Union" June 22, 2015, which is available at ec.europa.eu. A more detailed focus on the medium-term requirements of EMU reform is provided in Richard Baldwin and Francisco Giavazzi (2016) (eds.) *Rebooting Europe – How to Fix Europe's Monetary Union: View of Leading Economists* (London: Centre for Economic Policy Research), which is available as an eBook at www.VoxEu.org. The case for creating a sovereign debt-restructuring regime for the euro zone, which would operate in conjunction with the ESM is laid out in Chap. 1 of Giancarlo Corsetti et al. (2016) *Reinforcing the Euro Zone and Protecting an Open Society* (London: Centre for Economic Policy Research Press).

CHAPTER 6

The Global Financial Crisis and Inequality

The connections between global financial crisis and income/wealth inequality have been subject to much debate since the onset of the Great Recession. Certainly, the impact of the financial crisis on personal wealth and employment has raised concerns about increasing income inequality now more than was the case prior to the onset of the crisis, as reflected, for example, in the "Occupy Wall Street" movement that surfaced in late 2011. In addition, there has been much discussion about the role of inequality in precipitating the credit boom preceding the global financial crisis, as well as the role of the financial sector in exacerbating the long-term rising trend in inequality. It is therefore appropriate in assessing the lessons of the global financial crisis to focus on these issues, which is the purpose of this chapter. On the basis of the evidence available thus far, it appears that inequality and the global financial crisis have interacted in a mutually reinforcing manner. The growth of the financial sector was one factor (among others) that contributed to the worsening in income inequality prior to the crisis, which in turn played a role in the build-up of forces that gave rise to the financial crisis. To complete the cycle, the impact and effects of the financial crisis have further exacerbated the problem of income inequality.

In the first section of this chapter, I examine the main factors that have contributed to the long-term rising trend in income inequality, which clearly predates the global financial crisis, and the role of the financial

© The Author(s) 2017   147
A. Elson, *The Global Financial Crisis in Retrospect*,
DOI 10.1057/978-1-137-59750-2_6

sector in contributing to that trend. The discussion then turns in the second section to the question of why the issue of income inequality was less of a concern in mainstream economics before the financial crisis than it has been since. The explanation for this issue has something to do with the dominant framework of macroeconomics and policy design examined in Chap. 3. The third section of the chapter looks at the question of how the problem of income and wealth inequality may have contributed to the onset of the crisis, again, not as the primary factor but as one among others that were discussed in Chap. 2. The concluding section of the chapter considers how some of the financial reforms that are under way may contribute to an improvement in income distribution or at least reduce the adverse impact of the financial sector on income inequality in the future.

THE FINANCIAL SECTOR AND INCOME INEQUALITY

The rising trend in income inequality in the advanced countries, and in the United States in particular, has been under way for some time and roughly coincides with the onset of economic and financial globalization that expanded from the late 1970s. Because of data limitations, economists have tended to focus on income inequality as distinct from wealth inequality. Income inequality is commonly measured using the Gini coefficient, which measures the share of total income accruing to different percentiles of the population, with zero indicating perfect equality of income distribution and one indicating maximum inequality. In the United States, income inequality has followed a U-shaped curve since the mid-1930s, with its Gini coefficient falling from a peak of around 0.50 in 1933 to an average of around 0.37–0.39 during the post-WW2 period through the early 1980s. Since then, it has steadily risen to around 0.44 in 2007, just prior to the crisis, and further to 0.46 by 2013.[1] The United Kingdom has followed a broadly similar U-shaped pattern, although it has not been as deep, nor have the measured Gini coefficients been as high as in the United States. The United States is somewhat unique among the OECD countries in that it now has the highest level of inequality among the group according to this measure, except for Chile and Mexico.

Other measures of income inequality trace out a picture of deterioration similar to that of the Gini coefficient. For example, the share of income accruing to the top 1 percent of the income scale in the United States has also followed a U-shaped pattern, falling to a share of around 8 percent by around 1980 and then rising to one of nearly 20 percent in

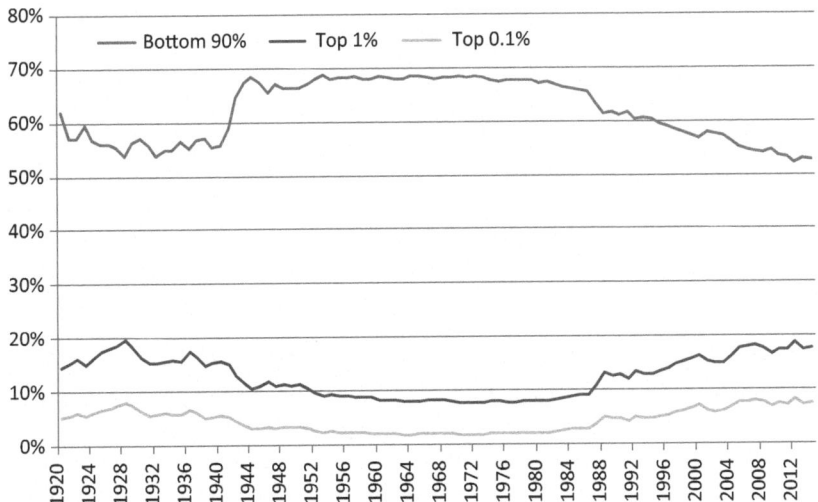

Chart 6.1 Share of income by population group in the United States (*Source*: The World Wealth and Income Database (www.wid.world))

2013, about the same as it was on the eve of the Great Depression (see Chart 6.1). Notably, there was a steady erosion in the income share of the bottom 90 percent of the income scale during this same time period in the growth of financial globalization from 67 percent in 1980 to 54 percent in 2007, a trend which has continued since the global financial crisis. In line with these trends, the earnings of the top decile of the income scale as a ratio of median earnings has risen from an average of around 1.75 in the mid-1960s to nearly 2.50 in 2013.[2]

Thanks to the work of Emmanuel Saez and Thomas Piketty, readers now have access to a unique cross-country database on wealth inequality, which has been developed from national tax records for the last 100 years. The publication of Piketty's book *Capital in the 21st Century* in 2014 caused a sensation not only because of the clarity and starkness of its findings but also because the timing of its publication coincided with greater public awareness of the problem of inequality among the advanced countries, which had been dramatized by the effects of the global financial crisis. These data pointed to a U-shaped pattern of inequality in wealth in the United States, which was more striking than in regard to income, as measured by the share of wealth concentrated among the top 0.1 percent of the population. In 1929 on the eve of the Great Depression, this share was 25 percent, which then dropped fairly steadily to around 7 percent in 1978. Since then, however, the trend in this measure of wealth concentration has reversed course, rising to nearly 18 percent in 2007 and then to around 22 percent by 2012, close to where it was in 1929. In 2012, what is stunning to see is that the share of wealth accruing to the top 0.1 percent of the population is virtually the same as that accruing to the bottom 90 percent of the distribution, thus having eliminated over time a difference in shares between these two groups that was as high as 26 percentage points in favor of the latter group in 1978 (see Chart 6.2).[3] Within these overall trends, what is of more immediate interest for purposes of this book is an understanding of the factors that have contributed to the rise in inequality since the late 1970s and the role that the financial sector in particular may have played, which are discussed below.

At the level of workers' income, there are a number of trends that have become more marked with the passage of time, which have suppressed the growth in wage income. One manifestation of these trends is that from around 2001 the share of labor income, as distinct from capital income, in total income has been declining. For a number of years since around

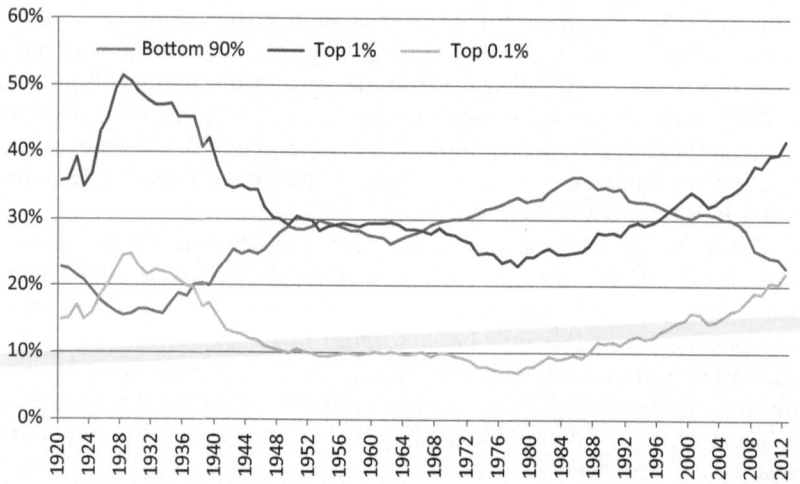

Chart 6.2 Share of wealth by population group in the United States (*Source*: Emmanuel Saez and Gabriel Zucman "Wealth Inequality in the US" (www.gabriel-zucman.eu/uswealth))

1980, the share of labor income in total national income was fluctuating around an average of 62–65 percent. In fact, from the 1960s, with the early development of economic growth theory, one of the assumed constants of the steady state, according to Nicholas Kaldor, was that the share of labor would remain relatively fixed over time, which in fact it did for a number of decades after Kaldor's assertion. However since around 2001, this share dropped to around 55 percent by 2013, contradicting that prediction. While a definitive explanation for this change is still being developed, a number of contributing factors have been identified. One is the divergence between real wage gains (or hourly compensation of workers) and productivity growth. Between 1948 and 1978, these two series tracked each other quite closely, as one would expect for an economy growing at or near its potential rate. However, for the next three decades from around 1980, there has been a growing divergence, with productivity growing by 74 percent and real wages growing by only 9 percent.[4]

While part of this divergence represents an acceleration in the growth of productivity, the data also reflect some compression of wage growth. The latter phenomenon has coincided with a steady decline in the share of manufacturing in the US economy over the past few decades that has accelerated with the impact of globalization and trade. A general trend toward the outsourcing of basic US manufacturing to countries with lower-skilled, lower-paid workers, such as China, has undoubtedly created downward pressure on manufacturing employment in the United States. A recent study has estimated that import competition from China during the period 1999–2011 reduced employment in manufacturing by an amount in the range of 2–2.4 million jobs. This trade effect has led to sustained unemployment and wage stagnation for displaced workers mainly because the US labor market has not been able to absorb these workers in other occupations, even though the demand for skilled labor resulting from trade with China has increased. Import competition from China has been growing for some time, with China's exports of manufactured goods rising from 2 percent of global manufactured exports in 1990 to 16 percent in 2011.[5]

The other important trend that has suppressed overall wage growth in the United States, while contributing to income inequality, is the divergence between wages for low-skilled and high-skilled labor as a result of technological change. The effects of skill-biased technological change, combined with a process of capital deepening, have now been well documented and have shown that the wages for skilled labor have increased while those for low-skilled labor have decreased, with the combined net effect of increasing wage inequality and reducing the overall share of labor income.[6] The declining share of manufacturing in the US economy and the compression of low-skill wages related to foreign competition have also occurred at a time of declining union membership, which had clearly been a factor in aligning real wages and productivity gains in the early post-WW2 years.

The financial sector has been an important contributor to the overall increase in corporate profits and the rising relative share of capital income, especially since 2000. It has also played a role in the growing divergence between income of the top 1 percent of the income scale and that of the rest of the population. One striking development has been the increase in the relative size of the financial sector in total GDP, rising from 2.8 percent in the 1950s to 7.6 percent on the eve of the global financial crisis. Such a rise is consistent with all the direct evidence we have for the growth of financial activity in the economy, such as credit outstanding in relation to GDP and the size of financial transactions, including in particular the growth of derivative trading, attendant upon the liberalization of the financial sector and the onset of financial globalization. While it is unquestionably the case that the growth of banking services and financial market activities is essential for the development of a modern economy, there may nevertheless come a point when this growth becomes counter-productive. In this connection, recent research has shown that the growth of the financial sector contributes to overall productivity and economic growth up to a certain point, after which it becomes a drag on total productivity. Such a point appears to have been reached in the period leading up to the financial crisis, with the case of Ireland and its surge in banking activity preceding its banking crisis in 2008 as a strong case in point.[7] According to one study carried out by International Monetary Fund (IMF) economists, the inflection point for the finance industry arises when the ratio of private sector credit to GDP rises above 100 percent of GDP, which would also be a signal of the increasing risk of a financial crisis.[8] All the countries most heavily involved in the pre-crisis housing bubbles and the aftereffects of the global financial crisis (Ireland, Portugal, Spain, the United Kingdom and the United States) clearly had exceeded that threshold.

More generally, the growth in financialization of the modern economy and the churning of transactions in financial markets related to derivative trading in mortgage-backed securities, collateralized debt obligations and credit default swaps prior to the financial crisis are other examples of potentially unproductive activities in the financial sector. Along with these trends, there is some evidence suggesting a growing inefficiency in the delivery of financial services, notwithstanding the positive benefits for efficiency in the financial industry associated with the ICT revolution. According to the work of Thomas Philippon, the cost of supplying US$1 of financing from the financial sector increased from around US¢20 in 1989 to US¢24 in 2011, a trend which coincided with a steady increase in the cost of financial intermediation.[9] Compared with the cost of other non-financial trading activities in the economy, Philippon concludes that the share of financial services in GDP is around 2 percentage points higher than it should be, signaling an annual resource misallocation of around US$280 billion. Some of this cost undoubtedly includes rents in the form of salary compensation and trading profits, as reflected in the lower tax treatment afforded to the earnings of private equity and hedge fund managers. It may also reflect rents accruing to too-big-to-fail (TBTF) financial institutions and the lower cost of their borrowing because of assumed bailout protection from the US government, which according to estimates of the IMF could be in the range of US$25 billion to US$50 billion annually.[10]

The finance sector has also contributed to the sharp increase in wage inequality discussed earlier. For example, between 1979 and 2005, managers in the finance industry increased their share in the top 1 percent of the income pyramid from 7.7 percent to 13.9 percent, and from 11 percent to 18 percent of the top 0.1 percent of the income groups.[11] As a result of these trends, the ratio of average wages in the financial sector compared with the average for non-financial sector workers rose from 1 in 1980 on a normalized basis to 1.7 in 2006. On the basis of these data, it is not difficult to understand some of the motivation for the Occupy Wall Street movement in the United States or the popularity among the millennial generation of concerns about income and wealth inequality raised by Senator Bernie Sanders in the US presidential campaign of 2015–16.

INEQUALITY AND MAINSTREAM ECONOMICS PRIOR TO THE CRISIS

While some economic research on issues of inequality was undoubtedly in progress prior to the financial crisis in terms of developing new data on wealth inequality (Piketty and Saez) and examining the factors behind growing wage inequality (David Autor of Harvard University), income inequality was not a significant part of the macroeconomic discourse or policy dialogue. In part, this lapse may be explained by the intense interest in the Great Moderation and the factors accounting for the success of macroeconomic stabilization. However, it may also have reflected certain conceptual biases in the economics profession that discounted the importance of income inequality as an issue of serious concern. This tendency is perhaps best captured by a statement by Robert Lucas, the dean of the new classical school of macroeconomics, who wrote in 2003: "Of the tendencies that are harmful to sound economics, the most seductive and, in my opinion, the most poisonous is to focus on questions of distribution.... the potential for improving the lives of poor people by finding different ways of distributing current production is nothing compared to the apparent limitless potential of increasing production."[12] Around a decade later, economists at the IMF argued convincingly on the opposite track that inequality matters for growth and its sustainability and that raising the income share of the poor is also good for growth.[13]

Lucas' statement reflected a long-standing belief among economists that there is an inherent trade-off in economics between efficiency (or maximum growth) and equity, as noted in Chap. 3, and that focusing policy on issues of equity would be detrimental to economic growth. Such a view was the basis for a belief in the power and efficacy of so-called trickle-down economics. This notion was also consistent with an important idea in macroeconomics of the post-WW2 era that improvements in the functioning of markets and price flexibility would bring about maximum social welfare and that this result was invariant to different sets of initial endowments or patterns of income distribution. While improving market efficiency provides a positive benefit for the economy, in isolation it ignores the fact that power relations within the economy related to the role of unions or the influence of large corporations can distort the role of market forces, thus frustrating the achievement of economic and allocative efficiency.

The focus on economic efficiency and competitive markets that is inherent in most macroeconomic modeling has also tended to ignore issues of equity or income inequality in that it builds on the notion that rewards to the factors of production (i.e., capital and labor) are determined by market forces such that wages result from the marginal productivity of labor while returns to capital are linked to its marginal productivity. These results are consistent with the objective of maximum social welfare noted earlier and thus can be considered "just" or "appropriate" from an economic perspective. Again, this result ignores the outcome of countervailing power relations in the economy and the appropriation of rents by different economic groups that can prevent the achievement of a desirable welfare objective.

Some readers of Thomas Piketty's recent book have argued that its statistical results and grand historical sweep show that modern finance capitalism leads inevitably to great inequality. This would be a mistaken reading. Some degree of inequality is integral to the functioning of a capitalist market economy and the incentives needed to promote investment and foster entrepreneurial activity. But the highly distorted picture of wealth inequality that Piketty and Saez have presented is another matter entirely. This result very much depends upon the "rules of the game" for the economy that result from the power relations and political forces in a given society, which determine the regulatory framework and institutional arrangements necessary for it to function. These rules may change over time as a result of the interplay of political forces (e.g., the coming of the Progressive Era and the New Deal in the United States), or wealth may be redistributed or extinguished as a result of extreme economic events (e.g., the Great Depression) and exogenous events such as war.

Prior to the publication of Piketty's book, one popular idea from the literature on economic growth was that over time market economies should display a tendency toward income convergence. This notion had both a statistical and a theoretical basis. The statistical foundation is best associated with the work of the Nobel laureate Simon Kuznets, one of the pioneers in the compilation of national accounts on a historical basis. In the mid-1950s, he propounded the thesis based on his statistical work that the process of economic growth should in its early stage lead to some inequality of incomes as workers migrate from rural agricultural areas where incomes tend to be low to urban industrial zones where wages and income tend to be higher. Over time, however, as this phase of industrial transformation is completed, the earlier rise in income inequality would be reversed with the growth of a large middle class attendant upon the spread of manufacturing and construction activity.[14]

The theoretical basis for a convergence of incomes in market economies over time comes from the neoclassical growth model. In its simplest formulation, this model posits that over time there should be a tendency for poorer countries to grow faster than rich ones as foreign direct investment flows from the latter group to the former group to benefit from the higher marginal productivity of capital in poor countries. Over time, this process will lead to a convergence of income levels between the two groups of countries or a catch-up phase. The same process takes place within countries as capital flows from richer regions to poorer ones, thus bringing about an increase in income levels in the poorer regions and a convergence of income levels more generally. At the global level, however, what we observe is not absolute convergence among countries as predicted by the neoclassical model but rather conditional convergence. The latter concept of convergence means that there is a tendency among countries that share a number of common elements such as culture, education or institutions, for income levels to converge. This tendency can be observed among different member states of the European Union or euro zone, as well as states of the United States. While this theoretical framework may help to explain a rise in the average or median level of income among a group of commonly situated countries or regions, it largely ignores the distorting effects on average income levels arising from large income gains for a tiny segment of the population.

THE ROLE OF INEQUALITY IN BRINGING ABOUT THE GLOBAL FINANCIAL CRISIS AND THE IMPACT OF THE CRISIS ON INCOME INEQUALITY

The origins of the financial crisis in the sub-prime segment of the mortgage finance market in the United States suggest that income inequality and the burden of debt on low- and middle-income families were important factors in the housing bubble that preceded the crisis. Both the decline in relative income levels of poor families and the relaxation of mortgage underwriting standards created a situation during the decade preceding the crisis in which workers' debt-to-income ratios were rising. As long as housing values were also rising during the bubble phase of the crisis and MBS received a strong demand from investors, this emerging problem of financial fragility was concealed. Growing inequality at the top of the income scale increased the savings among wealthy investors who became a prime target for the marketing of AAA-rated MBS. This pattern of increased borrowing at the bottom of the income scale and increased saving at the top was reflected in a tendency for consumption inequality to rise more slowly than income inequality in the years prior to the crisis. But once the housing bubble burst, the fragility of the financing arrangements linked to growing inequality came into full view, with the cascading effects described in earlier chapters of this book.[15]

The data on income inequality and household debt show a striking parallel in the period leading up to the financial crisis. According to data collected by Kumhof and Ranciere (2010), while the top 5 percent of the income distribution increased their share of total income from around 22 percent in 1983 to 34 percent in 2007, the ratio of household debt of all income groups to GDP rose from 49 percent to 98 percent.[16] When one excludes the top 5 percent of the income scale in the measurement of household debt, one can see a more than doubling in the ratio of household debt to family income for the same time period, with a particularly large jump in the period after 2000 when the housing bubble became more intense (see Chart 2.1).

In the aftermath of the financial crisis, there has been a heightened awareness of the problems of income inequality in the advanced countries, in part because of Piketty's book but also out of concern for the impact of the crisis on working class families. As a result, it became an important issue in the presidential campaign of 2015–2016 in the United States, at least among Democratic Party candidates. Income inequality has also become an important issue in macroeconomic policy discussions, as reflected, for example, in the debate as to whether the Fed's policy of quantitative easing (QE) has favored disproportionately the top 1 percent of the income scale because of its positive impact on financial asset prices (see below).

Since 2008, it is clear that the growing income inequality that was evident prior to the crisis has continued to widen. During the sharpest period of decline of the Great Recession in 2009, all income groups were affected by the large jump in unemployment and destruction in financial wealth. Thanks to the effect of social safety net expenditures, overall poverty rates did not increase significantly. However, since 2009, the recovery in income has largely favored the upper income groups. This tendency is captured by the simple fact that nearly 60 percent of the income gain in the United States during the period 2009–14 accrued to the top 1 percent of the income scale, and the top 0.1 percent in particular, according to data compiled by Emmanuel Saez.[17] In addition, it is noteworthy that in 2014, the income share accruing to the top 10 percent of the income distribution reached 50 percent, the highest share measured in Saez' database going back to 1917. It is also the case that wealth inequality has continued to widen since the onset of the crisis, as noted earlier. Prior to the crisis, the share of wealth held by the bottom 90 percent of the wealth distribution was on a declining trend because of the massive dis-saving associated with the increase in household debt. Following the crisis, this downward trend has continued. The major collapse in the value of low- and middle-income housing outside the urban centers of large metropolitan areas has more than offset any improvement in savings as working class families have struggled to lower the burden of their debt. In fact, the share of wealth of families in the bottom 90 percent of the wealth distribution fell by around 20 percent between 2007 and 2012 while that of the top 1 percent increased by 24 percent (see Chart 6.2).[18]

The other concern about income inequality that has been raised in the aftermath of the financial crisis is whether the policy of QE pursued by central banks in the advanced countries has contributed to the trends in inequality described above. The issue here is that by design QE is intended to lower the yields on long-term bonds in order to make borrowing more attractive, which also has the effect of increasing the prices of these assets. By a process of arbitrage, this effect carries over to the prices of other bonds outside the scope of the central bank's asset purchases, and stocks and foreign assets, as well, that may be part of investors' portfolios. Since these assets are disproportionately held by the upper strata of the income distribution, if not mainly the top 1 percent, the policy of QE taken in isolation has contributed to a widening of income or wealth inequality. It has also been argued that the Fed's policy of QE has tended to depress the yields on fixed income assets, which are important investments for middle-income and elderly groups. On this point, however, it needs to be recognized that the Fed has largely accommodated a decline in long-term interest rates and the "natural" rate of interest that has been under way for some time, as discussed in Chap. 4. Officials of the Federal Reserve have also pointed out that QE has had the effect of increasing home prices to varying degrees across different regions of the country while stimulating employment, both of which effects have tended to improve the income and wealth position of middle-income and working families. In sum, it needs to be recognized that QE and monetary policy, more generally, have had different portfolio and economic effects in the short-to-medium term, which are offsetting to some degree. Thus, it is largely an empirical matter as to what the net effect of QE has been on income distribution for that time frame. Over the long term, however, monetary policy should be neutral with respect to its effects on the real side of the economy, and income distribution in particular. Accordingly, one must look at factors such as globalization, technological change and power relations in the economy, as noted earlier, in explaining changes in income distribution.[19]

On the quantitative side, various studies have tried to measure the net impact of changes in asset prices occasioned by monetary policy on income or wealth distribution. In regard to equity prices, it is important to note that through the end of 2015 the value of the US stock market as reflected in the S&P 500 index was not much higher than it would have been by extrapolating the trend growth path that the index was on during the seven-year period ending in 2007. This implies that the index has largely recovered from its major collapse during the peak phase of the Great Recession when it lost 35 percent of its value. From this perspective, if there was any significant effect of the Fed's QE on the value of the equity market, it was to speed up its recovery compared to what it would have been in the absence of a stimulative monetary policy.

Some studies have tried to quantify the net effect of QE on wealth distribution by looking at its impact on different channels of influence. One study by two economists at the University of Massachusetts tried to quantify the net distributional impact of the Fed's QE in terms of gains in employment, the rise in asset prices and the lower cost of mortgage refinancing. On balance for the period 2011–13, the net effect of QE on these three variables was estimated to have been mildly reinforcing of income inequality.[20] In another study, in the context of the euro zone, two European economists attempted to measure the effects of a 10 percent increase in bond prices, equity prices and home prices associated with the QE policy of the European Central Bank on the net wealth position of the population of various euro area countries using a benchmark survey of wealth distribution for 2010. On balance, this exercise resulted in a moderate net reduction in wealth inequality, with broadly similar effects across the euro area countries. The increase in bond prices would be relatively neutral across the wealth strata while the impact of a home price increase would reduce income inequality because of its positive impact on the middle groups of the wealth strata, which would mildly offset the skewed effect of an increase in equity prices that would favor only the top 5 percent of the wealth distribution.[21] Further evidence on the impact of monetary policy and QE on wealth inequality was provided by a recent study by the Bank for International Settlements that showed that wealth inequality has indeed risen since the financial crisis in the United States, the United Kingdom and selected countries of the euro zone and that monetary policy has contributed to that trend through the positive impact of QE on equity prices. This effect was only measured to have been partly offset through the equalizing effect of increases in home prices.[22]

In general, one can argue from a conceptual point of view that monetary policy has a number of different economic effects that do not lead to an unambiguous case for its positive or negative impact on inequality in the short-to-medium term. Moreover, the quantitative studies that have been conducted do not allow us to reach a firm conclusion on this issue, as well.

THE IMPACT OF FINANCIAL REFORM MEASURES ON INCOME INEQUALITY

As recounted in Chap. 5, reform of the financial sector has been at the core of national and international efforts to deal with the problems that contributed to the onset of the global financial crisis. The main reform issues will be taken up again in Chap. 7, but at this stage it is useful to consider what impact some of these reforms might have on limiting the negative impact of financial sector activity on income inequality. In this regard, reforms in five areas could be considered: (1) the imposition of a tax on financial market transactions (FTT), (2) limits on executive compensation, (3) actions to terminate bailouts of large complex financial institutions that are deemed TBTF, (4) the separation of consumer finance protection from the normal safety and soundness regulation of banks and other financial institutions and (5) the termination of favored tax treatment for the compensation of hedge fund and private equity managers and for long-term capital gains. There are undoubtedly other aspects of the financial reform that will have potential effects on income distribution, but the ones discussed here are perhaps more important.

An FTT has a long history of debate going back at least to proposals emanating from a famous Yale economist, James Tobin, who proposed in 1972 a currency transactions tax to limit speculation in foreign exchange transactions. Since the global financial crisis, the FTT has again become a focus of debate. Most proposals suggest a tax expressed in terms of basis points ranging from 1 to 10, or 0.01 to 0.1, percent. Against the background of the global financial crisis, one advantage of an FTT is that it would likely reduce the amount of high-volume, speculative trading that can potentially be a destabilizing factor in financial markets and has been an element that helped to create inefficiencies in the financial sector and increase its size without commensurate social value, as discussed earlier in this chapter. Such a tax would also be highly progressive in nature as it would mainly fall on those individuals in the top one-fifth of the income distribution who account for most of the trading in financial markets.[23] One concern about an FTT is that it might lead to a shift of financial trading to offshore markets. However, it should be noted that an FTT already exists in a number of G20 countries (as well as Hong Kong and Singapore) and is scheduled to be introduced in 11 countries of the European Union in mid-2016. If such a tax were imposed in a coordinated manner among the main financial center countries, then transfers of trading from one country to another would be less likely to occur.

Executive compensation in the financial sector was clearly a factor contributing to wage inequality and excessive risk-taking on the part of financial institutions in the lead-up to the financial crisis. Generous bonus payments linked to high short-term trading profits were one among many factors that contributed to financial instability and unsound banking practices that preceded the crisis. Since the crisis, executive compensation has become the focus of international attention in an effort to limit the potential for future financial instability. In April 2009, the Financial Stability Board (FSB) adopted a list of *Principles for Sound Compensation Practices*, which were endorsed by the G20 Leaders at their summit in Cannes, France, in November 2011. This document sets out certain guidelines for the determination and reporting of fixed and variable components of executive pay and for the role of corporate boards in ensuring that the variable component linked to performance provides appropriate incentives for maintaining the solvency of the financial institution concerned. While these standards are voluntary for members of the FSB, they have been subject to the G20's peer-review process and periodic monitoring by the FSB. In most countries, executive compensation practices since the crisis have become an integral element of the supervisory process. In the case of the European Union, within its capital requirement directives governing the prudential rules for banks and other financial institutions, caps have been set for the relationship between the variable and fixed components of executive compensation. In the United States, guidelines have been set determining that bonus payments in the form of stock options become available only after a minimum period of three years.

The G20's focus on sound compensation practices has been a useful endeavor in focusing attention and outside scrutiny on the incentives for excessive risk-taking in financial institutions. However, it is not clear that it has had any effect in limiting the scale of executive pay in the financial sector, which has been a factor in driving increases in wage inequality. To deal with this aspect of executive compensation, changes in income tax policy are required, along with corporate reforms prohibiting the combined roles of Board Chairman and Chief Executive Officer in one person and the creation of independent or outside directors.

Ending the implicit bailout protection for TBTF financial institutions has been a key focus of financial reform efforts in the wake of the global financial crisis. Such protection generated a subsidy for these institutions in increasing their leverage through market borrowing that created rents in the form of higher compensation for their top executives. It also implied that any gains from risky behavior were privatized while any losses from such behavior were socialized in the form of taxpayer-funded bailouts. The two elements of financial reform that have been focused on ending TBTF protection are higher capital requirements for large complex financial institutions and the creation of a credible resolution mechanism to deal with their dismemberment in the event of insolvency. Both of these reforms have been strongly endorsed by the G20 at the international level and have been developed under the coordination of the FSB.

An increase in capital requirements and the capital-asset ratio of financial institutions is one of the most important changes that can be made to limit the risk of financial crises and the negative spillovers of bank failures. In this regard, it is striking to note that in the case of non-financial corporations a capital-asset ratio of 40 percent or more is common, whereas for financial firms prior to the crisis, ratios of 3 percent or less have been the norm. There is no reason why these ratios should be so different, and in fact prior to the creation of the Federal Reserve System, most banks were financed mainly by private equity. Since that time, the lender of last resort financing of the Federal Reserve, the creation of deposit insurance, the implicit government subsidies for borrowing by TBTF institutions and the favorable tax treatment of interest payments on loans have created powerful incentives for banks to increase their leverage. As a result of the crisis, the FSB has coordinated efforts to revise the Basel Capital Accord, which has resulted in a significant increase in the minimum bank capital requirements and the imposition for the first time of a minimum capital-asset ratio. The important question is whether these changes go far enough. Certainly in the case of the new minimum capital-asset requirement of 3 percent they do not, as this ratio still allows for a very high degree of leverage. Most of the advanced countries have set national requirements that are above this guideline; in the case of the United States, the Fed has stipulated a ratio of 4 percent for banks up to US$100 billion in assets and 5 percent for those above that threshold.

In regard to capital requirements, the Basel Committee has further refined the risk-weighted system of asset classification to determine minimum ratios while minimizing the link of risk weights to the ratings of credit rating agencies. This is an important change, given the gross failings of the agencies to apply strict objective standards in their evaluation of securitized instruments in the period preceding the global financial crisis. As a general rule, capital requirements have been increased with the strengthening of the basic tier-1 capital requirement (equity financing plus retained earnings) and the addition of a new capital surcharge for "systemically important" financial institutions. Some other innovations have been made that allow for the imposition of a counter-cyclical capital requirement, along with a new minimum liquidity requirement and loss-absorbing debt category. While these changes represent a significant improvement over the Basel II regime, a good case can be made that they do not go far enough (see Chap. 7).

In the other dimension of financial reform related to insolvency regimes, it seems that significant progress has been made. The FSB has established guidelines for the constitution of bank resolution frameworks that will facilitate the coordination of national efforts to deal with the insolvency of globally significant financial institutions, which was not possible in the immediate wake of the financial crisis. In the case of the bankruptcy of Lehman Brothers, for example, insolvency proceedings were initiated in more than 80 countries owing to its large network of international affiliates. In the United States, where the largest share of Lehman Brothers' financial operations was located, a bankruptcy plan covering claims of more than US$350 billion was approved in late 2011, but the processing of these claims was still under way as of mid-2016.[24] As the failure of Lehman Brothers was the immediate trigger for the global financial crisis with its negative spillover effects on financial markets, employment and poverty levels, the existence of an efficient resolution mechanism for large, systemically important financial institutions, distinct from the time-consuming bankruptcy framework for non-financial corporations, would go a long way toward eliminating the moral hazard of the implicit bailout protection for these institutions that existed prior to the crisis. In this way, high risk and unsound banking practices should be greatly reduced as managers and corporate directors will understand the consequences of failure of their firm more clearly. In the case of the United States, the initiation of stress testing as a regular feature of bank supervision along with the supervisory certification of "living wills" that large financial institutions are required to prepare to facilitate their dismemberment in the event insolvency should reinforce the objective of eliminating TBTF protection.

Another important change in regulatory practice since the crisis that has a potentially important impact on income distribution is the separation of the oversight of consumer finance regulation from normal micro-prudential regulation and supervision. Prior to the financial crisis, there was an increasing amount of fraud and abuse in the marketing of sub-prime mortgages, which contributed to unsustainable debt burdens for low-income homeowners. Even though the Federal Reserve well before the crisis had broad power to stop deceptive and unfair mortgage lending activity, in practice this authority was not exercised in the Fed's normal safety and soundness supervision of banks. In the case of other lenders outside the Fed's purview, either consumer protection laws did not apply or regulatory oversight was badly fragmented among a number of different agencies. In the aftermath of the crisis, a new Consumer Finance Protection Bureau was established in the United States in 2010 with the explicit mandate to regulate banks and credit unions under existing consumer protection laws. It also has the authority to pursue cases of unfair or predatory lending practices by credit card agencies and other lenders, as well as the operators of "Ponzi" schemes and illegal offshore investment scams.

A final area of financial reform that would have obvious implications for income distribution is the elimination of the special US tax treatment for executive compensation in the hedge fund and private equity business and for long-term capital gains. While no changes have yet been made in these areas since the crisis, they are receiving more attention in public policy debate. During the liberalized regulatory environment that preceded the global financial crisis, one of the benefits accorded to hedge fund and private equity executives as a result of intense lobbying was the favored tax treatment of their earnings. Instead of treating the earnings of these individuals as ordinary income for tax purposes subject to the normal progressive schedule of income tax rates, a special provision was included in the US tax code that designated their earnings as "carried interest", subject to the same favored tax rates as long-term capital gains, or roughly half the rate that would apply to high-earning professionals in other fields. This is an example of a pure rent created by distorted government action, ostensibly justified on account of the substantial risk undertaken by these financial managers to improve the functioning of financial markets. Even if this claim were true, it is by no means clear that it warrants a special tax subsidy from the government, especially in view of the inefficiencies associated with increased financialization of the economy and the potentially large social costs of high-risk speculative activity in financial markets preceding the crisis. In view of the concerns raised about executive compensation earlier in this chapter, other ways should be sought to increase the progressivity of taxes on very high-income earners either through an increase in marginal tax rates or through the elimination of exemptions, and tax loopholes and subsidies that favor the very rich.

The treatment of long-term capital gains also has a significant relationship with the financial industry as most of these gains for tax purposes are generated by financial market activity and apply to high-income individuals. One simple proposal under consideration in this regard is to lengthen the period for distinguishing short-term from long-term capital gains: from one year under current law to three or four years. The intent in this case is to lengthen the holding period of financial assets and reduce the incentive for active market trading.

Summary and Conclusion

A rise in income and wealth inequality has been under way in many advanced economies (and especially the United States) since the onset of globalization, with marked increases in the share of income and wealth accruing to the top 1 percent of the population. Prior to the global financial crisis, the financial industry played a role in exacerbating income inequality, which then became a factor in contributing to its onset. The financial sector also contributed to the growing share of capital (as distinct from labor) income in total national income and to the marked divergence between high-income and low-income wage earners. It is important to recognize that other factors such as the decline in union power, trade policy and technological change also played an important role in bringing about these changes in income distribution. Growing income inequality in the United States, which was the country at the center of the financial crisis, contributed to a sharp rise in debt-to-income ratios among working class families that participated in the housing bubble preceding the crisis.

Issues of income distribution and inequality were not a major concern among macroeconomic researchers and practitioners prior to the crisis, in large measure because of their intense focus on the promotion of growth and allocative efficiency, as well as the objectives and methods of macroeconomic stabilization. To a large extent, rapid economic growth was viewed as the most effective solution to poverty while a focus on redistributive policies was considered detrimental to growth. The economic effects of the financial crisis, along with the impact of a major study of long-term trends in income distribution by Thomas Piketty, have raised the profile of issues of income inequality in public debate and economic research. Since the crisis, income inequality has continued to rise as the income share of the top tier of the income distribution has recovered more quickly than the rest of the population.

Some commentators have alleged that the unconventional monetary policy of the major central banks has contributed to income and wealth inequality because of its positive effects on the prices of financial assets, which are held and traded more actively by individuals in the top tiers of the income distribution. Over the long term, it is unlikely that these effects will significantly influence income distribution, while in the short-to-medium term, it needs to be recognized that they are likely to be counter-balanced by the impact of stimulative monetary policy on reducing unemployment and promoting home ownership. Empirical studies focusing on the short-term effects of monetary policy on income inequality have not shown conclusive results.

A number of financial reforms undertaken since the crisis or under consideration can be expected to play some role in reducing income inequality in the future, as reflected in efforts to limit gains in executive compensation, to end bailout protection for systemically important financial institutions and to improve consumer finance protection. In this regard, attention should also be given to the imposition of a financial transactions tax and the suspension of favored tax treatment for income earnings in the asset management industry. However, major improvements in income distribution will require sustained efforts in tax reform, education policy and job training over a number of years.

Notes

1. These data are taken from Anthony Atkinson (2015) *Inequality – What Can Be Done* (Cambridge, MA; Harvard University Press).
2. These data are presented in Fig. 1.1 of Atkinson (2015), p. 18.
3. These data can be found in the database assembled by Emmanuel Saez and Gabriel Zucman (2015) for their paper "Wealth Inequality

in the United States from 1913: Evidence from Capitalized Income Tax Data" which is to be published in the Quarterly Journal of Economics and is available at http://www.gabriel-zucman.eu/ uswealth/.

4. These data were assembled by Lawrence Mishel et al. "Wage Stagnation in Nine Charts" Economic Policy Institute, January 6, 2015, which is available at www.epi.org.

5. These data are taken from Daron Acemoglu et al. "Import Competition and the Great US Employment Sag of the 2000s" Journal of Labor Economics vol. 34 (1), part 2 (January 2016); pp. 141–198.

6. This discussion draws from Ric Armenter "A Bit of a Miracle No More: The Decline in the Labor Share" Federal Reserve Bank of Philadelphia Business Review, Third Quarter 2015; pp. 1–9.

7. This discussion is based on the research of Stephen Cecchetti and Enisse Kharoubi "Why Does Financial Sector Growth Crowd Out Real Economic Growth?" BIS Working Paper 490 (February 2015).

8. Jean-Louis Arcand et al. "Too Much Finance?" IMF Working Paper #12/161 (June 2012).

9. Thomas Philippon "Finance vs. Wal-Mart – Why Are Financial Services So Expensive?" Report of the Russell Sage Foundation (November 2012).

10. These estimates were presented in the IMF Global Financial Stability Report 2013, ch. 3 "How Big is the Implicit Subsidy to TBTF Banks?"

11. These data are taken from a report by Joseph Stiglitz (2015) "Rewriting the Rules" of the Roosevelt Institute, New York (May 12, 2015), which can be accessed at www.rooseveltinstitute.org/ rewrite-rules/.

12. Robert Lucas "The Industrial Revolution: Past and Future" 2003 Annual Report Essay of the Federal Reserve Bank of Minneapolis.

13. Jonathan D. Ostry et al. "Redistribution, Inequality and Growth" IMF Staff Discussion Note SDN/14/02 (March 2014) and Era Dabla-Norris et al. "Causes and Consequences of Income Inequality: A Global Perspective" IMF Staff Discussion Note SDN/15/13 (June 2015).

14. Simon Kuznets' view of the economic growth process can be found in Kuznets (1955) "Economic Growth and Income Inequality" American Economic Review vol. 45(1), pp. 1–30.

15. One of the first books to link the global financial crisis to the financial fragility associated with rising inequality was Raghuram Rajan (2010) Fault Lines: How Hidden Fractures Still Threaten the Global Economy (Princeton, NJ: Princeton University Press). A more formal analysis and model of these links can be found in Michael Kumhof and Romain Ranciere "Leverage, Inequality and Crises" IMF Working Paper #10/268 (November 2010).
16. Michael Kumhof and Romain Ranciere (2010), op. cit.
17. See Emmanuel Saez "Striking It Richer: The Evolution of Top Incomes in the United States" June 25, 2015 (http://eml.berkeley.edu/~saez/saez-UStopincomes-2014.pdf).
18. Data on wealth inequality are drawn from the statistical work of Emmanuel Saez and Gabriel Zucman, as presented in "Wealth Inequality in the United States Since 1913: Evidence from Capitalized Income Data" NBER Working Paper #20625 (October 2014).
19. A number of the points raised in this paragraph were argued persuasively by Ben Bernanke, former Chairman of the Federal Reserve, in his blog of June 1, 2015 (www.brookings.edu/blogs/benbernanke).
20. Juan Antonio Montecino and Gerald Epstein "Did Quantitative Easing Increase Income Inequality?" Working Paper #407 Political Economy Research Institute, University of Massachusetts (October 2015).
21. Klaus Adam and Angiota Tzamourani "Distributional Consequences of Asset Price Inflation in the Euro Area" Deutsche Bundesbank Discussion Paper #27/2015.
22. Dietrich Domanski et al. "Wealth Inequality and Monetary Policy" BIS Quarterly Review, March 2016; pp. 45–64.
23. This estimate is based on a study of the Tax Policy Center, which prepared an analysis of various features of an FTT, including its distributional impact (Leonard Burman et al. "Financial Transactions Taxes in Theory and Practice" July 31, 2015, Tax Policy Center – Brookings and Urban Institutes, Washington, DC).
24. The Lehman Brothers' bankruptcy case is discussed in Michael J. Fleming and Asani Sarkar "The Failure Resolution of Lehman Brothers" Federal Reserve Bank of New York Economic Review vol. 20 (2), December 2014, pp. 175–206.

CHAPTER 7

The Quest for Financial Stability at the National and Global Levels

This chapter deals with two critical dimensions of the reforms that have been under way since the global financial crisis, where there are particular challenges. One of these is the area of financial stability oversight at the national level, which was sorely lacking in the years prior to the financial crisis. This is commonly referred to as macro-prudential supervision, as distinct from micro-prudential supervision that is focused on the safety and soundness of individual financial firms. The other dimension, which embraces financial stability oversight at the global level, is the reform of the international financial architecture (IFA), where again, as discussed in Chap. 5, there were serious shortcomings in the detection of, and response to, major financial imbalances and risks that were accumulating in the international financial system prior to the financial crisis.

THE OVERSIGHT OF FINANCIAL SYSTEM STABILITY

To a large extent, one could conclude that the global financial crisis reflected a major failure of financial stability oversight, both at the national and international levels. In the United Sates, for example, macroeconomic policy, and monetary policy in particular, was focused primarily on the achievement of low inflation and full employment consistent with GDP close to its potential level. The experience of the Great Moderation suggested that monetary policy was becoming increasingly more successful in the achievement of these goals. However, under the surface beyond the

© The Author(s) 2017
A. Elson, *The Global Financial Crisis in Retrospect*,
DOI 10.1057/978-1-137-59750-2_7

scope of the monetary authorities, growing imbalances related to high-risk financial activities were building, which led to a financial crash with devastating consequences. A centralized focus on systemic stability issues as part of the macroeconomic orientation of the monetary authority would have identified areas of concern where action was required. Of course, one of the difficulties for the Federal Reserve was that many of the problems leading up to the crisis were playing out in the "shadow" banking system outside the normal purview of its supervision.

Since the crisis, much attention has been given to the need for incorporating a macro-prudential or financial stability perspective into the activities of central banks in the countries most affected by the crisis. This is not a new issue and had been part of central bank deliberations during the early years of financial globalization when problems of international banking failures led to the creation of the Basel capital standards. It has also been part of the experience of central banks of a number of emerging market economies, often with a particular focus on exchange rate stability through the use of capital controls.[1] In the advanced countries, financial stability concerns receded as policy-makers' attention shifted to macroeconomic stabilization objectives and with the belief that financial liberalization could help to make the financial sector more self-stabilizing. The global financial crisis has shattered that belief and brought financial system stability concerns back to the forefront of central bank policy discussions.

Prior to the crisis, as noted in Chap. 4, a dominant frame of thinking about monetary policy and financial stability was conveyed by the phrase "lean and clean". This phrase was meant to convey the notion that monetary policy should "lean against the wind", in the sense that it should be tightened soon enough in the upswing of a business cycle to avoid overheating and inflation. This posture together with proper supervision and risk management within the financial sector was thought to be the best protection against the failure of one or more financial institutions. However, if a bank failure did occur, it was imperative to deal with its resolution (or "cleaning") promptly to avoid contagion with other financial firms. This was the approach adopted by the Federal Reserve in the late 1990s in dealing with the failure of the hedge fund Long-Term Capital Management, as recounted in Chap. 3.

In addressing recent concerns about financial system stability, it is important to understand what is meant by financial system stability or a macro-prudential perspective and how to operationalize this dimension of central bank policy. Two questions are paramount. Can financial system stability be addressed through the normal tools of monetary policy or does it require separate instruments? If the latter, how do they need to be coordinated with the central bank's regulatory or supervisory functions?

The simplest way to think about financial system stability is to consider how resilient the financial system is to external or exogenous economic shocks, such as a sharp fall in the price of oil or a major stock market index, significant changes in the yield curve or an increase in the risk premium on government debt. However, it is also true that financial systems because of their interconnectedness and network of relationships display emergent properties that cannot be detected by the traditional focus of micro-prudential regulation and supervision on the safety and soundness of individual banks. In these conditions, the resilience of the system can be tested by an endogenous shock, as distinct from the kinds of exogenous shocks mentioned above, such as the failure of a major financial institution or problems in the housing finance segment of the system. The global financial crisis was an example of financial system instability caused by a series of endogenous shocks and emergent properties of the system that were not well understood by the regulatory authorities, not just in the United States but also in other advanced countries.

Should financial system stability be added to the macroeconomic policy objectives of the Federal Reserve and other central banks? In a direct sense, yes it needs to be a central concern of the monetary authority in terms of gauging the risks of a crisis in the financial system from either endogenous or exogenous sources, and the obvious threats such events can pose to its macroeconomic objectives. In addition, the central bank policy-makers need to be alert to the possible impact of monetary policy on the behavior of commercial banks, for example, in the upswing of a business cycle, if the stance of monetary policy is too accommodative and credit growth is accelerating. An example of the systemic stability perspective of monetary policy prior to the global financial crisis was the concern that monetary policy of the Federal Reserve was too relaxed during the expansion phase of the housing bubble, as judged by the extent to which the actual level of the federal funds rate was well below the policy rate that would have been appropriate according to the calculation of the well-known "Taylor Rule" (see Chap. 4).

If it is clear that financial system stability needs to be a principal concern of the central bank consistent with its regulatory and monetary policy responsibilities, there is still debate as to whether or not it is appropriate to use the standard tools of monetary policy to deal with issues of systemic stability. There may be situations in which the objectives of financial stability coincide with the macroeconomic policy objectives of the central bank and changes in its policy rate can deal with both objectives at the same time. For example, in the case of a credit boom, where there might be growing concern over inflationary pressures, as well as undue risk banks may be assuming without adequate provisioning, an increase in the central bank's short-term policy rate can help to address both concerns. However, there may also arise cases where the central bank has adopted a relaxed monetary stance in the interest of promoting a more rapid recovery from recession and yet its low-interest-rate policy has induced excessive risk taking on the part of some financial institutions in a specific sector of the economy. In such a case, the macroeconomic and financial stability objectives are in conflict and an increase in the central bank's policy rate to deal with stability concerns runs the risk of delaying or cutting off the economic recovery. A recent example of this case was provided by the Swedish National Bank (Riksbank) in 2010–11 when it raised its policy rate by 175 basis points to deal with a credit boom in housing, at a time when the country was still struggling to recover from the spillover effects of the global financial crisis. It quickly became evident that this action on the part of the Riksbank had a significant dampening effect on the economic recovery as reflected in a decline in output and employment, at which point the central bank authorities decided to reverse course.[2] This example also shows that interest rate policy is a blunt instrument that cuts across many different sectors of the economy and cannot be targeted at one sector or activity in particular. In the example just given, the central bank should address financial stability concerns with the use of its monetary policy tools only if, for example, the benefits of forestalling a financial crisis with its severe negative effects on the aggregate economy outweigh the costs of derailing an economic recovery, either in the short term or the long term.[3]

Given the possible dilemmas for the use of monetary policy tools to deal with systemic stability issues, there has been much discussion on the range of macro-prudential tools that central banks have at their disposal. Some of these are quite specific, such as the application of limits on the debt-to-income or debt-to-value ratios connected with borrowing by individual persons, households and firms. These limits can be applied to specific sectors of activity or types of financial institutions. The application of these kinds of tools would have been appropriate during the housing bubble in the United States prior to the global financial crisis, but they were not available to be used by the regulatory authorities. Another specific tool that can be imposed on banks is dynamic loan provisioning that can be helpful in dampening credit expansion during the upswing of a business cycle, as requirements for increasing provisions against possible loan losses are raised at a time when credit growth is more buoyant and then relaxed during the downturn of the credit cycle. The application of these specific tools of macro-prudential regulation is still being analyzed and tested across many countries in regard to the timing of their application, the magnitude of the measures to be introduced and their coordination with monetary policy.[4]

A major focus of macro-prudential supervision in the wake of the global financial crisis is on the problem of dealing with systemically important financial institutions (SIFIs) or too-big-to-fail (TBTF) institutions. While there is unanimous agreement that the implicit government subsidies and protection for such institutions need to be removed in a way that is credible to their shareholders, creditors and financial markets more generally, it is not yet clear that the requisite institutional or regulatory changes have been put in place. In this area, macro-prudential supervision needs to be closely aligned with micro-prudential regulation and with the agency in charge of bank resolution in an event of insolvency to contain the large negative externalities of the failure of a SIFI.

In the micro-prudential area, supervisors must be concerned with the safety and soundness of large complex financial institutions, but they also need to understand its network of relationships with the broader financial system at home and abroad in order to be able to gauge the potential impact of its failure. In this regard, under the Dodd-Frank legislation, SIFIs in the United States are required to prepare resolution plans or "living wills" for approval by the Federal Reserve and Federal Deposit Insurance Corporation (FDIC), which would explain the various components of the firm's business operations, including its asset and liability structure, and how these could be closed down if necessary in the event of insolvency either by means of a bankruptcy proceeding or bank resolution process. These plans are intended to avoid the cumbersome, lengthy and highly disruptive proceedings of the Lehman Brothers' bankruptcy. Thus far, through the end of 2015, only one of the plans submitted by eight SIFIs had been judged by the Federal Reserve and FDIC to be satisfactory. If this new resolution mechanism is not credible, which is an open question since it has not yet been tested in the United States or in other advanced countries, then financial markets will not be convinced that

TBTF protection has been removed. An additional complication is that SIFI resolution mechanisms need to be coordinated on an international basis. This requirement has not yet been satisfied, although the Financial Stability Board (FSB) has prepared guidelines for the design of such mechanisms among its members in order to facilitate their joint operation should the need arise, which is a likely future eventuality given the strong international connections among SIFIs globally.

One regulatory innovation with both a micro-prudential and macro-prudential dimension that was introduced in the wake of the crisis, as noted in Chap. 4, was the initiation of "stress tests" for all large banking institutions and not just the more limited groups of SIFIs. These tests are designed to gauge the extent to which the tier-1 capital or equity position of a bank would be threatened and reduced in the event of an extreme economic or financial shock, including the failure of a SIFI. Over time, different scenarios have been prepared by the regulatory authorities for these annual stress tests, which the banks must incorporate in their internal risk models to determine the degree to which their equity would be affected. The results of these exercises are reviewed by the bank supervisors, and if they indicate a high risk of a significant loss of capital, steps must be taken by the bank in question to alter its business operations or strengthen its equity holdings. Since the time these stress tests were introduced in 2009, they have become an important and essential component of the supervisory process in the United States.

Another key innovation in macro-prudential regulation that is not yet fully implemented is related to the revised Basel Capital Accord (Basel III) that was approved by members of the FSB and disseminated in 2010. Basel III represents a significant improvement over the regime that was in place prior to the financial crisis with its obvious defects that contributed to the onset of the crisis, as discussed earlier in this book. In addition to an increase in the core tier-1 capital requirement, Basel III has introduced an additional capital conservation buffer of up to 2.5 percent of risk-weighted assets. In the event this buffer is eliminated by a bank's losses, such an event becomes a trigger for a mandatory increase in its capital holdings sufficient to restore the buffer. The new accord also allows for the introduction of an additional counter-cyclical capital requirement of up to 2.5 percent, which regulators can impose to moderate bank credit expansion during the upswing of a business cycle and reverse in the downswing. Such a requirement would be similar in its effect to that of dynamic loan provisioning noted earlier. A further innovation in Basel III is the introduction of an incremental capital requirement of 1.5 percent of risk-weighted assets exclusively for SIFIs. Finally, Basel III incorporates for the first time an overall leverage ratio of capital to the total, as distinct from risk-weighted, assets of a bank of 3 percent. This number, however, implies a very high leverage ratio of 33, which in the light of the financial crisis must be considered to be too relaxed. But, as in the case of all the new components of the capital accord, this is a minimum ratio, which country authorities can increase if they wish.

In addition to these modifications of the basic capital requirement, Basel III has established a new liquidity requirement for banks to ensure that they can liquidate certain of their assets to meet depositor or creditor withdrawals and a "stable net funding ratio" to ensure that banks are not overly dependent on very short-term liabilities (e.g., overnight repurchase agreements or commercial paper) that can evaporate in periods of stress. Finally, Basel III introduces a requirement for banks to issue certain bonds that are convertible to equity in the event of a crisis and can add to their "total loss-absorbing capacity". In practice, such bonds have been designated as contingent convertible bonds.

All the changes described above are important improvements in the Basel Capital Accord and address both the micro-prudential and macro-prudential needs of the regulatory authorities. However, these various new requirements are being phased in over a number of years, as stipulated by the FSB, and thus their full operational impact across the advanced countries will not be known until the end of the decade. Accordingly, it is not safe to say when, and if, the problem of TBTF will be removed and to what extent the oversight of financial system stability in the countries most affected by the global financial crisis will be strengthened.

In the latter regard, there are also questions about whether appropriate institutional reforms are being made to strengthen the macro-prudential dimension of bank regulation. In the United States, for example, a clear demarcation of institutional responsibility for macro-prudential regulation is lacking, while the oversight of financial system stability is shared among different agencies. Within the Fed, which has responsibility for the super-vision of most banks and, since the crisis, also SIFIs, regulatory policy is defined by the Board of Governors, while monetary policy is the respon-sibility of the Federal Open Market Committee (FOMC). However, these two bodies are not well defined, as all the seven members of the Board of Governors are also members of the FOMC, while presidents of the regional Federal Reserve banks (which conduct supervision on behalf of the Fed), who rotate as voting members of the FOMC, do not participate in the discussions on regulatory policy of the Board of Governors.[5] A more serious defect is that regulatory practice and supervision in the United States continues to be very fragmented among a number of different agencies. Under the Dodd-Frank Reform Act, instead of unifying or simplifying this institutional structure, the decision was made to create a new coordinating body, the Financial Stability Oversight Council (FSOC), under the chairmanship of the Secretary of the Treasury, which comprises representatives of all the other regulatory agencies. Apart from the further complication of this arrangement, placing the FSOC under the lead of a senior political figure in the executive branch rather than a technocratic appointee similar to the Chairman of the Fed's Board of Governors is not a good idea.

By contrast, the United Kingdom has established a simpler institutional structure for its regulatory policy. Macro-prudential regulatory policy since the crisis has been clearly vested in the Bank of England, through the work of a new Financial Policy Committee (FPC) chaired by the Governor of the Bank, who also chairs its Monetary Policy Committee. The FPC comprises the representatives of the agencies outside the Bank of England with responsibility for supervising financial institutions, as well as three outside members including currently a former vice-chairman of the Federal Reserve Board of Governors. In the case of the euro area, macro-prudential regulatory policy for banks and credit institutions has become the joint responsibility of each of the national central banks of the euro area in coordination with the European Central Bank (ECB) under the Single Supervisory Mechanism that was created in 2014. The ECB also coordinates with the European Systemic Risk Board of the European Union, which was created in 2011 in the oversight of financial system stability at the level of the European Union.

With all the changes in Basel III, one can raise two questions of concern: (1) Has it become too complicated? (2) Does it go far enough in reducing the risk of future financial crises? On the first question, a good case can be made in the affirmative. When the first Basel Accord was agreed in 1988, the agreed rules were encompassed in a document of 30 pages; however, for the Basel II regime 14 years later, the revised agreement was described in a document of around 350 pages. The most recent revision (Basel III) is laid out in more than 600 pages, which has required more than 1000 pages of documentation for its conversion into local rule making in the United States and the United Kingdom.[6] On top of this, the provisions of the Dodd-Frank Act in the United States are spelled out in 848 pages and call for the specification of more than 400 separate administrative rules by various regulatory agencies, which could involve more than 10,000 additional pages of documentation. Apart from the fact that the rule making for the Act has not been completed as of mid-2016, or six years since its enactment, one has to worry about the administrative costs involved in the implementation of these rules by the banks and their supervision by the regulatory agencies, as well as the burden these rules have placed on bank operations in the United States.

Notwithstanding the complexity of the regulatory changes that have been made since the financial crisis, a second question naturally arises as to whether they go far enough in reducing the risk of another crisis of the magnitude experienced in 2008–09. In this case, unfortunately, the answer is no. As noted before, the new capital-asset ratio has been set at 3 percent or the equivalent of a leverage ratio of 33, which was typical of the most vulnerable firms before the crisis. This is admittedly a minimum guideline, and the United States, for example, has set its own ratio at 4 percent for banks with assets of up to US$500 billion and at 5 percent for banks above that threshold, still generous amounts. However, if this leverage ratio was meant to act as a real constraint on the size of financial institutions and eliminate the problem of TBTF, it should have been set at a much higher number. Neel Kashkari, who was in charge of the Temporary Asset Relief Program of the US Treasury in 2009 and was appointed as the president of the Federal Reserve Bank of Minneapolis in late 2015, has suggested that the leverage ratio should be set in the range of 4 or 5 to 1.[7]

As for the capital requirements of the Basel III Agreement, one can also argue that they may still be too low. With the new agreement, the minimum tier-1 capital ratio for banks on a comparable basis has been raised from around 1 percent of risk-weighted assets prior to the crisis to 8.5 percent by 2019 and to 11 percent in the case of SIFIs. This is a significant increase. However, there is no intrinsic reason why banks should not be asked to issue more equity and less debt in order to finance their operations. The higher the share of equity on the balance sheets of the banks, the safer they will be as shareholders will have more "skin in the game" and thus will have a greater incentive to make sure that the banks they own are not undertaking excessively risky activities. At present, as discussed in Chap. 3, banks are benefitting from three government subsidies, which make it more attractive for them to increase their leverage or reliance on debt financing. One is the benefit that commercial banks enjoy from a government guarantee or insurance for their customers' deposits. In the absence of an appropriate schedule of insurance rates that forces banks to internalize the costs of their behavior in terms of individual or systemic failure, government deposit insurance can be an inducement to risky lending activity, including that supported by leverage. This characterization applies to the operations of the FDIC of the United States prior to the global financial crisis, which was even rebating to banks some of the fees they had paid for insurance because of the large size of the insurance fund.[8] The second subsidy is the tax deductibility of interest payments on debt, which creates an artificial incentive for banks to rely more on debt than equity in financing their investment and lending activities. The third subsidy arises from the implicit government guarantee of banks that are deemed to be TBTF, which lowers their cost of market borrowing. The presence of these subsidies, along with the absence of constraints on executive compensation, provides a powerful set of inducements for banks to take on more leverage while placing more of a burden on bank supervision to counteract their artificial incentives. Thus the "moral hazard" that these subsidies create for banks and the potentially high social cost of their failure that have not been internalized by the banks should be offset through higher capital requirements.[9]

One perceived problem for banks in issuing more equity is that an increase in shares will dilute the value of stock for existing shareholders and reduce the rate of return on equity for all shareholders. Under present practice, the lower the equity share of banks and the higher their leverage, the larger will be the return on equity for a given yield on assets. In this scheme of things, investors require or expect a higher rate of return to compensate for the higher risk they bear as owners of the bank or financial institution with high leverage. However, with a higher share of equity on the liability side of the balance sheet, a bank would assume less risk in its operations and shareholders would be satisfied with a lower rate of return for a more secure portfolio of investments and a safer financial institution.[10] It is also the case that since the financial crisis, higher reserve requirements for banks have not been associated with a reduction in bank credit to GDP ratios or a significant increase in the intermediation (net interest) margins for global SIFIs in the United States and Western Europe.[11]

In the light of the above considerations, it can be argued that bank capital requirements as defined in terms of risk-weighted assets should be much higher than they are set to be under Basel III. The revision of the Basel Capital Accord still allows banks to rely extensively on leverage and does not eliminate the problem of TBTF. As a result, the large gains from risky behavior remain fully internalized for banks, while the large externalities of individual or systemic failure involve a potentially heavy social cost in terms of tax-paid government bailouts or the perverse economic effects of a financial crisis. The only way to eliminate this large asymmetry of results is to increase the core equity requirement for banks. Professor Anat Admati of Stanford University, who has been a staunch and persistent advocate of higher capital requirements for banks, has argued that they should be in the range of 20–30 percent.[12] Other analysts have shown that a minimum risk-weighted capital ratio of 20 percent would have been sufficient to cover the loan losses associated with 85 percent of the banking crises in OECD countries since 1970. Such a level would reduce the likelihood of a crisis from once every 20 years to once every 100 years.[13] Apart from the significant improvement in the safety of banks that such an increase in capital requirements would produce, it would also virtually eliminate the problem of TBTF or at least reduce the likelihood of a financial crisis to a once in a century event. A risk-weighted capital requirement of 20 percent would be roughly double the current capital-asset and leverage ratios to be maintained by banks in the United States. An even simpler solution would be to operate with only an capital asset ratio or leverage ratio and set that requirement in the range of 20–25 percent, as discussed earlier. With a higher capital requirement for banks, however, it needs to be recognized that there is a risk of regulatory arbitrage as financial intermediary activity shifts to the "shadow" banking system where regulatory requirements have typically been lower. Thus it is important as the process of regulatory reform unfolds that the perimeter of micro-/ macro-prudential regulation be expanded.

REFORM OF THE INTERNATIONAL FINANCIAL ARCHITECTURE

The intensive work that has taken place in revising the Basel Capital Accord reflects the area or dimension of the IFA where perhaps the greatest reform activity has been focused since the outbreak of the crisis. This is appropriate given the major weaknesses in financial regulation that preceded the crisis and the obvious defects of the Basel II regime, which countries were implementing prior to its outbreak. However, there are other areas of the architecture where reform efforts are needed as well, which are briefly discussed in the remainder of this chapter. Each of these reforms should help to improve the IFA with a view to reducing the risks of financial globalization and the likelihood of future crises. The dimensions of the architecture where additional reforms are needed are as follows: the governance of the global system, international policy coordination, the international lender of last resort (ILOLR) mechanism and sovereign debt restructuring.

Global Governance

There are important issues related to the governance of the IFA that affect both its legitimacy and effectiveness where further reform is required. These relate to the coordination and oversight of the IFA and clarification of the roles of the FSB and International Monetary Fund (IMF). Since the outbreak of the global financial crisis, the G20 has assumed de facto responsibility for the political oversight of the IFA and the coordination of its operational agenda. In effect, the G20 is playing the same role that the G7 did prior to the crisis. Neither of these two groups, however, operates on the basis of any institutionalized authority as does, for example, the Security Council or the P5 (China, France, Russia, the United Kingdom and the United States) within the United Nations. Both the G7 and G20 represent self-selected groups and as such can be perceived as lacking legitimacy. The G7 represented the largest shareholders in the IMF, although this was not the criterion that determined its existence or membership; the G7 also shared a common commitment to an open trading and financial system within the post-WW2 political order as supported by institutions such as the IMF, World Bank and the World Trade Organization. The members of the G7 and the United States in particular decided on the membership of an expanded G20 following the East Asian financial crisis for purposes of overseeing reforms to the IFA that would be of benefit for developing and emerging market countries. It was the UK prime minister (Gordon Brown at the time) who took the lead in calling for a meeting of the G20, rather than the G7, at the heads-of-state level in late 2008 to coordinate a response to the global financial crisis, which was followed up by semi-annual meetings over the next two years. Such action was fortuitous, as it led to a rapid and united response to the crisis that helped to restore confidence in the capacity of the major economic powers to avoid a repeat of the Great Depression.

Notwithstanding the positive role that the G20 played in limiting the damage from the global financial crisis, one can easily challenge the legitimacy of this group as there are no clear rules that determine either its overall size or membership. As noted before, the G20 comprises more than 20 members, with Spain as a permanent guest member and 3–4 less developed countries invited to attend its meetings as temporary guest members on a rotating basis. By contrast, the membership of the International Monetary and Financial Committee (IMFC) of the IMF and the Development Committee for the World Bank, which are of roughly the similar size as that of the G20, are grounded in the treaty provisions of these two organizations with clear rules for membership on the basis of quota or voting shares in these two organizations. A further complication in the governance arrangements for the IFA is that the finance ministers and central bank governors of the G20 usually meet on a quarterly or semi-annual basis to help prepare the economic agenda for the annual heads-of-state summit and to follow up on their past commitments, even though the membership of this group has a close similarity to that of the IMFC and Development Committee. This large redundancy in committee structure leads to a duplication of work and tends to diminish the importance of the institutionalized committees of the IMF and World Bank. One important governance reform would be to merge the G20 with the IMFC at the ministerial level and convert the IMFC into an International Monetary and Financial Council in order to give it more authority. The membership of the G20 at the heads-of-state level could be changed to conform to that of the IMFC. Consistent with its more elevated status, the IMFC should also assume responsibility for overseeing the work of the FSB in order to solidify its key coordinating role in the IFA and to ensure closer coordination in its work with that of the IMF.[14]

As noted earlier in this chapter, the FSB has assumed an important coordinating role in driving global financial regulatory reform since the financial crisis. Like the G20, it developed out of the Financial Stability Forum that was formed at the same time to oversee efforts to establish international standards and codes for financial practices in an effort to help eliminate the conditions that gave rise to emerging market financial crises. Following its conversion to the FSB in April 2009, it has become the body responsible for coordinating the changes in international financial regulation, as well as other infrastructural aspects of the international financial system, such as accounting practices, the trading of derivatives and solvency reform. In view of this responsibility, it is appropriate and convenient to designate the FSB and the IMF as the twin pillars of the IFA. Accordingly, it is critical for the governance of the IFA that these two organizations be well coordinated. At an institutional level, this is supported by the fact that the IMF is represented in the meetings of the FSB, as is the FSB in the meetings of the IMFC and G20. The IMF and FSB also collaborate in the preparation of an "early warning" risk assessment of the international financial system for the meetings of the IMFC. The two organizations have also agreed to have the FSB's peer review of its members' regulatory practices provide inputs into the Fund's Financial Sector Assessment Program on a mandatory basis each five years. One obvious shortcoming, however, in the ability of the FSB to carry out its work is that it has a very limited secretariat (less than 50 staff), while its main leadership role is filled on a part-time basis by one of the central bank governors who sits on its governing council, instead of a permanent, full-time executive. Accordingly, the staffing and organizational structure of the FSB need to be strengthened in order to fulfill its role as one of the two pillars of the IFA.

Another defect in the governance of the IFA is that neither the FSB nor the IMF has a clear mandate for overseeing the international financial system or global financial stability. The Articles of Agreement of the IMF provide a clear mandate for the IMF to oversee the international monetary system through its responsibilities to monitor member countries' exchange rates systems and practices and their foreign reserve management. However, the IMF does not have a similar mandate to monitor or oversee the international capital transactions or capital controls of its members. In 1998, as noted earlier, a proposal was considered by its membership to extend the Fund's surveillance responsibilities to capital account transactions of its members, with a view to promoting capital account liberalization as an objective of IMF membership, as is the case for current account liberalization, but this reform was not approved in view of the capital account problems which the Asian crisis countries were facing at the time. Such an amendment should be reconsidered with a view to making explicit an institutional responsibility within the IFA for oversight of global financial stability. Such a reform would be consistent with giving the IMFC or a newly instituted IMF Council an institutional role in coordinating the work of the IMF and FSB, as suggested earlier.

International Policy Coordination

In late 2008 and early 2009, the G20 Leaders Summit played an important role in promoting a coordinated fiscal response to the evolving global financial crisis, which was followed by an attempt at international policy coordination in the macroeconomic arena through its peer review Mutual

Assessment Program (MAP), for which the IMF served as the technical secretariat. The MAP was closely coordinated with the IMF's Article IV consultation or macroeconomic surveillance procedure and was most intense during the period 2009–11. While this exercise was useful in promoting a common understanding of the global economic setting and a mutual understanding of each participant's national policy perspective (policy cooperation), it is generally the view that the MAP was not successful in bringing about significant adjustments of major countries' macroeconomic policy program (policy coordination). It is also the case that over time, the central focus of the G20 on its MAP has been diverted to a number of other issues of global concern, with the result that its impact on economic policy coordination has largely dissipated. This has created a vacuum within the IFA that needs to be filled. The IMF is the logical institutional choice for supporting a revitalized policy coordination process, especially with an enhanced role for the IMFC or IMF Council.

Since the crisis, the IMF has reformed its surveillance procedures with a view to strengthening its oversight of member countries' macroeconomic policies and prospects, as well as its analysis of the global economy through a variety of reports that could provide the essential technical inputs for effective policy coordination at the international level. This reform was articulated in the IMF's Integrated Surveillance Decision of 2012, which established the basis for coordinating the Fund's traditional bilateral consultation or macroeconomic surveillance exercises with a new multilateral consultation procedure, which would build on the informal multilateral consultation exercise that was attempted without success in 2006–07. The decision also incorporated an understanding that the spillover effects of policy adjustments by the systemically important countries should be taken into account by the national authorities and evaluated in the Fund's country surveillance exercises. As a result, the IMF has experimented with a variety of new reports examining the global impact of macroeconomic policies among the major economies (External Sector Reports) and their particular impact on emerging market and developing countries (Spillover Reports), as well as reports to support a multilateral consultation procedure, although such a procedure has not yet been invoked in view of the MAP exercises of the G20.

Since the crisis, it seems clear that the technical expertise of the IMF has been enhanced and that it is ideally suited to play the role of a facilitator for policy coordination at the international level. The problem is that there have not been many instances of successful policy coordination in the past. As noted earlier in Chap. 5, the G7 countries were successful on three occasions in the 1980s in addressing issues of currency valuation, but these experiences involved a select group of advanced countries dealing with a specific issue of important national interest. There also was implicit agreement within the group on the means to bring about currency depreciation or appreciation. The multilateral consultation exercise of 2006–07 involved a more heterogeneous group of countries, which convened not on their own initiative but rather at the behest of the IMF Managing Director. An additional problem was that there did not exist at the time a common understanding or agreement among the countries involved on the sources of the global imbalance problem and the role each country played in bringing it about. The G20 exercise on fiscal stimulus in 2008–09 was a good example of policy coordination mainly because of the crisis conditions at the time and the consensus that existed on the policies needed to confront it.

In mid-2016 another moment existed in which international policy coordination by way of fiscal stimulus should have been attempted. Eight years following the onset of the crisis, economic recovery had not been fully achieved, and the advanced countries were well below their stated inflation objective of a 2 percent annual target, despite a prolonged period of monetary ease. In the conditions of weak demand that existed, it would have been appropriate for the major countries to coordinate a package of fiscal expansion to stimulate economic activity in a more direct way, especially at a time when the cost of government borrowing was so low.[15] One of the major countries could summon the G20 to take up this issue (e.g., China, which is the host of the Leaders Summit for 2016) and call on the IMF to play a more active role than in the past in proposing different scenarios of fiscal stimulus and assessing the policy trade-offs for each of the major countries in formulating a program of tax cuts and/or expenditure increases.[16]

As a possible alternative option to fiscal stimulus that was discussed in Chap. 4, the disbursement of what has been called "helicopter money" has been proposed, by which is meant that the central bank would purchase government debt on a permanent basis in order to finance a program of direct government transfers to each citizen or taxpayer.[17] Such a program would likely be inflationary, but it is not clear that it would be more beneficial for the economy than a concerted program of public investment in infrastructure that would have positive multiplier effects on economic activity in a more sustained manner. Recourse to helicopter money would also pose a risk to the operational independence of the central bank(s) involved in the exercise, as it is equivalent to direct central bank financing of fiscal operations.

Since the onset of the crisis, the primary tool that countries have been using to stimulate economic recovery has been monetary policy, first via a sharp reduction in policy rates to zero and then with the tools of forward guidance and quantitative easing. Since mid-2014, a number of central banks in Europe have also experimented with negative short-term policy rates, and as of mid-2016 their deposit rates ranged from minus 0.4 percent for the ECB to minus 1.25 percent for the National Bank of Sweden. (Over the same time period, yields on the medium-term debt of a number of European governments have shifted into negative territory.) As a general matter, the various attempts in the use of unconventional monetary policy adjustments, as noted in Chap. 4, have had some impact on lowering long-term interest rates and raising asset prices, but it is not clear that there has been a significant effect on consumer and investment spending. At the same time, these adjustments may have induced more risky behavior on the part of investors in the search for higher returns while weakening the position of banks through a compression of interest rate spreads and of insurance companies through a reduction in their asset yields.

As of mid-2016, the major countries were embarked on very different programs of monetary stimulus or normalization, which has raised the risk of disruptive currency movements and an undue degree of appreciation of the US dollar thus posing a serious impediment to sustained recovery in the United States. In these circumstances, a strong case can be made, as in regard to fiscal policy, for policy coordination among the major currency countries to bring about a rebalancing among the dollar, pound, yen and euro and less volatility in international capital flows. Raghuram Rajan, the former Governor of the Reserve Bank of India, has made an interesting proposal for new "rules of the monetary game" under which the spillover effects of a country's monetary policy actions would be evaluated by the IMF for their negative, neutral or positive economic impact on other countries, building in effect on its Integrated Surveillance Decision of 2012 (noted earlier). If these policies violated certain pre-established norms or codes for appropriate policy conduct, collective sanctions would be imposed by the Fund membership.[18]

International Lender of Last Resort Mechanism

The global financial crisis revealed that the IFA does not yet have an effective ILOLR mechanism. To a large extent this gap had already been confirmed by the behavior of self-insurance of the part of the major emerging market economies as reflected in their substantial reserve accumulation in the years prior to the crisis and the emergence of regional reserve funds, such as the Chang Mai Initiative for the ASEAN+3 countries and the Latin American Reserve Fund. During the crisis, the Federal Reserve essentially played the major role of an ILOLR through its bilateral swap network on a scale much larger than in the past. However, this was an ad hoc arrangement, and it is not clear by what criteria countries were selected to participate in the swap program and how the size of their access to dollar funding was determined. In February 2010, the swap program was terminated, but in May of that same year it was reinstated on a temporary basis for the Bank of Canada, the Bank of England, the Bank of Japan, the ECB and the Swiss National Bank. It is also significant to note that along with the Federal Reserve, other major central banks (the Bank of England, the Bank of Japan, the ECB, the People's Bank of China and the Swiss National Bank) established swap networks for selected countries facing liquidity demands for obligations denominated in their national currency.[19] Altogether, 12 advanced and 9 emerging market countries were selected for these swap arrangements in the wake of the global financial crisis.

Along with the Federal Reserve, the IMF played a secondary role as an ILOLR via three mechanisms, as described in Chap. 5. First, with the agreement of the G20, the IMF disbursed the equivalent of around US$250 billion in Special Drawing Rights (SDR) in August 2009 that was tantamount to an increase in foreign reserves for all its members. This was the first time that SDRs had been allocated or issued at a time of global financial stress and represented in effect an attempt to re-allocate some of the existing pool of global foreign reserves to countries that had a need for international liquidity. Second, the IMF negotiated quick disbursing regular standby arrangements with 18 developing and emerging market countries during the first 12 months of the global financial crisis. Finally, the IMF revised its emergency lending facilities, the Flexible Credit Line (FCL) and the Precautionary and Liquidity Line (PLL) and approved access under the FCL for Colombia, Mexico and Poland on a contingent basis (none of the three countries actually requested disbursements) and for Macedonia and Morocco under the PLL. Access to the FCL and PLL was limited to these few countries essentially because of the policy requirements attached to both. For the FCL, the IMF must be fully satisfied that member countries requesting access have "very strong" macro fundamentals and policy frameworks, whereas for the PLL, the requirement is for "sound" fundamentals and frameworks, a qualitatively lower, but still high, bar for many countries. For access to the PLL, the Fund may require policy adjustments as a condition for access.

Notwithstanding these efforts in the wake of the crisis to enhance the role of the IMF as an ILOLR, a global financial safety net involving the IMF, central bank swap networks and regional financing arrangements has continued to expand on a very decentralized basis without a clear coordinating framework and with varying degrees of access, effectiveness and predictability, especially for emerging market and developing economies.[20] As a result, there has been a continued sharp expansion in self-insurance by these countries through foreign reserve accumulation. Gross foreign reserves amounted to around US$12 trillion at the end of 2015, two-thirds of which were held by emerging market economies, compared with around US$7 trillion in 2007 and US$2 trillion in 2000. At the same time, the global financial safety net expanded from around US$500 billion in 2007 to nearly US$4 trillion at the end of 2015.[21]

To improve the ILOLR mechanism, a number of reforms could be introduced to deal with crisis situations. First, the IMF should establish a practice that subject to a vote of, say, 70 percent of the membership, it will make further allocations of SDRs in times of global financial market stress upon the recommendation of its Managing Director.[22] Such a practice would also help over time to increase the role of SDRs in the international monetary system, which was the original intent of its creation in 1969 but has not been fulfilled because of the very few allocations in limited amounts that had been authorized prior to 2009. Second, the G20 or IMFC should establish an agreement with the major central banks to link the triggering of their bilateral swap networks with a decision of the IMF to allocate SDRs at times of turmoil in the international financial system. At the same time, the IMF should allow either the FCL or PLL or both to be accessed up to a certain multiple of a member's quota on an unconditional basis, subject to a process of pre-qualification. This process would establish the extent of access for each member through a rating of each member country's macroeconomic polices determined at the time of the Fund's annual Article IV consultation exercise, which would become a standard procedure for all countries.[23] To finance such access, it could be established that the Fund would draw, if needed, on its contingent resources under the New Agreements to Borrow as it did to finance normal lending under its regular facilities during 2008–10. Access to regional reserve facilities could also be coordinated with emergency access to Fund facilities. Unconditional access to IMF resources on an emergency basis under a reformed FCL/PLL would match the liquidity provision that was made available to a relatively select group of countries under the central bank swap network. The combination of SDR allocations, bilateral swap networks and unconditional access to an emergency facility of the IMF would represent, if triggered on a coordinated basis, an important step in creating a more fully functional equivalent of the LOLR mechanism at the international level in times of crisis.

A Sovereign Debt-Restructuring Mechanism

The global financial crisis has revealed another gap in the IFA in respect to the restructuring of sovereign debt. This is not a new idea, as at the beginning of the last decade, in the wake of a number of emerging market financial crises, a serious effort was made to create a sovereign debt-restructuring mechanism (SDRM) attached to the IMF, but the proposal was rejected in 2003 as a result of strenuous resistance by the international financial community and some of the major countries including the United States.[24] What was agreed instead was a more decentralized or so-called contractual approach in which standard sovereign bond contracts would include special "collective action" clauses. These clauses would allow a majority of creditors in the event of default to negotiate with the debtor government and agree among themselves on the terms of a restructured bond contract, which would be binding on any holdout creditors who were not willing to agree to the new terms. Notwithstanding a recent improvement in the legal terms of these clauses, there have been two problems in sovereign debt restructuring since these new clauses were introduced. First, a substantial share of sovereign debt contracts remain in place that do not carry the revised collective action clauses, and second, there continues to be a strong tendency for governments to delay bond restructuring even when it is clear that their foreign debt is unsustainable. In these circumstances, macroeconomic adjustment programs end up being unduly burdensome because of the debt service payments that must be accommodated through a severe program of fiscal consolidation.

The experience of Greece with the "Troika" since 2010 clearly fits into this category. Unfortunately, the IMF made an exception to its own rules on "exceptional access" to allow Greece to borrow, and then later on, when a debt-restructuring agreement was introduced, the debt relief came "too little, too late". As a result, in 2016, Greece was facing the need for a new debt-restructuring program.

Another extreme case has been that of Argentina, which defaulted on US$80 billion of its foreign debt in 2001. In 2005, it presented to its bondholders on a "take it or leave it" basis a proposal for debt restructuring with a severe "haircut" of around 70 percent in the face value of the debt. These terms were accepted by a majority of the bondholders, but there were a number of holdout creditors who did not agree, including certain private sector "vulture funds" that had purchased pre-2001 Argentine debt in the secondary market at very deep discounts. As a result of continuous litigation by this minority group of holdout creditors, Argentina effectively had been excluded from borrowing in the international capital markets until a new government came to power in early 2016 with a firm desire to reach agreement with these creditors on the basis of the terms of repayment that proved to be much more favorable than those offered in 2005.

In both of these cases and many others, the existence of the equivalent of an international bankruptcy court for sovereign debtors would facilitate and accelerate the messy process of sovereign debt restructuring in a manner that would ultimately be agreeable to both sides of the debt renegotiation. One particular problem that an SDRM would help to overcome is the issue of how to aggregate different classes of bonds issued in different legal jurisdictions and currencies, as well as other forms of debt. In addition, an SDRM would be useful in addressing problems arising from the availability of credit default swaps for sovereign debt. These derivatives have complicated debt restructuring as the process of renegotiation may become more difficult when one of the parties has a non-transparent interest in default and may not be willing to bargain in good faith.[25]

One advantage of having an SDRM associated with the IMF, although there may be other feasible institutional arrangements, is that the Fund can provide an independent, technical judgment on debt sustainability to guide the restructuring process. In addition, it can provide the equivalent of "debtor-in-possession" financing, which would be linked to a "stay" on debt service payments as the restructuring process is being carried out.[26] In this respect, the existence of an SDRM would help to reinforce the traditional posture of the IMF that it should not commit significant amounts of its own resources in situations where the debt sustainability of the country in question cannot be affirmed with a high degree of probability.

SUMMARY AND CONCLUSION

Many reforms in financial regulation and financial stability oversight have been undertaken at the national and global levels in the aftermath of the global financial crisis in an effort to reduce the likelihood of future crises. At the national level, the crisis has shown that a focus by central banks on achieving the macroeconomic objectives of low inflation and full employment is not sufficient to maintain financial stability and that a new macro-prudential regulatory oversight function focused specifically on the stability of the financial system is required. Much debate has taken place on how to incorporate a macro-prudential perspective into central banking practice and coordinate it with monetary policy and the traditional micro-prudential regulation/supervision of individual banks. There may be situations where monetary policy tools can achieve both macro-prudential and macroeconomic objectives, as in dealing with a credit boom, but in other cases these objectives will not coincide. In such cases, there are a variety of separate macro-prudential tools that can be applied to specific sectors or categories of financial institutions. A major focus of macro-prudential policy needs to be placed on the regulation of SIFIs, which prior to the crisis were considered to be "too big to fail". For this purpose, new resolution procedures have been developed in the advanced countries to deal with their actual or potential failure, including their participation in annual "stress tests" and the preparation of resolution plans or "living wills".

In addition to the specification of macro-prudential oversight, the G20 has sponsored a major overhaul of the Basel Capital Accord that was completed in 2010. This revision introduced a number of new features in the structure of capital requirements for banks, which increased their overall level while differentiating between large and small banks and introducing a counter-cyclical feature. The new regime also established a new leverage ratio and specific liquidity and funding requirements for banks to reduce their vulnerability in periods of financial stress. Notwithstanding these improvements, a strong case can be made that the overall capital requirement and leverage ratio should be at least double the new stipulated levels.

International financial regulation has been one of the most active areas of reform of the IFA since the global financial crisis. However, other areas need to be addressed, including its governance and the relationship among the G20, the FSB and the IMF. International policy coordination also needs to be improved. The G20 proved to be effective in the immediate wake of the crisis, but since then, its effectiveness in this area has waned as its agenda has expanded. At present (mid-2016), there are important issues of monetary and fiscal policy coordination where action is required. The IMF can play an important role in promoting policy coordination and in discouraging countries from implementing policies that have negative spillover effects on other countries, but it lacks the power to enforce its policy recommendations on member countries except when they request the use of its financial resources.

The IFA also lacks a strong ILOLR mechanism. In response to the crisis, a number of ad hoc financing arrangements were introduced by the major central banks, the G20 and IMF, which should be regularized and coordinated more closely in the future. As a result, the global financial safety net involving countries' own foreign reserves, the IMF, central bank swap networks and regional financing arrangements has become highly decentralized.

Finally, an SDRM should be established in order to bring about a timely and orderly process of debt relief in cases where it is clear that a government cannot maintain or achieve debt sustainability. The recent experience of Argentina and Greece has shown that the current contractual approach to debt restructuring is not working.

NOTES

1. Past experience in the use of macro-prudential regulation is examined in Eugenio Cerutti et al. "The Use and Effectiveness of Macro-prudential Policies: New Evidence" IMF Working Paper #15/61 (March 2015).
2. This episode was discussed in a conference paper by Lars Svensson at the Federal Reserve Bank of Boston on September 30, 2015 entitled "Monetary Policy and Macro-prudential Policy: Different and Separate", which can be accessed at www.bostonfed.org/macroprudential2015/paper/svensson.pdf.
3. For an extended discussion on the issue of monetary policy and financial stability, see IMF "Monetary Policy and Financial Stability" IMF Policy Paper (September 2015).

4. One recent study in this arena is Stijn Claessens "An Overview of Macro-prudential Tools" The Annual Review of Financial Economics 2015 (7); pp. 397–422.

5. An additional concern is that the private commercial banks in each of the 12 regional Federal Reserve districts are the majority shareholders in their corresponding regional Federal Reserve Bank. This arrangement creates a potentially strong conflict of interest for each Bank in carrying out its regulatory/supervisory responsibilities.

6. The data on the page count of Basel rules are taken from Andrew Haldane "The Dog and the Frisbee" A Speech at the Federal Reserve Bank of St. Louis Economic Policy Symposium (August 31, 2012).

7. This proposal was put forward at a conference of the Hutchins Center on Fiscal and Monetary Policy at the Brookings Institution on February 16, 2016.

8. The flaws in the US system of deposit insurance prior to the financial crisis are discussed in Viral Archaya "Systemic Risk and Deposit Insurance Premiums", which was published on the VoxEU.org blog of the Center for Economic Policy Research (September 4, 2009).

9. One attempt that has been made in the United Kingdom to limit the extent of this "moral hazard" was to establish a "ring-fence" that would separate essential retail banking activities from wholesale investment banking operations of large banking groups by means of separate capital, liquidity and funding requirements, as well as corporate governance arrangements. This proposal was advanced by the Independent Commission on Banking (so-called Vickers Report) in 2011 and enacted into law in 2013, with full effect to take place by 2019. A similar proposal was made in the Liikanen Report for EU banks in 2012, which was adopted by the European Commission in its proposals for Bank Structural Reform issued in January 2014. As an alternative to "ring-fencing", in the United States, the Dodd-Frank Wall Street Reform and Consumer Protection Act of 2010 prohibited commercial banks from making speculative trades in financial assets using funds from their own accounts (so-called proprietary trading) under what has come to be known as the Volcker Rule, named after the former chairman of the Federal Reserve (Paul Volcker) who advocated it. After much delay, this restriction became effective in September 2015.

10. These arguments have been persuasively advanced by Anat Admati et al. (2010), op. cit. in Chap. 3.

11. These results are reported in Stephen Cecchetti "The Jury Is In" Center for Economic Policy Research Policy Insight Report #76 (December 2014).

12. An extended discussion of Professor Admati's position can be found in Anat Admati and Martin Hellwig (2013) *The Bankers' New Clothes: What's Wrong with Banking and What to Do About It* (Princeton, NJ: Princeton University Press).

13. These estimates are presented in Stephen Cecchetti and Kermit Schoenholtz "Bank Resilience: Yet Another Missed Opportunity", which was published in their Money, Banking and Financial Markets blog (November 30, 2015).

14. This reform in the governance of the IFA was first proposed in Elson (2011), op. cit. in Chap. 5. A similar and more recent proposal was advanced by Malcolm Knight in "Reforming the Global Architecture of Financial Regulation: The G20, IMF and FSB" CIGI Papers #42 (September 2014).

15. Professor Lawrence Summers has been a strong advocate for such a policy for a number of years and has been joined recently by recommendations of both the IMF and OECD.

16. In February 2016, the IMF made a strong appeal for concerted G20 action on a fiscal stimulus and structural reform agenda through one of its customary surveillance reports for a quarterly meeting at the finance minister/central bank governor level (see IMF "G20 Surveillance Note on Global Prospects and Policy Challenges", February 26, 2016). Unfortunately, this call for action was not taken up by the G20 finance ministers and central bank governors when they met in Chengdu, China during July 23–24, 2016.

17. The case for "helicopter money" has been forcefully made by Adair Turner, the former head of the UK regulatory authority, in his 2015 book *Between Debt and the Devil: Money, Credit and Fixing Global Finance* (Princeton, NJ: Princeton University Press).

18. This proposal is put forth in Prachi Mishra and Raghuram Rajan "Rules of the Monetary Game" Reserve Bank of India Working Paper 04/2016 (March 2016).

19. These swap networks are discussed in a paper by William Allen and Richhild Moessner "Central Bank Cooperation and International

Liquidity in the Financial Crisis of 2008–09" BIS Working Paper #310 (May 2010).

20. Two papers that provide a good description and analysis of the global financial safety net are IMF "Adequacy of the Global Financial Safety Net" IMF Policy Paper (March 10, 2016) and Ed Denbee et al. "Stitching Together the Global Financial Safety Net" Bank of England Financial Stability Paper #36 (February 2016).

21. These data are taken from p. 14 of the IMF report cited in footnote 20.

22. This change would require an amendment to the Fund's Articles of Agreement, which specify that SDR allocations require the affirmative vote of governments representing 85 percent of the voting shares in the institution (including that of the United States which holds 16 per cent). The proposed amendment should also specify that decisions on allocations could be made at the level of the Fund's Executive Board or IMFC instead of only by its Board of Governors (i.e., member government finance ministers or central bank governors). A further significant change worth including in such an amendment would be to allow countries to exchange SDRs directly with issuers of the reserve currencies that comprise the SDR basket (i.e., dollars, euros, pounds, yen and yuan). Such a change would help to expand international liquidity at times of global financial stress as distinct from current IMF practice that only allows countries to exchange SDRs with countries that hold foreign reserves denominated in these currencies, which in effect serves to re-allocate existing liquidity to countries that need it. For more on this latter proposal, see Edwin Truman "The IMF as International Lender of Last Resort: What Future?" Real Time Economic Issues Watch of the Peterson Institute for International Economics (October 12, 2010).

23. Edwin Truman (2010), op. cit. in footnote 22, has been one of the proponents of this pro-qualification proposal.

24. The effort to establish an SDRM as part of the second reform of the international financial architecture is described in Elson (2011), op. cit. in Chap. 5. The IMF's formal proposal to establish an SDRM was presented in Anne Krueger "A New Approach to Sovereign Debt Restructuring" IMF, Washington, DC (April 2002).

25. The issues surrounding debt restructuring and the case for an SDRM were presented in a policy brief by Joseph Stiglitz et al.

"Frameworks for Sovereign Debt Restructuring", an IPD-CIGI-CGEG Policy Brief (November 17, 2014). In September 2015, the UN General Assembly approved "Nine Basic Principles on Sovereign Debt Restructuring Processes" by a large majority of countries, with the exception of Canada, Germany, Israel, Japan, the United Kingdom and the United States (see Joseph Stiglitz and Martin Guzman "A Step Forward for Sovereign Debt", Project Syndicate blog, November 9, 2015).

26. For one proposal that would combine sovereign debt restructuring with IMF financial assistance, see Committee on International Economic Policy and Reform "Revisiting Sovereign Bankruptcy" Brookings Institution (October 2013).

CHAPTER 8

Toward a Rethinking of Macroeconomics

As suggested in previous chapters, the global financial crisis and its aftermath have engendered a vigorous debate about the inherent stability/instability of the aggregate economy, the failings/limitations of the predominant conceptual framework for macroeconomic analysis (or new macroeconomic consensus/NMC) prior to the crisis and the appropriate fiscal and monetary policy responses to the crisis. These issues have not yet been resolved and will undoubtedly continue to draw debate in academic and policy settings in the years to come. The purpose of this chapter is to summarize some of the main points in the debate on the first two issues listed above; the third issue was already discussed in Chap. 4. In the light of the discussion on the first two points, the chapter then goes on to indicate two fields of analysis which offer promising alternative views of the aggregate economy that warrant further exploration within a more pluralistic vision of macroeconomics, namely behavioral economics and complexity theory. The chapter closes with a brief assessment of the post-crisis demand for more pluralism in the teaching of economics, which has been driven to a large extent by student dissatisfaction with the relevance of mainstream economics in elucidating the causes and effects of the crisis.

© The Author(s) 2017
A. Elson, *The Global Financial Crisis in Retrospect*,
DOI 10.1057/978-1-137-59750-2_8

Does the Economy Conform to Keynesian or Neoclassical Principles?

As discussed in Chap. 3, this question is part of an old debate in macroeconomics that was sparked by intellectual responses to the Great Depression (such as Keynes' *General Theory*), which has been given new life by recent efforts to understand the causes and effects of the global financial crisis. At its most basic level, the debate centers on whether the aggregate economy follows a steady-state growth path subject to periodic, exogenous shocks and is inherently self-stabilizing or whether it is inherently unstable, subject to endogenous shocks that can cause significant departures from an established growth path that require extraordinary government intervention to enable the economy to resume its growth along a path that may be different from the one it was on.

Prior to the crisis, proponents of these two worldviews tended to fall into two intellectual camps, with the first characterized as orthodox and the second as heterodox. The first camp was largely centered in neoclassical economics and the New Keynesian macroeconomic paradigm that was described in Chap. 3, whereas the second was quite diverse and covered a range of approaches that might be described as old Keynesian, post-Keynesian, Marxist or some other eclectic group. However, since the crisis there has been much debate within the neoclassical or mainstream camp of macroeconomics about these two paradigmatic approaches, which has led to challenges and some rethinking of the NMC. This rethinking has led not only to revisions and extensions of basic dynamic stochastic general equilibrium (DSGE) modeling but also to an examination of some of the basic assumptions within the NMC. My aim in this chapter is to suggest how some of the facts of the crisis have led to new thinking about macroeconomic behavior, which is likely to lead over time to a re-assessment and possible modifications of the NMC.

One striking example of the impact of the crisis on macroeconomic thinking is to consider how views of the likely path of potential GDP in the United States have changed in a downward direction since the crisis. In the accompanying chart (Chart 8.1), one can see the significant downward revisions of potential GDP that have been made by the US Congressional Budget Office since 2007. In that year, potential GDP was forecast to grow at a compound annual rate of 2.6 percent through 2017, roughly in line with the growth rate of real GDP during the period 2000–07. However, since then, that forecast has been significantly downgraded

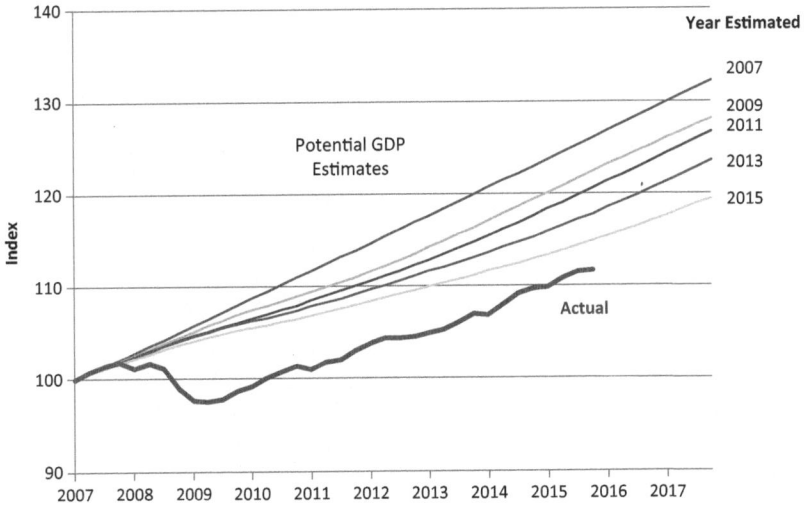

Chart 8.1 Potential GDP estimates and actual GDP for the United States (in constant dollar index format with 2007 = 100) (*Source*: US Congressional Budget Office and US Bureau of Economic Analysis)

during each of the subsequent two-year periods shown in the chart in the light of the actual pace of economic recovery, which has been slower than anticipated at the time each of those projections was made.[1] Potential GDP depends on a number of structural factors in the economy, such as labor productivity, demographic changes, the stock of capital and level of investment. The fact that there has been a downward revision on the order of 10 percent in the trajectory of potential GDP since the crisis began suggests that there has been a permanent loss in the productive capacity of the economy since the outbreak of the crisis. More specifically, one could explain this result in terms of the significant decline in the pace of investment, the stock of capital and the labor force participation rate that has been observed since 2007. These developments would constitute prima facie evidence for the instability hypothesis of the economy discussed earlier, according to which the economy can be permanently damaged by a severe downturn that causes it to deviate from the growth path that it was on prior to the recession.

In the same spirit, another interesting set of facts to consider is presented in Chart 8.2. This chart displays two trend lines for the US economy:

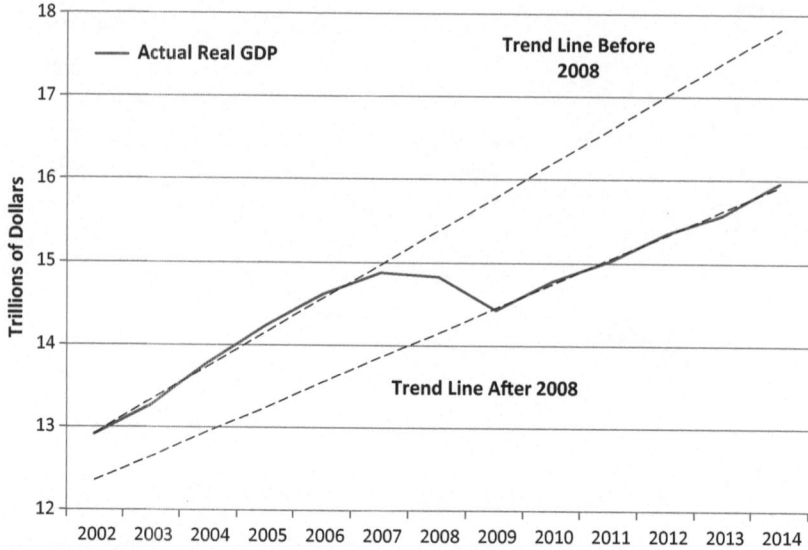

Chart 8.2   Real GDP for the United States with trend lines before and after 2008 (in trillions of 2009 dollars) (*Source*: International Monetary Fund World Economic Outlook Database)

one is the trend that the economy was on prior to the crisis based on its trajectory during the 2000–07 period; the other is the trend line for the economy since the bottom of the recession in mid-2009. What is striking about this chart is that these two lines do not reach any point of convergence in the future; instead, we observe a growing divergence between them. This divergence between the two lines means that not only has there been a downward shift in the projected growth path of the economy, suggesting a permanent loss in its productive capacity, but there has also been a reduction in the slope of the lower trend line, suggesting a slower rate of growth for the economy compared to what it was prior to the crisis. Again, this chart would suggest prima facie evidence against the view of the economy as a self-stabilizing mechanism. The experience of the euro area since the beginning of the crisis has revealed an even sharper pattern in terms of the downward adjustment in the trend growth of its GDP and the outlook for potential GDP.

One idea that has been advanced to account for the downward adjustments in aggregate economic behavior we can observe in both of these charts is known as "hysteresis", which was referred to earlier in Chap. 4. This term, which was borrowed from physics as are many of the notions behind the workings of neoclassical equilibrium dynamics, was first used in the mid-1980s to convey the idea that a sustained economic downturn may cause permanent damage to the productive capacity of the economy. This damage arises because of the loss of skills and attachment to the labor force associated with a relatively long period of unemployment and a reduction in investment, the stock of capital and productivity due to poorer growth prospects. With the emergence of the Great Moderation, this concept tended to fall into disfavor in mainstream macroeconomic analysis. However, in a recent paper, the two economists who invented this term in the mid-1980s (Olivier Blanchard and Lawrence Summers) have re-examined the issue of hysteresis in the light of the global financial crisis and other recessions, not only for the US economy but also for 22 other advanced countries. Their findings show that two-thirds of the recorded recessions were followed by a lower level of output in relation to the pre-recession trend and that roughly half of those cases were characterized by a lower rate of growth in output, much in accord with the evidence presented in Chart 8.2.[2] Thus, the issue of hysteresis continues to be a relevant policy concern.

In connection with the notion of hysteresis, it is interesting to consider a heated debate that surfaced during the first quarter of 2016 among academic economists regarding the potential macroeconomic impact of US presidential candidate Bernie Sanders' government expenditure program. This program was designed in part by Professor Gerald Friedman of the University of Massachusetts. In short, what the program claimed to accomplish was a significant increase in GDP and employment by 2020 above the baseline projections of the Congressional Budget Office for that year, which were based on its latest outlook for potential GDP in late 2015.

Initially, the top-line claims of this plan were criticized by four previous Chairs of the Council of Economic Advisors under former Democratic Party Presidents (see Letter to Sanders, New York Times, February 17, 2016). Subsequently, in a paper by one of those economists (Professor Christina Romer), the analysis behind the initial critique of Senator Sanders' plan was explained in more detail.[3] Essentially, the dispute between Professor Friedman and his critics comes down to an evaluation of how much of an impact on potential GDP can an expanding economy have under the impulse of an increase in public and private spending over the medium to long term. The baseline trend for potential GDP that the proponents and critics of the plan used was the latest trajectory of potential GDP displayed in Chart 8.2 above, which has been significantly downgraded by the effects of hysteresis. But can these effects be reversed? In the short term, surely not, but over a ten-year period, certainly yes, at least to some degree. In this respect, Professor Friedman could have drawn on the argumentation of two mainstream economists (Bradford Delong and Lawrence Summers), who advocated in 2012 for the fiscal stimulus of a public investment program at a time when interest rates were extraordinarily low in order to raise actual output closer to its estimated potential prior to being downgraded due to the effects of hysteresis.[4]

While it is likely that the projected size of the reversal in potential GDP envisaged in Sen. Sanders' plan is probably overstated and the potential inflationary effects of his plan underestimated, it is also the case that there is very little or no allowance for such a reversal in the critique referred to above by Professor Romer. In that critique, the trajectory of potential GDP over the coming decade is essentially fixed and unaffected by any of the elements in Sanders' program, whereas Professor Friedman argues that over time that trajectory can be revised upward, thus reversing at least some of the downward adjustment that has occurred since the outbreak of the financial crisis.[5] Such an effect under Senator Sanders' plan would only be feasible with a well-targeted public investment program on infrastructure and technological development, something that has been recommended by a large group of mainstream economists and incorporated to a significant degree in the Sanders' economic program.

Another example of the rethinking of macroeconomics that has taken place in the light of the crisis is the re-examination of certain key assumptions of the behavior of economic aggregates over time. In the first view of the world noted earlier, the main economic aggregates such as production, consumption, investment and unemployment evolve over time according to the so-called ergodic principle, that is, they are stationary in a statistical sense, which means that when they deviate from some trend they tend to revert to that trend with a certain regularity, thus exhibiting "mean reversion"; in this case, shocks to the data have transitory effects. In the alternative view of the world, these aggregate time series are non-stationary, or in statistical terms they display a "unit root", such that the position of the trend line around which they fluctuate may shift over time; in this case, shocks to the data have permanent effects. Expressed in this way, it would seem that some of the controversy over the stability or instability theses expressed earlier could be resolved through a series of statistical time series tests of major economic aggregates. In fact, this has been the subject of much analysis and debate over the past 30 years or so, with the ascendancy of the new classical macroeconomic paradigm, which has been re-examined in the light of the Great Recession. The current consensus in this area seems to be that the main macroeconomic aggregates do tend to exhibit a unit root.[6] These results tie in directly with the concept of hysteresis as applied to the behavior of actual and potential GDP that was presented in the two charts discussed above.

Within the academic community, there has been much debate about the current state of macroeconomics as a result of the financial crisis that goes beyond the issues examined above. At one level, economists within the New Keynesian tradition have been making adaptations to the DSGE modeling framework in order to incorporate explicitly the effect of financial sector variables and financial frictions on the real economy in ways that would help to account for the origins and impact of the financial crisis.[7] At another level, however, other mainstream economists have expressed reservations about the single-minded attachment of many macroeconomists to the DSGE framework, with calls for more eclecticism in the selection or development of models to account for the complex variety of phenomena in the actual behavior of aggregate economies. One such criticism was leveled by Professor Robert Solow, a Nobel laureate from MIT, in his testimony at a US Congressional Hearing on July 20, 2010:

"I do not think that the currently popular DSGE models pass the smell test. They take it for granted that the whole economy can be thought about as if it were a single, consistent person or dynasty carrying out a rationally designed, long-term plan, occasionally disturbed by unexpected shocks, but adapting to them in a rational, consistent way. I do not think that this picture passes the smell test. The protagonists of this idea make a claim to respectability by asserting that it is founded on what we know about microeconomic behavior, but I think that this claim is generally phony. The advocates no doubt believe what they say, but they seem to have stopped sniffing or to have lost their sense of smell altogether... The DSGE school populates its simplified economy – remember that all economics is about simplified economics just as biology is about simplified cells – with exactly one single combination worker-owner- consumer- everything-else who plans ahead carefully and lives forever. One important consequence of this 'representative agent' assumption is that there are no conflicts of interest, no incompatible expectations, no deceptions.

This all-purpose decision-maker essentially runs the economy according to its own preferences. Not directly, of course: the economy has to operate through generally well-behaved markets and prices. Under pressure from skeptics and from the need to deal with actual data, DSGE modelers have worked hard to allow for various market frictions and imperfections like rigid prices and wages, asymmetries of information, time lags, and so on. This is all to the good. But the basic story always treats the whole economy as if it were like a person, trying consciously and rationally to do the best it can on behalf of the representative agent, given its circumstances. This cannot be an adequate description of a national economy, which is pretty conspicuously not pursuing a consistent goal. A thoughtful person, faced with the thought that economic policy was being pursued on this basis, might reasonably wonder what planet he or she is on."[8]

Given the academic prestige of the economist who wrote this criticism, it is a very damning statement, especially in view of the fact that MIT is one of the centers for the New Keynesian DSGE paradigm. More generally, there has been much debate since the financial crisis that goes to the heart of the main macroeconomic paradigm in terms of its basic methodology. One particularly vocal critic of the micro-foundations of the New Keynesian paradigm is Professor Lars Syll of Malmo University in Sweden, whose thinking parallels that of American professors such as Kevin Hoover of Duke University.[9] Syll's challenge, which is not new in the history of economics but newly expressed since the crisis, is that the micro-foundations revolution in macroeconomics depends too strongly on an axiomatic hypothetic-deductive or reductionist mode of thinking that is based on unrealistic assumptions (e.g., atomistic, independent representative agents) and leads logically to conclusions that are not directly applicable to the real world. A reductionist mode of thinking is meant to convey the idea that once one specifies some assumptions about economic behavior and the behavioral relationships underlying economic aggregates to be explained, then certain conclusions can be drawn directly from this logical structure.

As Professor Solow notes in the quote above, all models in natural science and economics are simplifications of the real world by necessity, in order to isolate a particular aspect of reality for specific analysis. However, if the assumptions made in those models bear no relation to reality, one can question whether the conclusions or implications drawn from those models are applicable to the real world. Of course, Milton Friedman in his famous essay "On the Methodology of Positive Economics" argued precisely in favor of the deductivist approach to economic modeling as exemplified by the DSGE framework, if it gave rise to predictions that are relevant for understanding economic reality. One example, however, of an implication of the standard New Keynesian framework that is clearly unrealistic is that over the medium term, unemployment in the normal statistical sense of the term cannot exist, as at any point in time the level of employment is determined by the voluntary and rational choices of firms and workers. For example, if there is a negative shock to the economy that leads it to deviate below its normal growth path, this event will cause a decline in production and a fall in real wages. Since the real wage determines the choice of laborers for work or leisure, they will choose more leisure instead of work until the real wage level is restored to its normal or equilibrium level. This implication is obviously hard to square with the high and sustained levels of unemployment of the Great Recession and the effects of hysteresis that it caused.

Another critique that has been raised by Professor Syll and others suggested earlier is that the economic aggregates of the DSGE model are assumed to behave in accordance with the principle of ergodicity noted earlier, such that they are stationary and stable stochastic processes that can be well represented as predictable statistical outcomes, similar to the case of a normal distribution of random events or a coin toss. Such an assumption is inherent in the notion of "rational expectations" according to which the "representative agent" of DSGE models is expected to behave. In this sense, these models assume that the future can be determined on the basis of quantifiable risk related to the pattern of past economic developments. In other words, the probability distribution of likely events in the future is known strictly on the basis of their past behavior. But, as Keynes pointed out many years ago, such an assumption cannot be squared with the fact that the future is fundamentally uncertain and unknowable. Accordingly, any prediction is subject to a large margin of error, with "fat tails" of extreme events, instead of the "thin tails" of a normal probability distribution assumed in DSGE models. The assumption of quantifiable risk, as distinct from unquantifiable uncertainty, was one of the problems underlying the use of value-at-risk (VAR) models by financial analysts prior to the financial crisis.[10]

Another criticism of the standard macroeconomic paradigm that has been advanced in the wake of the crisis is its excessive dependence on elaborate mathematical modeling. This critique can be found in the writings of eminent mainstream economists such as Olivier Blanchard, Paul Krugman and Paul Romer. First, it needs to be recognized that the development of theory by means of mathematically based model building is a fundamental and legitimate element in economics' claim to be a science, along with data analysis and statistical testing. The use of mathematical concepts and reasoning in economic models can be viewed as a rigorous check on the logical consistency and validity of conclusions derived from a given theory, as well as a means of deriving certain implications that would not be evident from a purely verbal explanation and discourse. However, the critics above have argued that many macroeconomic theorists have become too wedded to the derivation of mathematical proofs and theorems in the sense that they have adopted assumptions that were too limited and unrealistic solely because of their mathematical tractability and have reached for certain results that were appealing mainly because of their mathematical elegance. In the words of Paul Krugman, writing about the failings of mainstream economics prior to the crisis in the <u>New York Times Magazine</u> (9/2/09), "...the economics profession went astray because economists as a group mistook beauty clad in impressive mathematics for truth." Paul Romer leveled in 2015 an even stronger indictment of many academic economists for their "mathiness", claiming that they have misused mathematical formulations that do not bear close scrutiny, simply as a means of giving academic respectability to a preferred theory or political view of the world, thus undermining the scientific legitimacy of the profession.[11]

Another challenge to the use of mathematics in macroeconomics has come from Olivier Blanchard, formerly of MIT and the Chief Economist of the International Monetary Fund during 2008–15. His critique is that the mathematization of macroeconomics as represented by DSGE modeling has restricted economists' analysis of certain processes and phenomena in the "dark corners" of aggregate economic behavior when normal activity breaks down and the economy malfunctions as during a financial crisis and its aftermath, again simply because these events were not "tractable" from a mathematical modeling point of view. As suggested above, the mathematical techniques typically used (e.g., DSGE models) are best suited, according to Blanchard, for a world where economic fluctuations are well behaved and self-correcting, as required, for example, by the rational expectations hypothesis. Implicit in this modeling structure was an assumption of linearity, namely that shocks had proportional effects on the economy, as suggested by a linear algebraic expression, which was convenient because of its mathematical tractability. Non-linear effects with positive feedback mechanisms were not typically incorporated in such models, even though these represent the kind of phenomena that occur in the "dark corners" of the economy.[12] As a relevant example of such phenomena from the financial crisis, Blanchard points to the perverse public debt dynamics of the euro zone in 2009–10, when threats of insolvency led to large jumps in risk premia on public debt, which then created a positive feedback mechanism or "doom loop" in the sense of further worsening the debt burden of the government and also weakening the financial position of banks that held government debt as part of their assets. These sudden shifts from solvency to insolvency or jumps from a "good" equilibrium prior to the crisis to a "bad" equilibrium after the crisis are examples of multiple equilibria that depart from the normal concept of a stable equilibrium, on which much of macroeconomic theory is premised.

ALTERNATIVE ECONOMIC VISIONS OF THE WORLD

While much "soul-searching" has taken place within the economics profession since the financial crisis on the state of macroeconomics, there has been renewed interest in at least two fields of economics that stand in contrast to the premises of the NMC. One is behavioral economics, and the other is complexity theory. Both of these specialties have been actively developed since the 1980s but have attracted new adherents since the financial crisis. It is not my intention to try to summarize each of these fields, for which there is a large literature, but rather to call attention to some of the key differences they have with respect to the basic assumptions of the NMC and ways in which they can contribute to a better understanding of macro-financial events.

The field of <u>behavioral economics</u>, and behavioral finance in particular, has been posed as an alternative to neoclassical economics and the micro-foundations of the NMC, mainly because of its challenges to the assumption of perfect rationality in those fields.[13] These challenges are based on the notion that in studying economic behavior and phenomena one should draw on the insights of psychology and sociology in understanding how individuals and groups actually make decisions and choices. This is obviously important because many situations arise where time constraints or circumstances or simple biases in human perception and thought processes make it abundantly clear that an assumption of pure rationality with all the complex, forward-looking calculus it may imply is simply not realistic.

Expressed in this way, it seems odd that behavioral economics would be considered a sub-specialty within the field of economics rather than part of its core, as it is based on the idea that in understanding economic activity, one should try to understand how individual agents actually make decisions rather than assume a priori a certain kind of cognitive behavior or decision-making process. In part, this arrangement reflects the fact that the neoclassical paradigm has been the dominant framework for economic analysis for a far longer period of time than behavioral economics has been in existence and has proved itself useful as providing an idealized benchmark and a highly developed analytical framework for understanding or explaining many kinds of economic activity. The distinction between the two fields also arises because of a basic difference in methodological approaches. Behavioral economics is based on the results of laboratory experiments or elaborate data studies in trying to understand human decision-making and economic outcomes and follows an inductive approach similar to that used in the natural sciences. By contrast, neoclassical economics, as suggested earlier in discussing the NMC, follows a deductivist approach, whereby a limited set of basic assumptions about optimizing behavior on the part of economic agents is adopted as axiomatic and certain implications for economic outcomes are derived as logical conclusions to serve as a theoretical framework for understanding economic phenomena observed in the real world. This may be a useful initial approach in thinking about economic problems, but the lesson of behavioral economics is that it needs to be supplemented by the use of experimental and evidence-based techniques in order to reach sound conclusions about problems in the real world.

At the present time, however, it is hard to define a unified framework of behavioral economics wholly separate from neoclassical economics, as one of its main reasons for existence has been to explain anomalies in economic outcomes that cannot be accounted for by the neoclassical paradigm. Alternatively, whether and how in the future the behavioral approach becomes gradually integrated with the neoclassical approach will depend on the extent to which the latter tries to incorporate the results of the more experimental and data-driven analyses of behavioral economics.

For the purposes of this book in understanding the financial crisis, the distinctions discussed above apply equally as well in the field of finance in comparing behavioral finance with the implications of the efficient market theory of finance (EMH). The obvious point of departure is the housing bubble and credit boom, which preceded the global financial crisis and the financial crisis itself, which together represented a major break-down or departure from the EMH. So too was the dot-com bubble of the late 1990s, although its collapse had less damaging consequences for the economy as it was not propelled in the same way as the housing bubble by massive increases in leverage linked to very short-term funding (e.g., overnight commercial paper). In thinking about the housing bubble and the ensuing financial crisis, it is interesting to note that economists such as Keynes and Minsky, who both spent much of their lives trying to under-stand financial booms and busts, offered interpretations of these events similar to the approaches of specialists in behavioral finance well before it became a defined field of study.[14] Keynes is often quoted for his description of stock market events as analogous to "beauty contests" where market participants are guided more by what others think or are expected to do rather than by careful financial analysis. He also famously described invest-ment behavior as guided by "animal spirits" or the psychological outlook and expectations of investors instead of rational calculations of rates of return and the cost of capital or the "marginal efficiency of capital".

Similarly, Minsky, as noted earlier in Chap. 2, considered cycles of credit boom and bust as inherent in the financing of capitalist systems as banks typically initiate credit booms by taking on greater risk in their loans and investments in search of higher yields. This process can ultimately develop into what he called "Ponzi finance", whereby loans are made to borrowers who cannot generate cash flows to pay down their past credits simply in order for them to sustain ever higher amounts of debt service. At some point in this process, outside investors realize that the project sup-ported by Ponzi finance is unsustainable and they begin to withdraw their support, at which point a "Minsky moment" occurs and the project and its financing collapses, with negative consequences for banks, investors and the broader economy. This explanation of a credit cycle can be easily applied to the sub-prime housing credit boom and the associated surge in securitized instruments.

More recently, behavioral specialists such as Robert Shiller of Yale University have expanded our understanding of financial markets by show-ing that as a general proposition there is far more volatility in stock market returns than is consistent with the EMH. He has also advanced the thesis that bubble phenomena are inherently social processes that are guided by positive feedback loops and often propelled by information cascades gen-erated by news media.[15] This image stands in marked contrast with that of the EMH in which individual agents operate independently in response to new information to assess the intrinsic value of traded securities on the basis of rational expectations. Shiller has tried to incorporate in his work the insights of psychologists such as Daniel Kahneman and Ivan Tversky, who demonstrated through laboratory experiments the biases with which individuals make decisions in the face of uncertainty, which, among other things, formed the basis of what they called "prospect theory". This theory, in simple terms, postulates that individuals evaluate the risks involved in financial gains and losses asymmetrically because of a strong sense of loss aversion. Accordingly, they display behavior that is risk seeking in order to avoid losses and risk avoiding in the presence of gains. These behavioral tendencies can help to explain financial market outcomes that are quite distinct from the predictions of the EMH.[16]

As a more general proposition, Professor Richard Thaler of the University of Chicago, which is the home of the EMH, has pointed to the "impossible trinity" of the EMH, namely that it cannot be simultaneously true that investors are rational, asset prices are equivalent to intrinsic values and the financial intermediation sector accounts for 8 percent of GDP.[17] The size of the financial sector suggests that there may be significant rents in financial activity and large profits from speculative/high-frequency trading, which is inconsistent with the EMH; it also suggests that there are substantial gains to be made from the search for information and arbitrage activity to take advantage of the facts that prices do diverge from intrinsic value for periods of time and that it is possible to "beat the market". If the EMH were strictly true, there would be no gains from the search for information as all relevant information would be immediately reflected in the prices of financial assets, yet the fact that much time and money are allocated to this search in the world of financial markets suggests that there are gains to be made.

As in the case of behavioral economics, there is no single unified framework of behavioral finance as there is for the EMH, as up to now it has existed mainly for purposes of explaining anomalies that cannot fit within the efficient markets framework. In that sense, the EMH remains a useful benchmark for thinking about financial market behavior under a set of simple, idealized assumptions, but it needs to be supplemented by the insights of experimental psychology and evidence-based studies to account more fully for financial booms and busts.

The field of complexity economics also provides a useful counterpoint to the main macroeconomic paradigm. Instead of focusing on the conditions under which the aggregate economy will be in general equilibrium, as in the NMC, complexity economics views the economy as a complex, dynamic, constantly evolving mechanism that is out of equilibrium as economic agents interact with each other and adjust their behavior on a continuing basis as a result of those interactions and in response to new or unexpected developments.[18] Expressed in these simple terms, complexity economics is based on a more realistic vision of the aggregate economy than that of the NMC, which to an important extent has been limited in its approach by what was mathematically tractable. As a result, the latter has been defined by the methodological individualism of its microfoundations as reflected in its focus on the behavior of a "representative agent" for purposes of explaining aggregate economic outcomes, which by its very nature rules out the consideration of heterogeneous agents and their interactions that are an essential reality of economic life. The NMC, with its focus on the determinants of equilibrium, comes out of a tradition of economic thinking that was based on notions of physics derived from classical mechanics and thermodynamics, whereas complexity economics is more similar to notions of evolutionary biology, with its focus on process and change. Both schools of economic thinking and their scientific analogue are theoretical, but the former is more mathematical than the latter.

Another striking difference between the two approaches to understanding the aggregate economy is that the NMC relies on negative feedback effects and linear relationships among economic agents to understand the determination of equilibrium in a closed system, whereas complexity economics builds on the idea of positive feedback and non-linear effects to account for economic change through time in an open system. The reductionist approach of the former school implies that macroeconomic outcomes can be accounted for by the aggregation of individual economic agents' behavior; by contrast, the alternative school envisions an economic system with "emergent" properties whereby macroeconomic outcomes cannot be understood simply as a result of individual agents' behavior, but rather they need to take account of their interaction along with the positive feedback and non-linear effects of those interactions. Curiously, as many writers have noted, Adam Smith's vision of the economy in the *Wealth of Nations* has more in common with the view of the economy as a complex evolving system with emergent properties than it does with the NMC. The mystery of the "invisible hand" whereby socially beneficial outcomes could be the result of individuals and firms acting in their own self-interest was in modern terms an illusion to an emergent property of the economic system that was not evident by consideration of the nature of microeconomic behavior. Prior to the financial crisis, the emergent properties of complex adaptive systems had sometimes been used as a framework of understanding certain economic phenomena as the result of the workings of a self-organizing mechanism.[19]

In some respects, the vision of complexity economics speaks to the concerns of macroeconomists such as Olivier Blanchard, as noted earlier, in his reference to the "dark corners" of macroeconomic behavior where the standard models do not apply and cannot account for different kinds of extreme economic events, such as the sudden emergence of a financial crisis and the "doom loop" of a jump in sovereign debt risk premia and potential insolvency in the banking sector. These phenomena reflect the outcome of positive feedback mechanisms and non-linear relationships in the economy.

The economics of complexity is also useful in understanding certain aspects of economic development, which by its very nature is a process of dynamic structural change. This process has not been well explained by the neoclassical growth model and its offspring, in part because of their focus on determining a country's path of steady-state economic growth, which largely obscures its structural transformation over time from an agricultural to an industrial and to a service-based economy. Using the insights of complexity economics, two economists at the Harvard Kennedy School of Government (Ricardo Hausmann and Cesar Hidalgo) have explained the stages of economic development in terms of the evolving business and labor capabilities of a country as reflected in the growing sophistication or complexity of a country's trade relations with other countries.[20] The metrics these authors have developed through careful data analysis of cross-country trade patterns provide a reliable predictor of a country's level of per capita income and prospects for future growth. More generally, complexity economics views technological change as a key driver of structural change in the economy over time, as the invention of new machines or processes sets in motion further inventions and changes in business practices and institutions as a result of the responses of economic agents and their interactions in adapting to these inventions. In pointing to the importance of technological change as a driver of economic growth, complexity economics and the neoclassical growth model obviously share something in common. However, the latter framework does not attempt to show how structural change in the economy results from technological improvements, as its main focus of attention is on the elements of an aggregate production function made up of labor, capital and total factor productivity.[21]

Andrew Haldane, the Chief Economist of the Bank of England, has suggested that the approach of complexity economics can be important in dealing with the effects of the global financial crisis and minimizing the risk of similar events in the future.[22] In his view, a systems-theory approach needs to be adopted at each layer of financial sector regulation: beginning with the micro-prudential perspective on the operations of large complex financial institutions or systemically important financial institutions, then proceeding up to the macro-prudential perspective on financial system stability and then further to the global financial perspective covered by the international financial architecture. At each of these three layers, there are important, complex networks of financial relationships and inter-dependencies that need to be understood from a regulatory perspective if systemic stability is to be maintained. This goal can only be achieved if an effort is made through detailed data collection to understand the nature and density of these networks and the manner in which a shock in one node or edge (i.e., link) of the network can be amplified through positive feedback effects or non-linear relationships to such a degree that a financial crisis could emerge.

At this stage in the development of economic thought, it is not possible to define a fully fleshed-out alternative paradigm to the NMC rooted in complexity theory. However, it seems clear that this theoretical approach offers a valid and useful framework for conceptualizing many different aspects of macroeconomic behavior in a manner which is more realistic than the NMC. On these grounds, further work in understanding the aggregate economy as a complex adaptive system should be encouraged in order to gain insights from other disciplines and allow for a more pluralistic approach in the study of economics.

How Has the Global Financial Crisis Influenced the Teaching of Economics?

Just as the global financial crisis has triggered calls for new approaches and reforms in macroeconomic theory and research, so too has it triggered calls for reform in the teaching of economics. Interestingly, these appeals have come from the top down (i.e., teachers) as well as from the bottom up (i.e., students) and have been focused on both the general education of economists at the undergraduate level and the more specialized training of economists at the graduate level.

Two of the student-led reform groups started in the United Kingdom and have gradually attracted student affiliations in other countries: One is the Post-Crash Economic Society (PCES) that was started at the University of Manchester at the end of 2012, and the other is the International Student Initiative for Pluralism in Economics (ISIPE) that was founded in 2014 and now has affiliates in over 30 countries. In April 2014, the PCES released a report with a foreword by Andrew Haldane of the Bank of England, who was cited earlier, criticizing the dominant focus on neoclassical economics in the training of economists in the United Kingdom and the economics curriculum at the University of Manchester, in particular.[23] The ISIPE group has made a strong appeal for teaching economics from both orthodox neoclassical and heterodox perspectives.

What is common in all these initiatives is a call for a broader base of training in economics that goes beyond the foundations of neoclassical economic theory and includes economic history, the history of economic thought and the methodology of economics to counter what is viewed as a tendency to teach economics mainly as an abstract, value-free and purely quantitative exercise governed by unchanging rules of behavior applicable to all economic agents of any time and place. This tendency could be countered by a greater emphasis on the role of institutions in economic activity and the major historical debates among economic thinkers in the teaching of macroeconomics. There is also an appeal to balance the predominant emphasis on deductive modes of analysis to explain certain "stylized facts" observed by economists with a more inductive approach, which relies on evidence-based techniques of data analysis, case studies, historical analysis and experiments as a basis for generating certain hypotheses or different theories to account for the patterns observed in real-world economic events.

A good example of the latter approach is the landmark study by Thomas Piketty on the development of wealth and income inequality in the United States and selected European countries since the late nineteenth century, which was discussed in earlier chapters.[24] Based on his detailed analysis of historical tax records, Piketty has pieced together over a period of 20 years a clear and similar U-shaped pattern of inequality in these countries during the twentieth century, which he explains from a variety of historical, literary and sociological perspectives. He then posits a simple set of relationships (or "fundamental laws" of capitalism) among wealth (or the capital stock), the rate of savings, the return on capital and economic growth to develop a unifying conceptual framework that can account for the quantitative results that he derives and also form a basis for making certain predictions about the path of income inequality in the future.

Piketty's work is also striking as he views it as an antidote to the prevailing mode of mainstream economics, notwithstanding his own professional development at the London School of Economics and teaching affiliation with MIT early in his career. In the introduction to his study (*Capital in the 21st Century*), he writes:

> The discipline of economics has yet to get over its childish passion for mathematics and for purely theoretical and often highly ideological speculation, at the expense of historical research and collaboration with other social sciences. Economists are all too often pre-occupied with purely mathematical problems of interest only to themselves. This obsession with mathematics is an easy way of acquiring the appearance of scientificity without having to answer the far more complex questions posed in the world we live in…The truth is that economics should never have sought to divorce itself from the other social sciences and can only advance in conjunction with them. (p. 32)

The tone and direction of these remarks are very much in harmony with the post-crisis critiques of macroeconomics discussed earlier (including that of Paul Romer in his concern with "mathiness") and the student-led appeals for more relevance to real-world problems in the teaching of economics.

Building on these ideas, organizations such as the Institute for New Economic Thinking (INET), which was founded by the philanthropist George Soros in 2009, have begun to sponsor new course curricula for the teaching of economics. One of these is the CORE-ECON project (The Curriculum in Open Access Resources in Economics) directed by Wendy Carlin of University College London, which is in the process of completing a series of training modules for first-year students in economics (www.core-econ.org). Professor Carlin has also revised her own textbook in macroeconomics with her co-author David Soskice to cover in greater detail the role of monetary and financial institutions in the modern economy in order to deal with the fallout from the global financial crisis.[25] Another interesting example of INET's open access course promotion is a graduate-level course in microeconomics ("Microeconomics for the Critical Mind"), which comprises videotapes of the main lectures and workshops from a recent course delivery at the New School for Social Research in New York City. What is striking about this course is that while it is rooted in the mainstream neoclassical approach to microeconomics based on a widely used textbook by Mas-Colell, Whinston and Green, the lectures (and the reading list) devote a considerable amount of time (and space) to examining the history of economic thought and controversies surrounding the main theoretical concepts and approaches presented in the text, as a supplement to the axiomatic-deductive theorizing of microeconomics.[26]

SUMMARY AND CONCLUSION

The global financial crisis has triggered an active debate about the validity and applicability of the mainstream macroeconomic paradigm, the potential contribution of alternative theoretical frameworks to the understanding of macroeconomic phenomena and the need for different approaches in economics education.

The mainstream macroeconomic paradigm or NMC based on DSGE modeling comes out of an intellectual tradition that views the economy as a self-stabilizing mechanism. However, the effects of the financial crisis and the Great Recession have raised challenges to that view, as reflected in persistent downgrades to potential GDP in the advanced economies and the projected timing of economic recovery. Recent research since the crisis has shown that the economy suffers permanent damage to its productive potential during major recessions (or "hysteresis") as a result of sustained unemployment and lost labor skills, deferred investment and decline in the capital stock. Debates during the recent presidential campaign in the United States about the potential recuperative effects of fiscal stimulus highlighted this important issue. While work has been undertaken since the crisis to introduce financial frictions explicitly into the theoretical framework of the NMC, many critics have argued that there are basic flaws in the "micro-foundations" of this framework and its emphasis on mathematical rigor and precision, which limit its relevance to real-world macroeconomic problems.

The debate over the relevance of the NMC has triggered renewed interest in two fields of analysis that are viewed as capable of dealing with some of its shortcomings, namely, behavioral economics and complexity theory. The former has incorporated the insights of experimental psychology in trying to account for some of the anomalies in financial behavior that cannot be explained by, or are in conflict with, the efficient market theory of finance. In this regard, the thinking of past scholars who tried to understand the causes and effects of financial booms and busts, such as

Keynes and Minsky, was fully consistent with the framework of behavioral economics well before it became a specialized field of study.

Complexity theory views the economy as an evolving, complex and adaptive (open) system with emergent properties rather than a closed system moving from one equilibrium state to another or along a steady stationary trend. Instead of viewing the aggregate economy as the reflection of the actions of a single "representative agent" with perfect foresight, as in the NMC, complexity theory understands macroeconomic phenomena as patterns or emergent properties of a system in which heterogeneous agents are interacting with each other in the face of uncertainty and responding to new developments (e.g., innovations and technological change). The systems approach of complexity theory is also important for understanding financial networks at different levels of the national and international financial system and for gauging the potential for financial crises to develop as a result of non-linear effects associated with problems in certain edges or clusters within those networks.

The re-examination of the NMC has coincided with a re-assessment of the standard approaches in the teaching of economics. A number of new initiatives have surfaced since the financial crisis advocating more pluralism in economics education, a greater emphasis on economic history and the history of economic thought and a more inter-disciplinary and evidence-based approach in economic analysis and empirical work.

NOTES

1. The IMF has made similar downward adjustments in its estimates of potential GDP for the global economy and for the advanced economies, as presented in Chart 4.1 of this book; see also IMF (2015) World Economic Output (April), Chap. 3 "Where Are We Headed? Perspectives on Potential GDP".

2. This evidence is presented in Olivier Blanchard, Eugenio Cerutti and Lawrence Summers "Inflation and Activity – Two Explorations and Their Monetary Policy Implications" IMF Working Paper #15/230 (November 2015).

3. The debate between Professor Friedman and his critics has mostly played out in the blogosphere. Professor Friedman's explanation of the Sanders' Plan was presented on January 28, 2016 in an essay "What Would Sanders Do? Estimating the Economic Impact of Sanders Programs" (www.dollarsandsense.org). A critique by

Professors Christina and David Romer ("Senator Sander's Proposed Policies and Economic Growth") can be found at www.economist-stypepad.com on February 25, 2016. Professor Friedman's rebuttal ("Gerald Friedman Responds to the Romers on the Sanders Plan: Different Models, Different Politics") appeared on March 8, 2016 on www.nakedcapitalism.com. An interesting analytical and graphical examination of the two points of view by Professor Menzie Chin appeared on March 4, 2016 and can be found at www.econbrowser.com ("Visualizing Textbook and Alternative Explanations of the Friedman Analysis of the Sanders' Economic Plan"), as explained further in footnote 5 below.

4. Bradford Delong and Lawrence Summers, "Fiscal Policy in a Depressed Economy" Brookings Papers on Economic Activity 2012(1); pp. 233–297.

5. As a useful and interesting independent contribution to the debate, Professor Menzie Chin of the University of Minnesota demonstrated in a conventional textbook presentation of aggregate demand and supply curves (AS-AD) in his blog (www.econbrowser.com/ March 4, 2016) that the outcome of the debate depends on the shape of the short-term aggregate supply curve, the size of the output gap and the extent of any shift in the long-run aggregate supply line (LRAS). The possibility of a shift in the LRAS depends critically on the stimulus effect of additional spending on productivity gains. In the Keynesian tradition, such a result could be envisaged as the outcome of a multiplier-accelerator type model in which investment is dependent on the rate of growth in output.

6. For a recent summary of this debate and analysis, see David Cushman, "A Unit Root in Post-War US Real GDP Still Cannot Be Rejected, and Yes, It Matters" Economic Journal Watch vol. 13(1); pp. 5–45 (January 2016). A concurring position is expressed in "Roger Farmer's Economic Window" blog of April 16, 2015. Another recent analysis that confirms these findings using unemployment data is Paul Beaudry, Dana Galizia and Franck Portier "Is the Macroeconomy Locally Stable and Why Should We Care?" NBER Working Paper #22275 (May 2016).

7. A recent example of this literature can be found in Jesper Linde, Frank Smets and Rafael Wouters "Challenges for Central Banks' Macro Models" National Bank of Sweden Working Paper #323 (May 2016).

8. Prepared Statement by Professor Robert Solow for a Congressional Hearing on "Building A Science of Economics for the Real World", Committee on Science and Technology, US House of Representatives, July 20, 2010.
9. Professor Syll has attracted a large following through his blog "Non-ergodic, Realist and Relevant Economics", which can be found at https://larspsyll.wordpress.com
10. Notwithstanding the popularity of the EMH, it has long been established that stock-market returns follow a power-law distribution, which implies that extreme market events are much more likely than would be the case if they followed a normal probability distribution as assumed for the EMH. For a recent discussion, see Xavier Gabaix "Power Laws in Economics: An Introduction" Journal of Economic Perspectives vol. 30 (1); pp. 185–206 (2016).
11. Paul Romer "Mathiness in the Theory of Economic Growth" American Economic Review: Papers and Proceedings vol. 105 (5); pp. 89–93 (2015).
12. Olivier Blanchard "Where Danger Lurks" Finance and Development vol. 51(3); pp. 28–31 (September 2014).
13. Richard Thaler, past President of the American Economics Association (AEA), provided a very succinct and insightful overview of the field of behavioral economics in his Presidential Address of January 4, 2016, which can be accessed at www.aeaweb.org/webcasts.
14. The intellectual links among Keynes, Minsky and modern behavioral finance specialists are examined in a paper by Hersh Shefrin and Meyer Statman "Behavioral Finance in the Financial Crisis: Market Efficiency, Minsky and Keynes" Russell Sage Foundation (November 2011).
15. These hypotheses are examined in Shiller's book (*Irrational Exuberance*) that was published in 2000, just at the peak of the dot-com bubble.
16. For a discussion of how prospect theory has gradually influenced the work of economists interested in financial markets, see Nicholas Barberis "Thirty Years of Prospect Theory in Economics: A Review and Assessment" Journal of Economic Perspectives vol. 27(1); pp. 173–96 (Winter 2013).

17. This proposition about behavioral finance can be found in Richard Thaler's Presidential Address at the AEA Annual Meetings cited in footnote 13.

18. Many of the ideas expressed in this section have been adapted from W. Brian Arthur "Complexity Economics: A Different Framework for Economic Thought" Working Paper 2013-04-012 (2013) Santa Fe Institute (www.santafe.edu). An additional source of ideas about how complexity theory can contribute to macroeconomic analysis is Tony Dolphin and David Nash (eds.) *Complex New World: Translating New Economic Thinking Into Public Policy* (London: Institute for Public Policy Research) August 2012.

19. Paul Krugman has examined this concept in Krugman (1995) *The Self-Organizing Economy* (New York: Blackwell Publishers).

20. Cesar Hidalgo and Ricardo Hausmann "The Building Blocks of Economic Complexity" Proceedings of the National Academy of Sciences, vol. 26 (106); pp. 10570–10575 (June 2009).

21. One study that examines technological change as a driver of structural change in the economy from the vantage point of complexity economics is Eric Beinhocker (2006) *The Origin of Wealth: Evolution, Complexity and the Radical Remaking of Economics* (Cambridge, MA: Harvard Business School Press).

22. The ideas expressed in this paragraph are drawn from Andrew Haldane "On Microscopes and Telescopes", a speech delivered at the Lorentz Centre workshop on socio-economic complexity, Leiden, Netherlands (March 27, 2015), that is available on the website of the Bank of England (www.bankofengland.co.uk).

23. The report is "Economics, Education and Unlearning: Economics Education at the University of Manchester" and can be found at www.post-crasheconomics.com.

24. Thomas Piketty (2014) *Capital in the 21st Century* (Cambridge, MA: Belknap Press).

25. Wendy Carlin and David Soskice (2015) *Macroeconomics: Institutions, Instability and the Financial System* (Oxford, UK: Oxford University Press).

26. Andreu Mas-Colell, Michael Whinston and Jerry Green (1992) *Microeconomic Theory* (Oxford, UK: Oxford University Press).

CHAPTER 9

Conclusions and Lessons for the Future

The global financial crisis (GFC) of 2008–09 with its aftermath has been the most dramatic example of global booms and busts in the modern era of capitalism since the Great Depression. As a near cataclysmic event for the global economic and financial system, it has had profound implications for macroeconomic analysis, monetary and fiscal policy-making, regulatory frameworks and the reform of the global financial architecture. In this regard, it is likely to be considered in future years as a watershed event in terms of our understanding of financial globalization, financial markets and their effects on national economies. As discussed in previous chapters, much has been written since the crisis in an effort to understand its causes and implications for policy-making and regulatory reform, as well as for the teaching of economics. The purpose of this chapter is to identify a number of important lessons and conclusions one can distill from the crisis and its consequences with the benefit of hindsight and the analytical work that has been undertaken thus far, drawing on the content of previous chapters. In the paragraphs that follow, 25 key lessons and conclusions are identified and summarized under five general headings: (1) the financial sector and its regulation, (2) monetary policy, (3) fiscal policy, (4) the international financial architecture and (5) thinking about the aggregate economy. While these lessons are many in number, they are not intended to be exhaustive or complete. However, they deal with some key areas of macroeconomic theory and policy and the governance

© The Author(s) 2017
A. Elson, *The Global Financial Crisis in Retrospect*,
DOI 10.1057/978-1-137-59750-2_9

of the international financial system where conclusions held prior to the financial crisis have either been confirmed or modified in important ways. Undoubtedly, they will be refined and extended with the passage of time, as the full implications and effects of the financial crisis are further analyzed and understood.[1]

The Financial Sector and Its Regulation

1. One principal lesson about the financial system to be drawn from the GFC is that an unregulated financial sector can have a strong tendency to destabilize itself. The prime example of this phenomenon was the so-called "shadow" banking system in the United States, which was at the epicenter of the GFC. The "shadow" descriptor applied to this sector was intended to capture the notion that it played a similar role in financial intermediation as the traditional banking sector but within an institutional framework that was largely outside the perimeter of the government's regulatory and financial safety-net structure. It comprised mortgage originators, investment banks, money market funds and off-balance-sheet operations of large commercial banks.

At one level, the behavior of the "shadow" banking sector, which was largely a capital-markets-based system, exhibited many of the tendencies that were identified by Hyman Minsky in his analysis of financial crises, or "financial instability" hypothesis. Typically, in a period of relative macroeconomic calm such as that associated with the Great Moderation, Minsky noted that financial institutions begin to seek opportunities to take on activities involving higher risk in an effort to boost their returns. The presence of a bubble phenomenon such as in housing provides an ideal vehicle for generating higher profits for financial institutions. Housing itself can be an attractive form of collateral for supporting bank lending, and rising asset prices in the form of home prices can appear to justify continued lending. However, once the bubble of home prices bursts, often following a tightening of the monetary policy, loan defaults rise as homebuyers find themselves holding mortgages worth more than the value of their house and facing debt-service payments they cannot make because of an increase in lending rates. The banks begin to face losses because of the write-down of loans in default, which may threaten the solvency of one or more banks. At this point, depositor panic may set in and a banking crisis may ensue. This scenario based on Minsky's financial instability hypothesis describes almost exactly what occurred prior to the GFC, albeit within the framework of financial institutions operating outside the perimeter of the traditional banking system with excessive leverage and minimal capital.

At another level, the prelude to the GFC represented a perfect storm in the sense that there was a complete breakdown of the principal-agent relationships and counterparty risk assessments that are normally expected to function without government involvement as a stabilizing influence within an advanced capitalist system. These weaknesses, coupled with widespread fraud and abuse within the "shadow" banking system, created the conditions that gave rise to the GFC. In the context of the housing bubble that preceded the crisis, mortgage originators provided credit to households with minimal conditions, even when the lack of creditworthiness of the borrowers was clearly evident, with the prospect of selling these to willing buyers such as the government-sponsored agencies (Fannie Mae and Freddie Mac). These loans in turn were repackaged by investment banks as securitized instruments such as mortgage-backed securities (MBS), combining a mix of risk-weighted mortgages, or as collateralized debt obligations (CDOs), which combined tranches of different risk categories from various MBS. These instruments were given favorable ratings by the credit rating agencies under pressure from the investment banks, on which the agencies depended for their fees and business relationships. The CDOs and MBS were sold to individual or institutional investors, in many cases, without full disclosure by the investment banks of the quality of the underlying loan components. Other derivative instruments, such as credit default swaps (CDS), were sold by a large insurance company (the American International Group, or AIG) as a form of insurance against CDOs/MBS defaults without proper reserves and virtually no external supervision. These derivatives were sold not only to the purchasers of MBS and CDOs but also to speculators who wanted to profit from any default on the MBS/CDOs held by other investors. In these activities, boards of directors and equity owners exercised little or no influence on corporate managers as long as the value of their shareholdings was increasing. Finally, in the case of the large investment banks, which held many securitized instruments and derivative positions, accounting firms were willing to advise these banks on accounting maneuvers at the end of any reporting quarter that would conceal certain transactions in these instruments or temporarily alter their financial statements in order to reassure investors or financial analysts of their financial soundness.

Transactions in securitized instruments and CDS were common not only in the United States but also in the European Union as banks in Europe became eager buyers of MBS/CDOs (given their high credit ratings), often with cross-border funding secured from money market funds in the United States. The extreme fragility of these transactions is evidenced by the fact that the financing provided by money market funds and other "shadow" banking operators was typically provided in the form of overnight repurchase agreements against the collateral of MBS/CDOs. Once the quality and liquidity of these securitized investments were placed in doubt, as in late 2008, a system-wide panic and failure at the national and global levels became inevitable as investors sought to shift their assets to the safety of government securities.

2. Apart from the idiosyncratic nature of the "shadow" banking system, a clear lesson from the crisis is that the pattern of events that gave rise to the financial crisis followed a familiar sequence based on the experience of other countries that had experienced a banking or financial crisis during the age of financial globalization. These crises had typically developed in the context of a housing or stock market bubble involving the speculative build-up of asset prices, following a liberalization of the financial sector and the failure of the government to put in place adequate supervision of the institutions operating in that sector. One important action of the US government in liberalizing the financial sector, which helped to set the stage for the financial crisis, was the repeal in 1999 of the Glass-Steagal legislation that was introduced after the Great Depression. That legislation had separated commercial and investment banking operations in the financial sector and prohibited commercial banks from engaging in equity, bond and derivative trading for their own account as a means of raising profits. Then at the beginning of 2004, the main regulator with oversight of the investment banks, namely the Securities and Exchange Commission (SEC), adopted a posture that these institutions should be allowed to determine their own capital requirements on the basis of their internal risk management systems without any regulatory oversight. Also in 2000, a decision was taken by the US Treasury Department and the Commodities Future Trading Commission that had the effect of removing over-the-counter (OTC) derivative transactions from any regulation or supervision. In addition, money market funds operated without any regulatory supervision, while AIG was able to take steps

that allowed it to select as its regulator a government agency with the weakest reputation for its supervisory activity (Office of Thrift Supervision), which was closed down after the crisis.

3. With the benefit of hindsight, it is clear that the structure and framework of financial regulation in the United States was woefully inadequate in the lead-up to the financial crisis. Apart from little or no regulatory oversight of the "shadow" banking sector, which operated with minimal levels of capital and high ratios of leverage, bank regulators largely ignored a growing problem of low capital-asset ratios of the commercial banks and their reliance on high levels of leverage, in part owing to a misguided belief in the self-disciplining power of financial market institutions. Another problem was revealed in the very fragmented and diffuse structure of regulatory agencies that exercised oversight of the financial sector in the United States. In this context, the regulatory reforms introduced through the revision of the Basel Capital Accord (Basel III) and Dodd-Frank legislation in the United States have been essential. In addition to strengthening the common core capital requirements for banks, with a special surcharge for systemically important financial institutions (SIFIs), these reforms have introduced a new macro-prudential or systemic stability perspective to regulatory regimes, along with leverage limits, special funding and liquidity requirements for banks, and the migration of OTC derivative trading to central clearinghouses. Resolution procedures for SIFIs have also been improved. Despite these reforms, capital requirements have become more complex and should be simplified and further increased along with the new minimum capital-asset ratio in order to eliminate the problem of too-big-to-fail institutions and reduce the high social cost of system bank failures. Financial regulation of the "shadow" banking system also needs to be strengthened. Unfortunately, the fragmented institutional structure of the regulatory regime in the United States remains a problem, notwithstanding the creation of the Financial System Oversight Council, while the availability of macroprudential tools available to the Federal Reserve is very limited.

4. The behavior of the financial sector as described in points 1 and 2 above supports a strong implication that financial markets are not efficient in the sense of avoiding extreme bouts of asset expansion or asset price inflation through the rational processing of information and appropriate discounting of future profits and dividends. The existence

of a housing bubble in the United States, as well as in Ireland, Portugal, Spain and the United Kingdom in the period leading up to the crisis, supported by a ballooning in the provision of credit to the private sector, is clear evidence of the potential inefficiency of asset markets. In addition, the fragile pyramid of risk that was built up around the housing bubble in the United States testifies to the poor judgment of investors in identifying and appropriately pricing that risk.

5. One has also learned from the financial crisis that the links from a collapse of an asset price bubble to a financial crisis and then to a severe recession can be very strong. Once the housing price bubble deflated in late 2006 and 2007, the balance sheet of banks weakened, with a drop in the value of collateral, a rise in loan delinquency and a decline in the value of securitized instruments. With the decline in the value of securitized instruments, sources of liquidity for banks dried up and banks began to cut back on their loans to other banks. In addition, the prices of other assets, that is, stocks and bonds, declined with the second-round effects on the balance sheet of the financial institutions. At this stage, at least three channels of influence took effect in bringing about a collapse in economic activity. From the side of the banks, the deterioration in their balance sheets led to a generalized decline in lending to households and businesses, which induced a significant "financial accelerator" effect on output. At the same time, the decline in the value of financial assets had strong wealth effects in dampening consumer and investment spending. A third channel operated through the effect of an increasing debt burden on banks and households, which reinforced the reduction in lending to businesses and spending by households. Emergency lending by the Federal Reserve and the Treasury Department had the effect of shoring up the liquidity and capital position of large financial institutions, but the US government failed to put in place a program that was of any significance to alleviate the debt burden of private households.

Monetary Policy

6. Prior to the crisis, a consensus seemed to have been reached among academic macroeconomists and policy-makers that a central bank regime focused on inflation targeting and a fiscal policy linked to fiscal rules, operating independently and with full transparency, would be the best guarantor of low inflation and sustained growth

in real GDP close to the economy's output potential. Most central banks in the advanced countries and leading emerging market economies were following an implicit or explicit regime of inflation targeting. Regimes of fiscal rules were less common, but important examples could be found in the Stability and Growth Pact (SGP) of the euro zone and the operation of stabilization or sovereign wealth funds in emerging market economies that attempted to smooth out the impact of commodity price volatility on fiscal performance. A clear lesson from the crisis is that this consensus was severely deficient. As noted earlier, a regime of inflation targeting was inadequate in that it essentially ignored the potential problem of systemic financial risk, while a framework of rigid fiscal rules in the euro zone has only reinforced the deflationary bias of a fixed exchange rate regime at a time of a global economic downturn.

7. Monetary policy has proven to be a very potent tool in forestalling a collapse of the financial system nationally and globally and in limiting the downturn in economic activity. The massive provision of liquidity by the Federal Reserve for US-based financial institutions and globally through a network of central banks swaps provided an essential lender of last resort mechanism in the wake of the crisis. This action was supplemented by capital infusions to banks by the US Treasury Department. At the same time, the rapid decline in policy lending rates on the part of the major central banks provided a brake on the drop in global economic activity. In retrospect, however, it is clear that there was no "playbook" or operations manual from emergency planning to guide the authorities. Nor were there any useful policy prescriptions to be drawn from the mainstream macroeconomic paradigm or new macroeconomic consensus (NMC; see below). The authorities responded to the crisis with a large degree of improvisation and experimentation, along with the benefit of some important lessons distilled from the experience of the Great Depression. A clear lesson for the future from this experience is that contingency plans and mechanisms need to be developed at the national and global levels for liquidity provision, bank resolution and recapitalization to deal with the possibility of major financial distress that can occur on a sudden basis in response to unexpected developments.

8. Once the zero lower bound in central bank policy rates was reached, we have learned that the major central banks can continue

to play an important role in promoting economic recovery through unconventional monetary policy in the form of "forward guidance" and "quantitative easing" (QE). The former activity has shown the strong signaling effect of central banks' announced policy intentions in shaping expectations in the financial markets about the future course of interest rates. With a similar objective, the latter activity has involved a substantial expansion of central bank balance sheets through the purchase of MBS and government securities with a view to bending the yield curve down at the medium-to-long-term range of interest rates in order to encourage borrowing and spending by the private sector. An important lesson in the use of QE, however, is that it needs to be closely coordinated with the public debt program of the finance ministry. During the period 2009–13, the impact of the Fed's QE program on reducing long-term interest rates was partially offset by the public debt management of the US Treasury Department which was substituting maturing short-to-medium government debt with long-term debt issues in order to lengthen its debt profile to take advantage of the low long-term yields in the financial markets.

9. One possible undesirable side effect of QE has been a generalized increase in financial asset prices, which has tended to favor the wealth position of upper income groups who typically are the major players in stock and bond markets along with institutional investors. It may also have induced a renewed search for yield on the part of financial institutions, reminiscent of Minsky's framework, especially at a time when the cost of funding balance sheet operations has been so low. While it seems clear that these unconventional policies have had some effect on lowering long-term interest rates and raising inflation expectations, their impact on increasing real economic activity has been less certain. Looking forward, it also remains unclear how long it will take for central banks in the advanced countries to raise their policy rates to positive levels in real terms and to normalize the size of their balance sheet positions and what impact, if any, this process will have on financial markets.

10. Another lesson from the crisis is that the announcement of major changes in monetary policy can have powerful effects on exchange rates through shifts in capital flows in anticipation of interest rate adjustments. With a zero lower bound on central bank policy rates,

the transmission mechanism for monetary policy has shifted from interest rates and asset prices to exchange rates. This dynamic was in full play during the second half of 2014 and early part of 2015, with a divergence in monetary policy plans among the Bank of Japan, the European Central Bank (ECB) and the Federal Reserve. During the eight-month period leading up to the commencement of QE by the ECB in early March 2015, as expectations of monetary tightening in the United States and monetary loosening in Europe were growing, the euro depreciated against the dollar by around 20 percent. At the same time, these shifts in monetary policy of the major central banks, and in particular the Federal Reserve, can have powerful spillover effects on interest rates and exchange rates of emerging market economies. The so-called "taper tantrum" in mid-2013 when the Federal Reserve announced, as part of its experiment in "forward guidance", its intention to begin to moderate its expansionary monetary policy stance was a prime example of this spillover effect. Uncoordinated actions by central banks in the timing of actions to loosen the stance of monetary policy have also raised concerns of "currency wars". These concerns show that the exclusive orientation of the monetary policy of the major economies to domestic economic objectives may not be optimal from a global perspective, contrary to a widely held view prior to the financial crisis. It thus raises the issue of whether closer policy coordination at the international level would be beneficial for purposes of dampening the volatility of capital flows and promoting greater financial system stability.

11. We have now learned that the zero lower bound for central bank policy rates is not absolute and thus an impediment to the emergence of negative market interest rates in nominal terms. This effect has been most clearly in evidence in the euro zone, where economic activity has remained depressed and expectations of inflation have been severely dampened. Beginning in September 2014, yields on a range of government notes and bonds for Austria, Belgium, France, Germany, Ireland, the Netherlands and Switzerland slipped into negative territory, and by the end of 2015 this trend had spread to an additional six countries of the European Union. In addition to the programs of QE by the major central banks, since mid-2014, the ECB and other central banks in Europe and Japan have experimented with negative policy rates on bank

deposits ranging from minus 0.4 percent for the ECB to minus 1.25 percent for the National Bank of Sweden as of mid-2016. The impact of negative policy rates on promoting economic activity remains unclear while it runs the risk of weakening the financial position of commercial banks through a compression of their interest rate spread or of inducing an increase in lending rates, contrary to the policy intent of the central banks, as banks attempt to resist that compression.

12. Notwithstanding the potency of monetary policy changes for achieving certain macroeconomic policy objectives, it is now clear that interest rate policy, together with individual bank or microprudential supervision, is not sufficient to maintain financial system stability. Accordingly, a consensus has developed that central banks need to add macro-prudential tools to their policy mix in order to minimize the risks of financial system instability arising, for example, from a rapid growth in bank credit and private sector indebtedness. What is still being tested, however, is which macroprudential tools (such as counter-cyclical capital charges, loan-to-value limits or debt-to-income limits) work best and in what situations, and whether and how these tools should be coordinated with interest rate adjustments.

FISCAL POLICY

13. In the same way that we have learned from the financial crisis about the potentially strong effects of monetary policy, so too has been the case for fiscal policy. The evidence for this lesson was particularly clear in the wake of an economic downturn when central bank policy rates had reached the zero lower bound. A strong consensus on the need for fiscal action was formed at the international policy level when the Group of 20 (G20) Heads of State agreed on a coordinated fiscal stimulus package in their first summit meeting in Washington in November 2008. Unfortunately, following this action, there was a fragmenting of this consensus, which has complicated the process of promoting economic recovery in the advanced economies. One fracture was created by the resurgence of a view from within the new classical school of macroeconomics that the expansion of fiscal policy through government expenditure would be counter-productive as it would be offset by a cut-

back in private expenditure (both investment and consumption). This effect is captured by the notion of "Ricardian equivalence", which postulates that the economic effect of an expansion of government expenditure, whether financed by current taxes or by borrowing, would be offset by a similar reduction in private spending as households and businesses seek to increase their saving to pay for the taxes now or in the future that are needed to keep the fiscal position in balance.

A second fracture in the early consensus on fiscal stimulus originated within the governments of the euro zone and the United Kingdom, which became pre-occupied with the mounting public debt associated with the impact of the GFC. Such thinking was bolstered by an academic view that government efforts to reduce public debt in situations where debt sustainability was in question could be stimulative for the economy. According to this view, fiscal austerity could be expansionary by restoring the private sector's confidence in the government's intent to stabilize the economy and making clear that an expansion in private consumption and investment would be subject to less risk of inflation or the complications of a government debt default. In the case of the euro zone, this thinking was reinforced by the rigidity of the fiscal rules under the SGP that set a target for government debt not to exceed a level equivalent to 60 percent of national GDP. In the United Kingdom, as well as in the United States, the reigning concern about the size of government debt was reinforced by a strong belief that the size of government spending in the economy needed to be reduced, regardless of the cyclical position of the economy. Nevertheless, in the euro zone, the United Kingdom and the United States, it is evident that when fiscal policy shifted from an expansionary to a contractionary stance in 2010, this change operated as a significant drag on economic recovery during the period 2010–12.

14. Notwithstanding the fracturing of a consensus on fiscal policy as the recovery phase following the GFC further evolved, we have learned that fiscal multipliers arising from fiscal expansion and contraction can be significantly positive, especially at times when the zero lower bound on interest rates is present. Prior to the crisis, the prevailing view was that such multipliers were small, weak and uncertain, which was consistent with the attachment to fiscal rules and reliance on automatic stabilizers on the revenue and expendi-

ture sides of the government budget. The debate about the size and significance of fiscal multipliers was influenced by an internal review by the International Monetary Fund (IMF) of its policy advice to countries seeking financial assistance in the wake of the crisis. As a result of the programs of fiscal consolidation that were implemented by borrowing countries, this study showed that economic contractions were greater than expected because the impact of efforts to reduce the overall government deficit on economic activity were significantly larger than projected. This result has been supplemented by more recent studies of the IMF and mainstream macroeconomists, which have shown that increased public investment spending on infrastructure can have significantly positive multiplier effects on aggregate output.

15. In the context of the euro zone, one clear lesson is that the use of fiscal policy to bring about an internal devaluation in order to restore competitiveness through a reduction in domestic wages and prices can result in a severe and sustained reduction in employment and output, especially if such an adjustment program is pursued under conditions when the public debt burden is unsustainable. This lesson applies clearly to the southern-tier countries of the euro zone, and to Greece in particular. The adjustment process for Greece would have been much more tolerable if it had its own currency and was able to use currency depreciation as a means of restoring its external competitiveness, as did Iceland, for example, which is not a member of the euro zone, in its adjustment program following a public debt crisis at roughly the same time as that of Greece. The public debt crises which Greece, Spain, Portugal and Cyprus experienced in 2010–11 have clearly revealed the burden of adjustment on countries tied to a fixed exchange rate regime, especially in the absence of a fiscal union and an agreement (or willingness) for surplus countries (such as Germany) to pursue an expansionary fiscal policy in order to ease the burden on countries (such as Greece) that need to reduce their fiscal deficit. Of course, Greece should not have been allowed to expand its fiscal deficit so far beyond the fiscal limits of the euro zone prior to the crisis, which it did in large part through misreporting and deliberate efforts to conceal the true nature of its fiscal mismanagement.

16. In connection with some of the lessons for monetary and fiscal policy noted earlier, it is now clear that unconventional monetary pol-

icy alone is not sufficient to promote a sound recovery of the economy and that a further boost to aggregate demand through a temporary expansion of fiscal policy is required. In view of the effects of "hysteresis" that are associated with a long and slow post-crisis recovery, it is also important to recognize that the initial fiscal and monetary response to a financial crisis needs to be very strong in order to minimize the negative impact of the crisis on output and employment. The challenge for fiscal policy-makers whether in the executive or legislative branches of government is that the use of fiscal policy for stabilization objectives needs to be framed within a medium-term plan for maintaining or reaching fiscal sustainability. An additional challenge for fiscal policy, as distinct from monetary policy, has always been that there can be significant lags between the points in the economic cycle when it would be seen as desirable to have fiscal stimulus and the time it could be designed, agreed upon and implemented. This issue has raised debate on whether more potent elements of automatic stabilizers need to be embedded in budget design. At the same time, it is clear that more empirical work and debate is needed in order to forge a consensus on the proper role of counter-cyclical fiscal policy in macroeconomic stabilization. This issue is particularly important in the context of the SGP of the euro area. It is striking to see such a divergence of opinion across the major economies on what should be the proper role of fiscal policy in the wake of a severe economic downturn, when there is much less disagreement on what the role of monetary policy should be.

The International Financial Architecture

17. One of the clearest lessons we have learned from the GFC is that the international financial architecture (IFA) is seriously defective. The IFA represents the institutional and informal arrangements that governments have put in place to provide stability to the international monetary system and to manage the systemic risks of financial globalization. The twin institutional pillars of the IFA, which have links with a number of other agencies and committees, are the Financial Stability Board (FSB) and the IMF. The former oversees work on standards for the infrastructural aspects of the IFA (accounting, banking regulation, financial market organization, etc.), while the latter has been the main forum for policy

deliberation and emergency lending to promote global stabilization objectives. Both the FSB and the IMF are expected to coordinate their activities with a view to monitoring global financial system stability. The political directorate that guides the IFA is the G20. To be effective, the IFA needs to provide essential public goods in regard to the oversight of systemic financial risk, the coordination of financial regulation, international policy coordination and an international lender of last resort (ILOLR) mechanism. In each of these four areas there were major shortcomings. Clearly the recent growth of financial globalization has exceeded the capacity of the IFA to guide or manage it.

18. In the regulatory field, the financial crisis demonstrated in a dramatic fashion that while the cross-border networks created by financial market institutions had become very dense, the regulatory perimeter of governments remained strictly territorial. This reality became evident, for example, in the aftermath of the Lehman Brothers' bankruptcy in which international operations of this investment bank were "ring-fenced" by multi-year insolvency proceedings in each country in which it operated. Prior to the crisis, the major effort in international regulatory cooperation was embodied in the Basel Accord for bank supervision, which was first agreed upon in 1988 on a voluntary basis by bank regulators from the G10 countries meeting in the Basel Committee on Bank Supervision at the headquarters of the Bank for International Settlements in Basel, Switzerland. That agreement (Basel I) established the minimum capital requirements for commercial banks according to risk weights for their assets, using ratings of credit rating agencies to determine the riskiness of different asset classes. The Basel Accord was revised in 2004 (Basel II) to introduce additional risk weights for the determination of capital requirements for most banks and to establish a new regime for larger banks based on their own internal risk models. This regime was already in place in the European Union at the time of the financial crisis but was still in the stage of early implementation in the United States, although bank regulators in the United States under pressure from the large banks had already adopted the Basel II approach for the determination of capital requirements for those banks. This feature of Basel II became a critical factor in laying the groundwork for the GFC as it led to a reduction in the capitalization of the large banks and an increase in their leverage.

As a result of the crisis, an expanded membership of the Basel Committee, which brought in the representatives of all the G20 countries, agreed in December 2010 on a revised Basel standard (Basel III). An important impetus for this revision came from the establishment of the FSB in 2009, comprising finance ministers and heads of regulatory agencies from the G20 countries. The new accord represented a radical revision of its predecessors in that it established a more rigorous definition of capital and raised the minimum requirement for all banks while introducing a new capital surcharge for the larger banks. It also put in place a new minimum capital-asset ratio requirement of 3 percent and minimum liquidity requirements for banks. While it is clear that improvements have been made to the Basel Accord, it can easily be argued that the minimum capital requirements are still too low and that the new capital-asset ratio still allows banks to operate with an excessively high degree of leverage (up to 33 to 1).

19. In the wake of the crisis, there has been some improvement in international policy coordination with the shift in the leaders' summit from the G7 to the G20 and its links to the IMF through the G20 Finance Ministers and Central Bank Governors. Prior to the crisis, the main continuous forum for international policy discussions was the IMF, which can provide an effective and highly competent secretariat for such discussions but does not have the power to enforce any agreement or commitment among its members. This limitation on the part of the IMF was evident in pre-crisis efforts to bring about macroeconomic policy adjustments by means of a multilateral consultative process among the major economies to deal with the problem of global imbalances. Immediately after the crisis, the forum for international policy discussions shifted to the G20 with the technical support of the IMF. Initially these efforts were successful, as suggested earlier in the design of policies to respond to the crisis. In this connection, a process of peer review on policy implementation (so-called Mutual Assessment Process) was instituted in 2009 to help reinforce policy commitments, but with the passage of time, this mechanism has weakened. In part, this outcome has resulted from the fact that the agenda for the G20 has been greatly expanded to cover a range of issues beyond international macroeconomic policy, each of which merits political direction at the highest level. The lesson from the crisis in this dimension of the IFA is that the major economies still need to find

a way to establish a mechanism of peer review with sanctions, for example, to reinforce key decisions in the international macro policy arena. Building on its post-crisis Integrated Surveillance Decision, the IMF should be given authority to recommend some form of collective action by its membership in the event a country's economic policies are judged to be a major threat to its own stability or to have serious negative spillover effects on other countries.

20. Another sign of the weakness in the IFA is the absence of a clear ILOLR mechanism at times of financial stress, such as during the GFC. The IMF is ideally suited to play that role, but it lacks a liquidity instrument that countries can easily access at a time of financial stress. The two emergency credit facilities that now exist (the Flexible Credit Line and Precautionary and Liquidity Line) require high standards of macroeconomic performance as a basis for pre-qualification, and access has only been granted to four member countries. During the recent crisis, the US Federal Reserve in effect served as the main ILOLR through its central bank swap network, but this was an ad hoc and temporary arrangement established for only 15 countries. The Fund played a secondary role in crisis lending, by providing conditional lending to 17 other smaller countries under traditional standby arrangements during the first year of the crisis.

One result of the absence of an ILOLR is that most emerging market economies have established their own contingent reserve facilities through the accumulation of high levels of foreign assets. This development was in full display in the years prior to GFC and was one factor in limiting the spillover effects of the financial crisis emanating from the advanced countries. This decentralization of the ILOLR mechanism has continued since the crisis, with a further build-up or expansion in bilateral swap arrangements and regional funding facilities, such as the Chiang Mai Initiative Multilateralization for the ASEAN+3 countries, and the Latin American Reserve Fund. However, the largest element of the global financial safety network has remained countries' own reserve facilities. This further decentralization of the ILOLR mechanism creates additional problems for coordination among its constituent elements that puts a greater premium for enhancing the emergency lending role of the IMF within the IFA.

21. In light of the adjustment problems of Greece, an important lesson from the GFC is that a sovereign debt-restructuring mechanism (SDRM) is required at the international level to deal with problems of debt sustainability of sovereign borrowers. The IMF established, in 2002, a policy that its financial resources should not be committed to support a country's external adjustment programs in cases where the country could not be judged to have a sustainable debt burden over the medium term. While this is a sensible policy on the part of the Fund, even though it was breached in the case of Greece under the pressure of its European members, no statutory mechanism or facility exists to promote debt restructuring in country cases where it is required. Since the failure of efforts to create an SDRM associated with the Fund in 2001–02, sovereign debt restructuring has proceeded on an informal and decentralized contractual basis through the device of the "collective action" clauses in sovereign debt contracts. The lessons of experience, including that of Greece, have shown, however, that debt relief by this approach has generally been provided on a "too little and too late" basis, which has frustrated rather than promoted successful medium-term adjustment programs. Moreover, the experience of Argentina has demonstrated that the current informal arrangements for sovereign debt restructuring can lead to very protracted negotiations, which do not restore a country's borrowing capacity in the face of holdout creditors.

THINKING ABOUT THE AGGREGATE ECONOMY

22. An important macroeconomic lesson of the crisis of 2008–09 is that it has put to rest any claims that national economies can be seen as equilibrium systems that have a natural tendency to self-correct. This is not a new idea in the history of economic thought and was, many decades ago, the focus of Keynes' famous *General Theory*. In the wake of the Great Depression, Keynes attempted to show that the conclusions of the classical school of economic thinkers beginning in the nineteenth century, which pointed to the ability of national economies to operate as self-equilibrating systems, were not true. In subsequent academic work, however, the framework of Keynes' thought was put aside for its lack of "micro foundations". Instead, a new school of macroeconomics (or NMC)

had come into ascendency in the period leading up to the crisis which reasserted the claims of the prior classical school regarding the inherent stability and self-correcting capacity of capitalist market economies. This new paradigm, based on the aggregation of independent "representative agents" operating under rational expectations, was grounded in a much more theoretically sophisticated and mathematically elegant framework than the classical school of Keynes' time. As a tool for policy analysis, the quantitative framework of the new classical and new Keynesian paradigm, which was defined in term of dynamic stochastic general equilibrium (DSGE) models, was widely used in a number of central banks and international institutions. Remarkably, however, prior to the crisis, these models basically ignored the financial sector on the premise that it was not subject to any frictions and did not have any enduring effect on the behavior of the real economy. Since the crisis, we have learned that these models cannot account for the medium-term effects of "hysteresis" associated with a major economic downturn such as the Great Recession, which has resulted in a sharp decline in the estimates of potential GDP for the countries most affected by the GFC, as well as a drop in their post-crisis rate of economic growth compared with trends prior to the crisis.

23. The mainstream macroeconomic paradigm grounded in DSGE models was also shown to be problematic in the light of the crisis in that it had failed to identify any significant risks in asset markets and financial market activity in the years prior to the crisis. Some critics have complained that the dominant framework for macroeconomic analysis was defective because it was unable to predict the crisis; however, such a criticism seems unrealistic given the inherent uncertainty that applies to major deviations from forecasts or extrapolations based on recent developments. Nevertheless, one can argue that macroeconomic analysts and modelers should have been able to identify economic or financial activities where significant risks were present and the potential for negative spillovers existed.

By the same token, the mainstream macroeconomic paradigm can also be criticized for its failure to provide any guidance for policy action once the crisis had erupted. Macroeconomic shocks of the magnitude experienced by the United States and other major economies were simply not within the normal range of calibration associated with the use of DSGE models. Some commentators have claimed that the actual policy response to the crisis, as expressed in central bank liquidity provision, monetary easing and fiscal stimulus, was perfectly consistent with the standard macroeconomic policy framework that can be found in economic textbooks (i.e., the IS-LM and aggregate demand/supply models). This may be true, but these approaches to macroeconomic analysis have very little direct association with modern DSGE models and mainstream academic macroeconomics prior to the crisis. Instead, they derive from the work that was first developed nearly 80 years ago by lead interpreters of Keynes' classic work (such as John Hicks).

The growing concern with the potential problem of "secular stagnation" as a means of explaining the slow and uncertain pace of economic recovery in the advanced economies since the GFC, as well as Japan's experience over the past two and a half decades, only reinforces the basic notion that modern capitalist systems are not inherently self-correcting.

24. An additional distinct but very important lesson from the GFC is that the global capitalist system is not neutral with respect to its impact on income distribution and, in fact, has been associated with a substantial increase in income inequality. At first glance, the two issues of the financial crisis and income inequality seem to be unrelated, as the former was related to the operations of financial markets, whereas the latter is related to structural factors in the economy. However, in the wake of the crisis, the impact of the economic downturn on long-term unemployment rates, real income gains and the increasing share of income accruing to the top one percent of the income distribution have heightened concern about the connection between economic and financial globalization and income inequality. Prior to the crisis, the issue of income inequality was largely ignored in macroeconomic policy debate, even though it had been a growing problem since the onset of economic and financial globalization from the late 1970s. Moreover, since the crisis, economic research has shown that there has been a strong correlation between the growth in the financial industry and rising income inequality.

As a general matter, issues of income distribution were not a major focus of economic policy and academic debate prior to the crisis. At a conceptual level, one could argue that the main conclusion of economic growth models was that there should be some convergence in income distribution within and across countries over time, as poorer regions and countries tended to grow faster than richer ones with the benefit of domestic or foreign investment and a higher marginal productivity of capital. A similarly benign view was held by many economists, which can be traced to the empirical work of Simon Kuznets in the mid-1950s, who postulated on the basis of historical national income data that over time, as industrialization proceeds, there should be an initial tendency for income distribution to deteriorate, which is then reversed as a growing middle class develops. More generally, under the influence of the NMC, the focus of macroeconomics shifted to near-term stabilization objectives of low inflation and full employment and to the role of competitive markets and the expectations of market participants in achieving these objectives.

An important influence on focusing attention on the problem of income inequality in the advanced countries was the publication, in 2014, of Thomas Piketty's analysis of income distribution, *Capital in the 21st Century*. Few if any studies of economic history in recent memory have had the impact on academic and popular debate as has this one. The detailed historical research summarized in this book has demonstrated that as an empirical matter, the growth of modern capitalist economies has been associated with a clear and sustained pattern of worsening income distribution since the middle of the last century, contrary to Kuznets' conjecture. This trend was particularly noteworthy in the two decades prior to the GFC. A number of factors have been at work in bringing about this change in income distribution, such as the decline in union power, the reduction in marginal tax rates at the top level of the income scale and in taxes on capital income and estates, the upward spiral in executive compensation and the impact of globalization on widening the dispersion between wages for unskilled workers and those for educated workers, especially in IT-related industries.

On a priori grounds, it may not be possible to determine conclusively whether modern capitalist systems have positive or negative effects on income distribution, as it depends largely on the institutional, legal and policy arrangements that underpin the market system at a given period in history. Thus it is largely an empirical matter. In this regard, the negative impact of the Great Recession of 2008–09 on incomes of the lower- and middle-class groups in the United States has attracted much attention and has been the focus of great concern in academic and policy circles. This problem is highlighted by the simple fact that nearly 60 percent of the gains in income since 2009 have accrued to the top 1 percent of the income distribution, according to research by Emmanuel Saez of University of California (Berkeley). It is also noteworthy that following a long period of relative stability, the share of labor income in total factor income started to fall after 2000 from an average of around 65 percent in that year to around 55 percent in 2013.

There were two developments associated with the financial crisis that could have contributed to the declining share of labor income. One was the explosive growth in executive compensation, which was characteristic of both the nonfinancial and financial corporate sectors. The other was the increasing share of financial services in national income, which reached a peak in the years prior to the financial crisis. As regards the latter factor, it needs to be recognized that the financial services sector is a vital component of a dynamic capitalist, market-based economy. However, studies have shown that after a period of growth, there is a turning point after which a further growth in the financial services has a negative influence on growth. According to some recent empirical studies, such a point was reached in the years prior to the crisis and may have reflected the churning of financial activity ("financialization") that was associated with momentum trading and the development of high-speed trading in stocks and bonds. This activity can be seen as a means of extracting rents from financial transactions that goes beyond the socially useful role of financial markets in the allocation of investment and management of risk associated with a well-functioning financial sector.

Some of the financial sector reforms initiated in the wake of the crisis (e.g., higher capital requirements and insolvency regimes for SIFIs) may help to prevent a further deterioration in income inequality. However, significant improvements in income equality will require time and a broad-based effort including income tax reform and changes in corporate governance, as well as adjustments in social and educational policy.

25. In the wake of the financial crisis, an important lesson that many economists have drawn is that the NMC needs to be modified. At the very least, the main framework of DSGE models should be expanded to take explicit account of the links between the financial sector and the real economy, and work has proceeded along this line. However, it is also important to expand mainstream economic thinking by incorporating the insights of other fields of economic

analysis such as behavioral finance and complexity theory. These areas of study have attracted attention in large part because they offer insights into financial and macroeconomic behavior that cannot be derived from the axioms and postulates of DSGE models. More generally, economists should be prepared to incorporate the insights from other fields of the social sciences in their efforts to understand and explain economic phenomena.

The failure of the current macroeconomic consensus to provide any guidance into the causes and resolution of the financial crisis has also raised concerns about the range and scope of topics to be included in the teaching of economics at both the undergraduate and graduate levels. While maintaining the intent of economics to operate as a scientific field of study, it is important that students be exposed to the history of economic thought and the main currents of economic history that have influenced the evolution of both neoclassical and alternative approaches to the study of economics. At the same time, greater emphasis should be given to the empirical techniques to support a more evidence-based approach to economic analysis.

***

On the basis of the 25 conclusions and lessons summarized above, one can argue that the GFC has had, and will continue to have, a significant impact on macroeconomic thinking and the design and implementation of macroeconomic policy in both national and global settings. In particular, it has also brought to the fore the continuing challenges of financial globalization and the need to strengthen the IFA. Since the financial crisis of 2008–09, countries have become more acutely aware of the vagaries of international capital flows and the potentially large destabilizing shocks that they can create for emerging market and advanced economies alike, reminiscent of the problem of "sudden stops" during the 1990s. In order to avoid an erosion in financial globalization and the global capitalist system it supports, it is imperative that members of the G20 strive to find ways to improve international policy coordination, the monitoring of global financial system stability and international financial regulation while creating a permanent ILOLR mechanism and SDRM with a view to securing the benefits of financial globalization and minimizing its disruptive tendencies.

As the global economic and financial system continues to become more integrated, the institutional arrangements of the international financial architecture need to be strengthened on a continuing basis in order to promote stability and minimize the risk of future global financial crises. Over time, improvements in the crisis-prevention capability of the IFA will require an increase in the authority and independence of an international financial institution such as the IMF in conducting its multilateral and member-country surveillance activities. In its multilateral surveillance, the Fund (in coordination with the FSB) needs to be able to assess the risks to global financial stability on a continuing basis, drawing on its periodic evaluations of major country regulatory frameworks and financial systems. At the country level, it needs to have the full support of its members in conducting its annual assessments of the soundness of their macroeconomic policy frameworks and their prospects for maintaining medium-term fiscal and external sustainability and in any future efforts to coordinate policy changes to deal with problems in the global economy where a multilateral solution is required. In this connection, member countries should be willing to impose penalties or sanctions on a country that does not cooperate with the Fund in making adjustments to its domestic financial or macroeconomic policies that pose a threat to its medium-term financial or external stability or that have significant negative spillover effects on other countries. This kind of reform in the Fund's mandate, however, can only be envisaged in a global system where each member country shares a strong commitment to a liberal and stable economic and financial order and a common understanding of the significant benefits that can flow from such an international arrangement. In promoting such a commitment, the G20 has an indispensable role to play.

NOTE

1. This chapter is a revised and extended version of an essay by the author entitled "What Have We Learned from the Global Financial Crisis and Its Aftermath?", which was published in World Economics Vol. 16(2), April–June 2015.

INDEX

© The Author(s) 2017
A. Elson, *The Global Financial Crisis in Retrospect*,
DOI 10.1057/978-1-137-59750-2